The
Innovation
Secrets of
STEVE JOBS

INSANELY DIFFERENT
Principles for Breakthrough Success

CARMINE GALLO

New York   Chicago   San Francisco   Lisbon   London   Madrid   Mexico City
Milan   New Delhi   San Juan   Seoul   Singapore   Sydney   Toronto

The McGraw·Hill Companies

For Vanessa, Josephine, and Lela—
My source of endless joy and inspiration

1 2 3 4 5 6 7 8 9 10 11 12 13 14 15   QFR/QFR   1 9 8 7 6 5 4 3 2 1 0

ISBN   978-0-07-174875-9
MHID   0-07-174875-X

This publication is designed to provide accurate and authoritative information in regard to the subject matter covered. It is sold with the understanding that neither the author nor the publisher is engaged in rendering legal, accounting, securities trading, or other professional services. If legal advice or other expert assistance is required, the services of a competent professional person should be sought.
> —From a Declaration of Principles Jointly Adopted by a Committee of the American Bar Association and a Committee of Publishers and Associations

Library of Congress Cataloging-in-Publication Data

Gallo, Carmine.
    The innovation secrets of Steve Jobs : insanely different principles for breakthrough success / by Carmine Gallo.
        p.   cm.
    ISBN 978-0-07-174875-9 (alk. paper)
    1. New products.   2. Creative thinking.   3. Technological innovations.   4. Success in business.   5. Jobs, Steven, 1955–   I. Title.

    HF5415.153.G35   2010
    658.4'063—dc22   2010029784

Interior design by THINK Book Works

The Innovation Secrets of Steve Jobs is in no way authorized, prepared, approved, or endorsed by Steve Jobs and is not affiliated with or endorsed by any of his past or present organizations.

McGraw-Hill books are available at special quantity discounts to use as premiums and sales promotions or for use in corporate training programs. To contact a representative, please e-mail us at bulksales@mcgraw-hill.com.

This book is printed on acid-free paper.

Contents

Acknowledgments

I am grateful to the readers around the world who made *The Presentation Secrets of Steve Jobs* an international bestseller. I was thrilled to hear your stories. I hope you find this new content equally as valuable. Your passion inspires me. I'd also like to thank analysts such as Rob Enderle and many others who enthusiastically endorsed the book on their blogs and Twitter posts.

My former editor at McGraw-Hill, John Aherne, was a big believer in this book from the beginning. In 2010, he chose to follow his heart and embark on what I'm sure will be a wonderful journey. Thanks for everything, John.

Everyone at McGraw-Hill is fantastic. Vice president and group publisher Gary Krebs brings energy, passion, and enthusiasm to his role. It has rubbed off on this author! The rest of the McGraw-Hill team is equally as passionate: Mary Glenn, Heather Cooper, Lydia Rinaldi, Ann Pryor, Gayathri Vinay, Joe Berkowitz, Allyson Gonzalez, and everyone involved in editing, design, production, sales, and marketing. You make a wonderful team.

As always, thanks to my literary agent, Ed Knappman, who has mentored and guided me through my writing career.

Special thanks to Tom Neilssen and everyone at BrightSight for finding opportunities for me to share my insights and content with others.

Nick Leiber at *Bloomberg BusinessWeek* deserves a thank-you. He edits my columns and shares my enthusiasm. He is a wonderful collaborator.

Fauzia Burke, Julie Harabedian, and the team at FSB Associates continue to provide a fresh perspective and unique insight into the always changing world of online marketing and publicity. Thank you for teaching me something new!

My wife, Vanessa, deserves extra special thanks for helping with endnotes, editing, and preparing the material for submission. She means everything to me. My children, Josephine and Lela, are always a source of inspiration, as is the rest of my family: Ken and Patty, Donna, Tino, Francesco, Nick, my mother, and, of course, my father, who continues to live in our hearts. I know he is smiling on us all.

Introduction

What the World Needs Now Is More Jobs—
Steve Jobs

I n an open letter to President Barack Obama, *New York Times* columnist Thomas Friedman challenged Obama to create more Jobs—Steve Jobs. "We need to get millions of American kids, not just the geniuses, excited about innovation and entrepreneurship again."[1] If you want more good jobs, Friedman argued, the nation must do a better job of fostering an environment where innovation is encouraged and allowed to flourish. In short, the country needs more people like Apple cofounder and CEO Steve Jobs. After all, thanks in large part to the revolutionary iPhone, one of the most innovative devices of the decade, Apple surpassed Microsoft in 2010 to become the most valuable technology company in the world. That's a stunning achievement for any company and especially remarkable for one that was started in a spare bedroom.

America faces a host of problems as it enters the second decade of the new millennium. Millions of people are out of work or losing their homes, often both. One in six Americans lives on food stamps, public education is in desperate need of a radical overhaul, and businesses in every corner of the country are struggling to keep their doors open. "Bookended by 9/11 at the start and a financial wipeout at the end, the first 10 years of this century will very likely go down as the most dispiriting and disillusioning decade Americans have lived through in the post–World War II era"; calling it "the Decade from Hell," *Time* noted that the best thing we could say about the decade was that it was over.[2]

The Great Recession spread to many parts of the globe, infecting countries that were already struggling with weak economies, strained infrastructures, environmental problems, and unimaginable poverty. Real progress in the decade ahead will require fresh, creative, and innovative ideas. The key is to keep innovating, said Microsoft cofounder Bill Gates. "During the past two centuries, innovation has more than doubled our life span and given us cheap energy and more food. If we project what the world will be like 10 years from now without continuing innovation in health, energy or food, the picture is dark," he said.[3] In the next decade, businesses and individuals must embrace the twin pillars of creativity and innovation. Failure to do so will stifle progress at a period in history when progress is vital.

The good news is that recessions often act as catalysts for innovation. According to IBM general manager Adalio Sanchez, "When you're in a situation where you've really got to be judicious, to do more with less, that really drives a need for innovation and a level of creativity that you might not otherwise have in normal times. Increased innovation doesn't always have to be about more dollars. It's about how you use those dollars."[4]

History shows that the greatest innovations have been introduced in periods of severe economic stress. A 2009 Booz & Company report noted, "Television, xerography, electric razors, FM radio, and scores of other advances were produced during the Great Depression. Companies such as DuPont, which in 1937 was generating 40 percent of its revenues from products introduced after 1930, pursued innovation not only to survive the Depression but also to set the stage for decades of sustained profitable growth."[5] The Booz & Company study found that legendary innovators were molded in times of stress. In the face of adversity, successful innovators played to their strengths and took bold actions as they sought new opportunities to create value.

Indeed, stress, conflict, and necessity seem to be nature's way of saying, "Find a new way." During a visit to Paso Robles, California, acclaimed as one of the chief up-and-coming wine-growing regions in the world, I entered a winery with a display of rocks on the bar. "What are the rocks for?" I asked. "Those are limestone samples that make up the soil around here," the woman said proudly as she poured samples of the winery's award-winning zinfandel. "To survive in this gravelly soil, the vine roots have to work extra hard to reach the water. As a result, the fruit clusters have more intense flavors, and as any winemaker knows, great wine begins with great fruit."

Stress isn't comfortable, but I'm convinced the same force that acts on vines is also working its magic on an entire generation of business professionals. Over the past two years, I have received hundreds of e-mails from men and women who have lost their jobs but who see the situation as an opportunity to follow their passion and create something new and innovative. The *Wall Street Journal* noted that a growing number of college graduates, faced with an unforgiving job market, have decided to forgo the corporate route entirely to start their own companies. It turns out that members of the Millennial Generation—often described as brash, spoiled, and impetuous—are creating meaningful start-ups at an unprecedented rate. I would not be surprised if ten years from now we discover that the "Decade from Hell" was actually the decade that inspired countless new products, services, methods, and ideas. In every corner of the world, tucked in garages, cubicles, labs, and classrooms, a new wave of innovators is working on breakthroughs in technology, health, science, and the environment.

"Our fright may be our salvation," wrote Rick Hampson in a piece for *USA Today*. "Americans often suspect they face the worst of times and, as a result, try harder to make the best of them. Whether it's the launch of Sputnik in 1957, the fall of Saigon in 1975, or the economic challenge from Japan in the 1980s, there's this persistent conviction that our best days are behind us . . . yet Americans' assumptions that they're at the brink is what save us from going over. Instead of underestimating challenges, we overreact. In a competitive world, it's a key to our success."[6]

Innovation is needed to lift the country from the doldrums— big, bold, and creative ideas to revive and rejuvenate desperate countries, struggling companies, and stagnant careers. Who better to provide a road map than *Fortune*'s "CEO of the Decade," Steve Jobs?

In October 2009, McGraw-Hill released *The Presentation Secrets of Steve Jobs: How to Be Insanely Great in Front of Any Audience*. It quickly became an international bestseller. But a funny thing happened on the way to the top. The title began landing on bestseller lists alongside legendary success and self-help books such as Rhonda Byrnes's *The Secret* and Stephen R. Covey's *The 7 Habits of Highly Successful People*. Readers began sharing stories of how they changed their approaches to their businesses and their careers as a result of what they learned in the book. In an article for *Java World*, a reporter wrote that she picked up the book to improve her presentation skills but discovered nuggets of wisdom that could help IT managers and CIOs become better leaders. I was gratified by the feedback. Clearly the book had impacted readers who were searching for success tools that went beyond giving better presentations. You're reading its companion. Although this book addresses the importance of communication (innovation means nothing if you can't get people excited about it), the content delves much more deeply into the principles that have guided Steve Jobs for much of his life—lessons that will help you unleash your potential in business and life.

Before we explore the principles that make Steve Jobs one of the world's most successful innovators, we must agree on a definition of innovation that applies to everyone, regardless of title or function: CEOs, managers, employees, scientists, teachers, entrepreneurs, and students. In a sentence: *Innovation is a new way of doing things that results in positive change.* It makes life better.

"There is wide agreement that innovation is the best way to sustain economic prosperity," economist Tapan Munroe told me. "Innovation increases productivity, and productivity increases the possibility of higher income, higher profits, new jobs, new products, and a prosperous economy. Once you open the curtains to the world economy, you see the sunlight. It's not all cloudy. We need to transform smart ideas that tackle and address real problems into products and services that everybody wants."[7] Munroe, along with Gates and Friedman, believes that innovation needs to be our new mantra.

"Innovation is a broad concept," says Munroe. "There's innovation with a 'small *i*' and innovation with a 'big *I*.' The 'big *I*' involves things such as building the Internet, the internal combustion engine, and the bar code. But innovation also includes small, continuous improvements that help you run your life better, help your small business grow, or improve your company's product or productivity."[8] These small innovations take place every day and make life better for everyone.

"Business as usual is a recipe for disaster," writes Curtis Carlson in *Innovation*. "Traditional professional training is not enough if you are to adapt and thrive in this tumultuous business world; you must also have new innovation skills. If you know how to create customer value, regardless of your particular enterprise, you have a much greater chance to succeed and remain employable over your full working years. Otherwise, you may become obsolete."[9] Carlson says it doesn't matter if you have an advanced degree in aerospace or if you're trained as a financial analyst, an accountant, or an insurance professional; your expertise must adapt to the new world. And adapting means new, creative ways of looking at existing and potential problems.

Creativity takes work. "Innovation isn't something you do once and then sit back and relax," said Munroe. Innovation is a commitment to continuous improvement on everyone's part. He offers the following example: "Let's take a small consulting business that offers economic forecasting. The first thing I would do if I wanted to be truly innovative would be to offer services that play to my greatest strengths. If my service was similar to five other firms in my region, I would innovate by setting myself apart in the following areas: providing better customer service, a higher quality of research, more unique offerings, better communication, clearer communication, and more user-friendly material that clients can use to take action." Munroe says one question will set you apart: *How can I help my clients or customers do better?* "Discovering an answer to that question is innovation," says Munroe.[10]

For many companies and individuals, repeating the same processes that triggered the global financial meltdown would simply lead to the same result. Making innovation part of your DNA means applying the Apple mantra to your business, your career, and your life—"Think Different." If your products fail to excite buyers, you need to think differently about reinvigorating your offerings. If your sales are plummeting, you need to think differently about improving the customer experience. If you spent the 2000s shuffling from job to job, you need to think differently about managing your career.

Thinking more like Steve Jobs might help businesses and educators. "Education in America could use a big dose of innovation," wrote *Rich Dad* author Robert Kiyosaki. "America's schools need to take a page from the businesses that have been created by entrepreneurs like Henry Ford and Steve Jobs. They've given us a road map. America's education system needs an injection of innovation— which is just what entrepreneurs do. We need two different public school programs: one for employees and one for entrepreneurs . . . training entrepreneurs is different from training people to be employees."[11]

This book will avoid the discussion of arcane and complex theories of innovation that are relegated to the dusty bookshelves of academia. "Most Ph.D. papers on the topic of innovation are dense and complex because they are not written for most people," one economist told me. "The papers are written by Ph.D.s for Ph.D.s. In many cases, the more obtuse the theory, the more esteemed the authors become in the eyes of their peers. I played that game for years."

Coming out of a global recession, we don't have time for games. What we need are practical tools and principles to help unleash the creative potential that lies within each of us. The principles you are about to learn are simple, meaningful, and attainable for any professional in any field of endeavor: CEO, manager, entrepreneur, consultant, creative professional, small business owner, teacher, doctor, lawyer, Realtor, consultant, stay-at-home mom, and yes, Ph.D.s who truly believe in using their research to better the human condition.

Innovation is often confused with invention. The two notions are complementary but different. The act of inventing means to design, create, and build new products or processes. Innovation starts with creative ideas that ultimately are translated into inventions, services, processes, and methods. Not everyone can be an inventor, but anyone can be an innovator. Are you a small business owner who came up with a new idea to convert visitors into buyers? You're an innovator. Are you a manager who created a fresh way to motivate your employees? You're an innovator. Are you an entrepreneur who reinvented your career after losing one too many jobs? You're an innovator. Are you a stay-at-home mom who discovered a way to revitalize your neighborhood pubic school? You're an innovator.

Innovation is something that average people do every day to live extraordinary lives. You will meet many of them in the pages to follow—men and women who are transforming businesses, communities, and lives by innovating the Steve Jobs way.

Studying innovation may keep your brain sharp, too. Scientists are finding that as we age, the stuff we know in our brains doesn't disappear; it simply gets lost in the folds of our neurons. As the brain ages, it gets better at seeing the big picture. Scientists say the trick is to keep those connections firing. Experts contend that the best way to jiggle the synapses is to expose yourself to people and ideas that are different, who challenge your way of thinking. Maybe a nineteen-year-old Steve Jobs had the right idea when he left the leafy suburbs of California to backpack around India with his pal Daniel Kottke. The trip made Jobs question many of the illusions he had about the exotic land: "It was one of the first times I started thinking that maybe Thomas Edison did a lot more to improve the world than Karl Marx and Neem Karolie Baba put together."[12]

Failing to find spiritual enlightenment on his journey, Jobs returned to his parents' house in Los Altos, California, determined to blaze a trail of his own. Jobs's path over the next three decades would lead to astonishing highs and spectacular lows, both in his personal life and in his professional life. He has experienced success, failure, and redemption, and, beginning in 2004, the man who once went to India for answers to life's most puzzling riddles found uncommon wisdom after surviving not one but two life-threatening illnesses. "Remembering that I'll be dead soon is the most important tool I've ever encountered to help me make the big choices in life," Jobs said.[13]

If, as Thomas Friedman believes, America needs more leaders like Steve Jobs, then we must look to "Steve" for guidance. Jobs is intensely private, but he has dropped many clues on his path to breakthrough success. All you have to do is look.

CHAPTER 1

What Would Steve Do?

**Innovation distinguishes between
a leader and a follower.**

—STEVE JOBS

nnovation is Apple's secret sauce, but cofounder and CEO Steven P. Jobs does not believe in "systems" to create innovation. Apple employees do not attend workshops to exercise their innovation muscles. You will not find Legos strewn about the Apple campus to spark innovation, nor will you see employees scouring the halls for items in a scavenger hunt as an "innovation consultant" leads them in a contrived team-building activity. In fact, Steve Jobs disdains trite exercises. "We don't think, let's take a class! Here are the five rules of innovation; let's put them up all over the company!" Jobs once told Rob Walker for the *New York Times*. Walker pressed Jobs during the interview and suggested that many people do try to create systems—or methods—to ignite innovation. "Of course they do," Jobs said. "It's like somebody who's not cool trying to be cool. It's painful to watch . . . It's like watching Michael Dell try to dance. Painful."[1]

This book takes the pain out of innovation. It is not intended to create a rigid, step-by-step method for innovation, since that's the last thing Jobs would recommend. It *is* intended to reveal the general principles that have guided Steve Jobs in achieving his breakthrough success, principles that can spark your imagination, enhance your creativity, help you develop fresh ideas to grow your business and career, and inspire you to change the world.

Although the principles are based on the model of legendary technology icon Steve Jobs, innovation isn't just about technology; it's about creating new ideas to solve problems. Famous French designer Philippe Starck, who is a fan of Jobs (and Jobs is a fan of his), once said that a "good" product is one that will help you lead a better life. In addition to designing stunning hotel lobbies in some of the world's most desirable locations, Starck has "democratized design" by designing common items with uncommon style, elegance, and simplicity, including bathroom scales, baby monitors, and dozens of other everyday products for retailers such as Target. If we use Starck's definition of "good," then Steve Jobs has been making good—very good—products for more than three decades. The same ethos that drives Starck inspires Jobs, who makes existing products (computers, MP3 players, and smartphones) more accessible, enjoyable, and pleasing to use. If the ideas in this book inspire you to build the next great gadget, that's wonderful, but more broadly, these principles will provide a framework to ignite your business and your career, ideas that will propel you further than you ever thought possible.

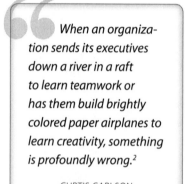

When an organization sends its executives down a river in a raft to learn teamwork or has them build brightly colored paper airplanes to learn creativity, something is profoundly wrong.[2]

—CURTIS CARLSON
AND WILLIAM WILMOT,
INNOVATION

The Steve Jobs Experience

How do we know what Steve Jobs has to say? After all, Jobs is one of the most reclusive CEOs on the planet. He is rarely seen in public, most Apple employees have never met him personally, he avoids regular appearances in the media, and he has created such a guarded compound at Apple headquarters that you'd think you had crossed the demilitarized zone into North Korea. Nevertheless, Jobs has had plenty to say since high school when he first met Steve Wozniak and began building computers in a bedroom of his parents' house. (Contrary to popular wisdom, Apple got started in a bedroom before moving to the kitchen and finally to the "garage" where the legend was born.)

While it requires thousands of employees to make Steve Jobs's vision a reality, at its center, the Apple experience is really the Steve Jobs experience. Few people are more closely associated with innovation than Jobs. A Google search for "Steve Jobs + Innovation" will generate more than 2.7 million links. A similar search using the name "Walt Disney" generates 1.5 million links, and "Henry Ford" generates just over a million links. I believe the people who conduct such searches are looking for more than a biography; they are searching for inspiration.

Innovation Secrets is not a biography of Steve Jobs. Instead, it seeks to uncover the principles that have led Steve Jobs to create boundless ideas that have truly changed the world—principles that you can apply today to unleash your potential. Consider it the ultimate field guide to breakthrough success in business and in life. The principles are derived from a thorough examination of Jobs's own words over the past three decades, insights from former Apple employees, experts who have covered the company for decades, and a wide range of business leaders, entrepreneurs, educators, and small business owners who have been inspired by asking themselves a simple question: *What would Steve do?*

The Big Hero

The *New York Times* Nobel Prize–winning economist Paul Krugman called the last decade "the Big Zero," because, in his opinion, "nothing good happened."[3] But something good did happen. From the ashes of the big zero rose the big hero, Steve Jobs. *Fortune* has credited Jobs for defying the downturn, cheating death, and changing the world. In a ten-year period that saw two recessions, financial scandals, a banking crisis, huge stock losses, and a reeling economy, Jobs posted win after win. He resuscitated Apple (the company was teetering on the edge of bankruptcy when Jobs returned in 1996) and radically reinvented the computer, music, movie, and telecommunications industries. Remaking one business in one's career is a rare achievement, but as *Fortune* points out, remaking four is unheard of. *Fortune* argued that Jobs's influence on global culture could not be underestimated. "Every day, several times a day, some student, entrepreneur, industrial designer, or CEO looks at a problem and wonders: What would Steve Jobs do?"[4]

The 2000s were all about Steve's success. Quarter after quarter, Apple set records for revenue and profits as sales of Macs, iPods, and iPhones exploded. By January 2010, Apple had sold 250 million iPods, commanding more than 70 percent of the MP3 market and changing the way people discover, purchase, and enjoy music. The company increased its share of the PC market to 10 percent, despite average selling prices well above those of other computer makers. Apple Stores had grown to number more than 280 and attracted some fifty million visitors in one quarter alone. In the short eighteen months since the introduction of the App Store on July 10, 2008, three billion applications had been downloaded for use on the iPhone and iPod Touch. Apple, which had started on April 1, 1976, had grown into a $50 billion company. "I like to forget that because that's not how we think of Apple," Steve Jobs said on January 27, 2010, "but it is pretty amazing." Since returning to Apple in 1996, Steve Jobs had created $150 billion in shareholder wealth and transformed movies, telecom, music, retail, publishing, and design. If you're looking for someone to model, it's fair to ask yourself, "What would Steve do?"

Wall Street values Steve Jobs for bringing Apple back to financial health. In January 2010, the *Harvard Business Review* named Steve Jobs the best-performing CEO in the world for delivering "a whopping 3,188% industry-adjusted return (34% compounded annually) after he rejoined Apple."[5] As of this writing, Apple has a larger market cap than Dell and HP combined. *TechCrunch* editor Michael Arrington, though, chooses to focus on what Apple means to the world beyond Wall Street. The world, he says, would have looked a lot different had Jobs not returned.

A World Without Steve Jobs

Jobs has spearheaded the development of some of the sexiest products on the planet: iMacs, MacBooks, iPhones, iPods, and most recently, iPad. "But the hardware isn't even the start of what Apple has done in the last 12 years," writes Arrington. "They've accelerated the pace of change in the music, film, and television industries and they've redefined the mobile phone." Had Jobs not returned, Arrington doubts that another CEO would have entered an already saturated MP3 market with the iPod. He questions whether anyone else would have launched the iPhone or the iPad. Even if you do not own these products, Arrington submits, your world would look a lot different had Jobs not been in it: "We'd likely still be in mobile phone hell. Chances are we still wouldn't have a decent browsing experience on the phone, and we certainly wouldn't be enjoying third-party apps like Pandora or Skype on whatever clunker the carriers handed us. Steve Jobs was also the man who nearly single-handedly disrupted the entire music industry. And it's amazing how many laptops and desktops today mimic the look and feel of MacBooks and iMacs. Without Steve Jobs, the world would be a less colorful place. The man is a living legend and deserves his place in history."[6]

Apple's influence was evident all across the exhibit floors of the Barcelona Mobile World Congress in February 2010, even though Apple was not an exhibitor. Competitors such as Samsung, Nokia, LG, and Research in Motion all introduced devices with touch screens and app stores, two innovations popularized by the iPhone.

Apple innovations touch your life every day. Perhaps you've never owned a Mac but you've upgraded to a PC with Windows 7. Upon the introduction of Windows 7, a Microsoft group manager caught some flak by announcing that the new operating system (OS) was inspired by Apple's OS X. Microsoft stripped out code to streamline the system and make it more efficient and stable—a very Apple-like thing to do. In addition, the manager said that what Microsoft attempted to do with its new operating system was to create a graphical look and feel similar to that of the Mac. Whether you're a Mac or a PC, Apple's innovations are all around you.

Someone suggested that matching Steve Jobs's success would be unattainable for most people. I will not insult your intelligence by claiming this book will turn you into a billionaire many times over like Steve Jobs, nor do I promise that it will help you invent the next iPod. A promise like that is akin to a high school coach claiming that he can teach a young athlete to shoot baskets like Michael Jordan. The odds that the kid will be the next Jordan are slim. That said, it is doubtless his skills will improve, and maybe that young athlete will go on to be a star in high school and college and, if he works hard enough, even get a contract worth millions of dollars to play in the NBA. He may never have the influence that Jordan had over the game, but he will have a far more successful sports career than the vast majority of high school athletes could ever hope to achieve.

Who Are Your Heroes?

I once heard that only 3 percent of people are committed to designing the life of their dreams. That sounds about right. Most people spend more time planning grocery lists than thinking about their future. Still, maybe the Great Recession has acted as a wake-up call, reminding people that they need to take control over their lives instead of leaving their futures in the control of others who may not have their best interests in mind.

Young people are looking for guidance, and many are looking to Steve Jobs. In a 2009 Junior Achievement survey, one thousand teenagers with ages ranging from twelve to seventeen were asked to rank the entrepreneurs they most admired. Steve Jobs topped the list with 35 percent of the vote. Oprah, skater Tony Hawk, the Olsen twins, and Facebook founder Mark Zuckerberg all received fewer votes. When asked why they chose Jobs, nearly two-thirds of those surveyed (61 percent) gave responses along the lines of "because he made a difference," "he improved people's lives," or "he made the world a better place."[7] Only 4 percent mentioned Jobs's wealth or fame as a reason for selecting him, leading one to believe that teens are more altruistic than adults give them credit for. Making a difference in the world seems to make a difference to American teenagers.

"You can tell a lot about a person by who his or her heroes are," Jobs said, explaining the famous "Think Different" television ad, which featured such notable innovators—and Jobs heroes— as Albert Einstein, Bob Dylan, Mahatma Gandhi, and Amelia Earhart.[8] The ad campaign debuted on September 28, 1997, less than a year after Jobs's dramatic return to Apple following an eleven-year absence. The Apple brand was tarnished, and Jobs's primary role was to revitalize Apple's image. Once Jobs approved the ad campaign, he did not sit on the sidelines as a passive observer. He immersed himself in every aspect of the campaign, reviewing the artwork every day. Jobs was also instrumental in getting permissions, picking up the phone himself to talk to Yoko Ono or the estate of Albert Einstein.

Actor Richard Dreyfuss read the voice-over narration for the television spot as black-and-white images of thinkers, scientists, and iconoclasts filled the screen. It's easy to see why Jobs took such an ownership role in the project—it was not because he thought the campaign would single-handedly revive Apple's fortunes, but because, in many ways, Dreyfuss was describing him: "Here's to the crazy ones . . . the ones who see things differently . . . they change things. They invent. They imagine. They explore. They create. They inspire. They push the human race forward."[9] The campaign meant a lot to Jobs because he was building his legacy, and, as with great innovators before him, he had pushed the human race forward.

Harvard professor Nancy F. Koehn puts Jobs in the same category as other major entrepreneurs of the last two centuries, men and women such as Josiah Wedgwood, John D. Rockefeller, Andrew Carnegie, Henry Ford, and Estée Lauder. They all share certain traits: intense drive, unflagging curiosity, and a keen imagination. "Jobs came of age in a moment of far-reaching economic, social, and technological change that we now call the Information Revolution," Koehn writes. "Wedgwood, the 18th-century British china maker who created the first real consumer brand, grew up in the Industrial Revolution, another period of profound change. And Rockefeller laid the foundations of the modern oil industry in the 1870s and 1880s, when the railroad and the coming of mass production where transforming the U.S. from an agrarian into an industrial society."[10] Koehn maintains that in a time of significant transformation, a lot is up for grabs. Innovators such as Jobs, Rockefeller, and the others seize these moments of disruption.

Revolution in the Air

Disruption was certainly in the air in colonial America in 1776 when fifty-six men, among the most innovative leaders of their time, added their signatures to a document that would ignite a revolution in America and spread to many parts of the globe. The Declaration of Independence put the power of government into the hands of the masses. As America celebrated its bicentennial, two men—Steve Jobs and Steve Wozniak—added their signatures to a founding document that would spark a revolution, putting computer power into the hands of everyday people. Just as Thomas Jefferson asserted a right of revolution—the idea that people have rights and that when a government violates those rights and conditions become intolerable, the people have an obligation to alter or abolish that government—Jobs and Wozniak took it upon themselves to change a system that in many ways had become intolerable. Computers were expensive, hard to assemble, and relegated to hobbyists, the elites. Jobs and Wozniak shared a common vision—to build a computer everyone could afford and use. "When we first started Apple we really built the first computer because we wanted one," said Jobs. "Then we designed this crazy new computer with color and a bunch of other things called the Apple II. We had a passion to do this one simple thing which was to get a bunch of computers to our friends so they could have as much fun with them as we were."[11]

Although the Altair 8800 was the first personal computer, *Time* magazine credited the Apple II with beginning the personal computer revolution. Just as happened in the revolution for independence, not everyone was confident that the computer revolution would lead to a better society. In the 1970s, some observers worried that computers would widen the divide between the haves and the have-nots given the expensive price points of early computers. Others expressed concern that people would lose the ability to think through problems or would become increasingly isolated from society. Of course, volumes could be written about the positive impact that computers have had on humanity, touching and improving our lives every day. One can argue that the forces behind the computer revolution would have led to the democratization of technology without Jobs and Wozniak, but it would be hard to refute the proposition that Jobs made it take flight. It takes confidence to start a revolution, confidence in your own skills and confidence that your vision will indeed advance society.

Seven Principles That Drive Steve Jobs

I believe it is possible to replicate the Steve Jobs experience in your business, career, and life, if you understand the seven principles that drive him. The same principles are at work behind other successful individuals and organizations. In the following pages you will learn how the world's most famous sushi chef, Nobuyuki Matsuhisa, applies the same principles to his award-winning recipes as Steve Jobs does to his award-winning creations. You will discover the one principle of innovation that sparked Jobs to create the Mac and sparked Rachael Ray to create thirty-minute meals. You will learn how John F. Kennedy applied a secret of innovation to inspire human's landing on the moon and how the same principle inspired the creation of the Mac. You will meet a group of stay-at-home moms who applied the same principle Jobs uses to inspire his team and made it work in revitalizing a deteriorating neighborhood school, and you will hear from former Apple employees who have started their own companies by tapping into the success principles they learned from their former boss.

I once heard the story of a grandmother who was trying to decide what to give her grandkids for Christmas. She wanted to give them something that would demonstrate her love and empower them long after she was gone. She bought four green apples and wrapped each in a gift box—one for each grandchild. The kids opened their gifts and found the apples. Tucked under the apple was a note offering a brand-new Apple computer. The note explained that like the real apple, each grandchild had, at his or her core, the seeds of greatness and that the new Apple computer would help them capture their true wealth. Their grandmother passed away, but the kids kept the accompanying note, referring to the gift as the "Apple experience."[12] Whether or not you own an Apple product, you can benefit from the gift that Steve Jobs has given the world: the secrets to innovation. Many business leaders, entrepreneurs, and former Apple employees have discovered the secrets and applied them to achieve breakthrough success. It's fine to ask yourself, "What would Steve do?"—but you will fail to get a good answer without first understanding the seven principles that guide his approach to business and to life.

The seven principles featured in this book will force you to think differently about your career, company, customers, and products. They appear in this order:

» **Principle 1: "Do What You Love."** Steve Jobs has followed his heart his entire life, and that, he says, has made all the difference.

» **Principle 2: "Put a Dent in the Universe."** Jobs attracts like-minded people who share his vision and who help turn his ideas into world-changing innovations. Passion fuels Apple's rocket, and Jobs's vision creates the destination.

» **Principle 3: "Kick-Start Your Brain."** Innovation does not exist without creativity, and for Steve Jobs, creativity is the act of connecting things. Jobs believes that a broad set of experiences broadens our understanding of the human experience.

» **Principle 4: "Sell Dreams, Not Products."** To Jobs, people who buy Apple products are not "consumers." They are people with dreams, hopes, and ambitions. Jobs builds products to help them fulfill their dreams.

» **Principle 5: "Say No to 1,000 Things."** Simplicity is the ultimate sophistication, according to Jobs. From the designs of the iPod to the iPhone, from the packaging of Apple's products to the functionality of the Apple website, innovation means eliminating the unnecessary so that the necessary may speak.

» **Principle 6: "Create Insanely Great Experiences."** Jobs has made Apple Stores the gold standard in customer service. The Apple Store has become the world's best retailer by introducing simple innovations any business can adopt to make deep, lasting emotional connections with its customers.

» **Principle 7: "Master the Message."** Jobs is the world's preeminent corporate storyteller, turning product launches into an art form. You can have the most innovative idea in the world, but if you cannot get people excited about it, your innovation doesn't matter.

You will find that two chapters have been dedicated to each of the seven principles. The first chapter within each principle reveals how that principle has driven Jobs's successful innovations, and the second chapter within each principle demonstrates how other professionals, leaders, and entrepreneurs have used the same principle to think differently in their personal and professional lives, enabling them to create and innovate in an impactful way. In these supporting chapters, the individuals and brands featured will challenge you to "think differently" about the following aspects of your life:

» Career (**Principle 1**: "Do What You Love")
» Vision (**Principle 2**: "Put a Dent in the Universe")
» Thoughts (**Principle 3**: "Kick-Start Your Brain")
» Customers (**Principle 4**: "Sell Dreams, Not Products")
» Design (**Principle 5**: "Say No to 1,000 Things")
» Experience (**Principle 6**: "Create Insanely Great Experiences")
» Story (**Principle 7**: "Master the Message")

These seven insanely different principles for breakthrough success will work only if, regardless of your title or job function, you see yourself as a brand. Whether you are an entrepreneur working out of a spare bedroom, a twenty-year veteran of an industry undergoing fundamental changes, a college graduate interviewing for that first job, or a small business owner looking for ideas to improve your enterprise, you represent the most important brand of all—yourself. How you talk, walk, and act reflects on that brand. Most important, how you *think* about yourself and your business will have the greatest impact on the creation of new ideas that will grow your business and improve the lives of your customers.

Steve Jobs is the CEO of two legendary brands—Apple and Pixar. But that's the Steve Jobs of today. Thirty-five years ago, he was assembling computers in his parents' house. Nobody viewed Jobs as a "brand" in 1976, but he did. Even at the age of twenty-one when Jobs and his pal Steve Wozniak were assembling printed circuit boards in the bedroom, kitchen, and garage of the home owned by Paul and Clara Jobs, young Steve saw himself as a brand. Jobs arranged for a corporate address by renting a mail-drop box in Palo Alto. He even hired an answering service so customers and vendors would think he was the owner of a legitimate business and not a young guy competing with his mom for access to the kitchen table. He wanted to "appear" bigger than he was because, in his own mind, he already was.[13]

Michelangelo is quoted as saying, "The greater danger for most of us lies not in setting our aim too high and falling short, but in setting our aim too low, and achieving our mark." Michelangelo, as with Jobs, could see things that others could not. Michelangelo looked at a marble block and saw David; Steve Jobs looked at a computer and saw a tool to unleash human potential.

What potential do you see in yourself? Imagine what you could achieve in business with the right insight and inspiration. Imagine where you could take your career if you had Steve Jobs guiding your decisions. *What would Steve do?* Let's find out.

Do What You Love

Have the courage to follow your heart
and intuition. They somehow already
know what you truly want to become.

—STEVE JOBS

CHAPTER 2

Follow Your Heart

Follow your bliss and the Universe will open doors for you where there were only walls.

—JOSEPH CAMPBELL, *THE POWER OF MYTH*

n 1972, Steve Jobs disappointed his parents when he dropped out of Reed College after only one semester. Reed is a small, liberal arts school in Portland, Oregon. In the 1970s, Reed was known for small classes, intelligent students, and an environment tolerant of different lifestyles and personalities. If you were a misfit in high school, you would have fit in at Reed.

Jobs's adoptive parents, Paul and Clara, were ready to spend their life savings to pay the expensive tuition bill at the private school. It was a commitment they had made to Jobs's biological mother, an unwed college student, seventeen years earlier. Neither Paul nor Clara had graduated from college. In fact, Paul had never graduated from high school. Jobs's birth mother signed the final adoption papers only when Paul and Clara promised that the baby boy would go to college. "After six months, I couldn't see the value in it," said Jobs. "I had no idea what I wanted to do with my life and no idea how college was going to help me figure it out. And here I was spending all of the money my parents had saved their entire life. So I decided to drop out and trust that it would all work out OK."[1]

Less than a decade later, Jobs, a college dropout, would be worth $100 million. In 1984, he and his business partner, Steve Wozniak, would be receiving the first National Medal of Technology from president Ronald Reagan. Jobs would go on to become a billionaire many times over, Disney's largest shareholder, *Fortune* magazine's CEO of the Decade, and a global icon whose influence over the computer, telecom, music, and entertainment industries would became legendary. Yes, it most certainly did work out.

A Font-ness for Calligraphy

Dropping out of Reed College set everything in motion for Jobs, but not for the reason you might think. Unlike his rival Bill Gates—another college dropout (he left Harvard to start Microsoft)—Jobs did not know what he wanted to do with his life. All he knew was that he was following his heart. "The minute I dropped out I could stop taking the required classes that didn't interest me, and begin dropping in on the ones that looked interesting," said Jobs.[2] For eighteen months, Jobs lived the stereotypical life of a 1970s college hippie, sleeping on the floor of his friends' dorm rooms, returning Coke bottles for grocery cash, and walking seven miles every Sunday to get a hot meal at a Hare Krishna temple.

If it sounds like a hard life, it wasn't. Jobs said he loved every minute of it because he followed his curiosity, letting his intuition guide his steps. Jobs's calling led him down a path that, at the time, seemed random and useless: he took a calligraphy course. Jobs had noticed posters around campus with beautiful typefaces, fonts, and styles. Reed had one of the best calligraphy departments in the country, and Jobs made a decision to pursue this beautiful art form—a decision that would change his life, not at the moment but in a way so profound that it would change the world.

"None of this [calligraphy] had even a hope of any practical application in my life," said Jobs. "But ten years later, when we were designing the first Macintosh computer, it all came back to me. And we designed it all into the Mac. It was the first computer with beautiful typography. If I had never dropped in on that single course in college, the Mac would have never had multiple typefaces or proportionally spaced fonts. And since Windows just copied the Mac, it's likely that no personal computer would have them. If I had never dropped out, I would have never dropped in on this calligraphy class, and personal computers might not have the wonderful typography that they do."[3]

Jobs took the calligraphy course for one reason: he found it fascinating. He did not know how the dots would connect in his life, but connect they did. Dots do not connect looking forward, Jobs would say. Dots connect only when you look backward. You must trust that, by following your curiosity, the pieces will ultimately fit.

It is likely your life would be different today had Jobs not taken that course. The Macintosh made personal computers accessible to everyone; it replaced command lines with color images and icons—the graphical user interface. It introduced a device called a mouse. In the hands of millions of creative "right-brain" people, Macintosh ushered in the era of desktop publishing, inspired new ways to teach students, and enriched the world immeasurably. And let's not forget that if it weren't for the success of Macintosh, Apple itself might have disappeared, Steve Jobs would have had nothing to return to in 1996, and the world would have been left without innovations such as the iPod, iPhone, iMac, Apple Store, and iPad. Even if you've never used a Mac, you can still thank Jobs for taking that calligraphy course—if he hadn't, your world might have looked very different from how it does today.

Jobs first told the calligraphy story publicly in 2005. It not only proved to be a turning point in our understanding of how Jobs develops insanely creative ideas but also contains the ultimate secret to success in business and in life: follow your heart. Do not dismiss this lesson as some fluffy, lightweight cliché. I assure you it's not. "What's the secret behind Jobs's creativity?" I once asked an analyst who has covered Apple for thirty years. "The calligraphy story tells you everything you need to know about what drives Steve Jobs," he said.

The Baron Way

Ron Baron heads a popular mutual fund company in New York City called the Baron Capital Group. The fund family has seven hundred thousand investors and $16 billion under management. Baron is an interesting guy. He's superwealthy (Baron purchased a home estimated at more than $100 million), and his annual investment conferences feature performers such as Elton John and Rod Stewart. Baron grew up in Asbury Park, New Jersey, and he has something else in common with another Asbury success story by the name of Bruce Springsteen: both have a grueling work ethic. Baron was able to turn $1,000 from shoveling snow and scooping ice cream into $4,000 by investing in the stock market.

Baron says his mantra is to invest in people, not buildings. "I recently read a commencement address that Steve Jobs made to Stanford's 2005 graduating class," Baron told the four thousand investors attending his annual conference on October 23, 2009. "I found it especially touching and on point regarding the sort of people in whom we invest," he said.[4] Baron recounted the story that Jobs told regarding the period of time when he resigned from Apple after a falling-out with the board, an event that left Jobs devastated. "The only thing that kept me going," Jobs said, "was that I loved what I did. The only way to do great work is to love what you do."[5] Baron closed with this thought: "It is our experience that the very best executives are the ones who are the most passionate about what they do . . . like Steve."

Over the last decade, Baron mutual funds have consistently outperformed the overall stock market, an accomplishment that very few funds can match. Baron's "gift" has been an uncanny ability to judge executives. That gift really comes down to character evaluation, judgments largely based on whether an executive and his or her management team have the passion to make their vision come true. That's "the Baron Way."

Two Steves with a Lot in Common

Steve Jobs has said that Silicon Valley, California, was a wonderful place to grow up. Not for the weather, the scenery, the schools, the proximity to the beaches or mountains, or any number of other things that make people fall in love with California. No,

Jobs thought Silicon Valley was a magical place because he was surrounded by engineers. Larry Lang was one of them. He lived down the street from Jobs. In a 1995 interview for the Smithsonian Oral History Project, Steve Jobs reflected on Lang and what it meant to grow up in early Silicon Valley:

> He was great. He used to build . . . these [electronic] products that you would buy in kit form. These Heathkits would come with detailed manuals about how to put this thing together, and all the parts would be laid out in a certain way and color coded. You'd actually build this thing yourself. I would say that this gave one several things. It gave one an understanding of what was inside a finished product and how it worked because it would include a theory of operation, but maybe even more importantly, it gave one the sense that one could build the things that one saw around oneself in the universe. These things were not mysteries anymore. I mean, you looked at a television set, you would think, "I haven't built one of those, but I could." My childhood was very fortunate in that way.[6]

Jobs had a "fortunate" childhood in that he could indulge in his passion for electronics, figuring out how things worked and how to make them better. He sought out friends with the same passion, including a young man named Steve Wozniak. "Woz" was five years older than Jobs and attending college while Jobs was a junior at Cupertino's Homestead High School, Woz's alma mater. They lived about a mile away from one another and were introduced by a mutual friend. "Steve and I got close right away," said Wozniak. "I remember Steve and I just sat on the sidewalk for the longest time, just sharing stories—mostly about pranks we'd pulled, and also what kind of

> " *I hope you'll be as lucky as I am. The world needs inventors—great ones. You can be one. If you love what you do and are willing to do what it takes, it's within your reach. And it'll be worth every minute you spend alone at night, thinking and thinking about what it is you want to design or build. It'll be worth it, I promise.*[7]
>
> —STEVE WOZNIAK, APPLE COFOUNDER "

electronic designs we'd done . . . We two Steves did have a lot in common. We talked about electronics, we talked about music we liked, and we traded stories."[8]

Jobs and the Woz shared a kinship that went well beyond their interest in electronics and their love of pranks. At its heart, their friendship was based on a mutual desire to do what they loved. According to the Woz, "I would design anything for free. I did all this stuff voluntarily, because I loved doing it. At college, people would want papers typed and I'd say: I'll type your paper. And I'd type it until four in the morning because I loved typing so much, and would never charge a cent. When you do things you love, you'll do them without worrying about money."[9]

Don't Settle

If you were lucky enough to have a rare conversation with Steve Jobs and you asked him what it takes to be a successful entrepreneur, what do you think Steve would say? You don't have to guess. He answered the question in 1995, in a rare interview with the Smithsonian Oral History Project:

> I think you should go get a job as a busboy or something until you find something you're really passionate about because it's a lot of work. I'm convinced that about half of what separates the successful entrepreneurs from the nonsuccessful ones is pure perseverance. It is so hard. You put so much of your life into this thing. There are such rough moments in time that I think most people give up. I don't blame them. It's really tough and it consumes your life. If you've got a family and you're in the early days of a company, I can't imagine how one could do it. I'm sure it's been done, but it's rough. It's pretty much an eighteen hour day job, seven days a week for awhile. Unless you have a lot of passion about this, you're not going to survive. You're going to give it up. So you've got to have an idea, or a problem or a wrong that you want to right that you're passionate about, otherwise

you're not going to have the perseverance to stick it through. I
think that's half the battle right there.[10]

Jobs says he was lucky, because he discovered what he loved
to do early in life. At thirty years of age, however, he got fired.
Following a power struggle, then Apple CEO John Sculley—whom
Jobs had brought in from Pepsi with the famous challenge, "Do
you want to spend the rest of your life selling sugared water or do
you want a chance to change the world?"—successfully convinced
the board to oust Jobs in May 1985. "What had been the focus of
my entire life was gone, and it was devastating," Jobs said.[11] Jobs
looked at the event as a public failure. He was humiliated. Then
something began to dawn on him: he loved what he did. He might
have been "rejected," but he was still in love. So, he started over
and began what he called the most creative period of his life, a
decade in which he launched several important innovations,
including a company that would revolutionize the entertainment
industry—Pixar.

Jobs summarized the importance of this creative period in his
life to a group of hopeful Stanford graduates in 2005:

> I'm convinced that the only thing that kept me going was that
> I loved what I did. You've got to find what you love. And that is
> as true for your work as it is for your lovers. Your work is going
> to fill a large part of your life, and the only way to be truly satis-
> fied is to do what you believe is great work. And the only way
> to do great work is to love what you do. If you haven't found it
> yet, keep looking. Don't settle. As with all matters of the heart,
> you'll know when you find it. And, like any great relationship,
> it just gets better and better as the years roll on. So keep looking
> until you find it. Don't settle."[12]

Most books and research studies on the topic of innovation
focus on arcane theories, methods, and techniques. In contrast, if
you study the life and words of Steve Jobs, the world's most exciting innovator, you find that innovation starts with something we
all have: passion. Capturing that passion and using it to transform

> *The money to me didn't really mean much. Pretty much I gave it all away to charities, to museums, to children's groups, to everything I could. It almost was like an evil to me. That was because it wasn't the motivation that I was after, and I wanted to remain the person that I would have been without Apple. So that's why I went back and did the teaching. I would have done teaching, were there no Apple.*[13]
>
> —STEVE WOZNIAK, APPLE COFOUNDER

ideas into products and services is where most world-changing innovations find their start. Passion is not a topic taught in M.B.A. classes, because it's not quantifiable—it doesn't fit easily into an Excel grid. Yet, Steve Jobs has repeatedly told us the secret to his success: do what you love.

Jobs once commented that, at the age of twenty-three, he was worth more than $1 million; one year later, his worth had soared to more than $10 million and went on to exceed $100 million by the time he turned twenty-five. Impressive though it may be, it wasn't important to him, because "I never did it for the money. Being the richest man in the cemetery doesn't matter to me. Going to bed at night saying we've done something wonderful—that's what matters to me."[14] What matters to you? If you pursue ideas with the goal of getting rich, you may have a small chance at succeeding. More likely, you'll give up when the inevitable hurdles arise. Jobs didn't give up when he got booted from Apple. He tried again because he could not imagine living a life without loving his work.

Innovation cannot occur in the absence of passion; without it, you have little hope of creating breakthrough ideas. Steve Jobs's secret to success—follow your passion—is so simple and intuitive that it's often overlooked or dismissed in grand management theories of innovation. Nevertheless, Jobs himself has emphatically reinforced this advice in his speeches, keynotes, and interviews.

Never underestimate the role passion plays in the success of your company, product, brand, or career. Is the passionate pursuit of a dream critical to your business success? Not necessarily. You may be very successful, at least financially, by following in the footsteps of others who made money in a particular industry. However, breakthrough innovation—the kind that moves society forward—will be much, much harder to achieve. Innovation occurs when someone is obsessively passionate about a particular subject, whether it be building computers that delight consumers, creating technologies that reduce the world's dependence on fossil fuels, developing lifesaving medicines, cultivating an exceptionally engaging workplace, or any number of other ventures that improve the human condition. The people who obsess over these ideas cannot imagine doing anything else. Thinking about the subject consumes them, energizes them, and ultimately inspires them to create breakthrough companies, products, and services.

If you still haven't found your passion, take Jobs's advice and keep looking. According to Jobs, your work is going to fill a big part of your life, and the only way to do great work is to follow your passion. If you haven't found it, don't settle. Steve Jobs did not discover his passion easily. He was obviously searching. Jobs attended nonrequired college classes, took trips to India, and even spent some time at a communelike apple farm in Oregon. Ultimately he married his love for electronics with his desire to put a dent in the universe. The result was a string of revolutionary devices that have impacted millions of satisfied Apple customers and investors, as well as countless millions of others who use Apple-inspired products. Find your passion. Once you do, you'll be on your way to creating insanely great ideas.

iLessons

1 What people do you know who have followed a passion? Study them. Are they coming up with creative and unique ideas? Do they seem to have more energy, enthusiasm, and excitement than others? Talk to them. You may get some insights on how they made a transition from working at something that didn't engage them to doing what they love.

2 Do you have interests outside of what you do for a living? If so, explore them. You may be surprised at how you can translate those passions into financial success.

3 Try something new this year. Take a course, read a book, or attend a conference that has nothing to do with your job.

CHAPTER 3

Think Differently About Your Career

Passions are irresistible. If you're paying attention to your life at all, the things you are passionate about won't leave you alone. They're the ideas, hopes, and possibilities your mind naturally gravitates to, the things you would focus your time and attention on for no other reason than that doing them feels right.[1]

—BILL STRICKLAND, AUTHOR, *MAKE THE IMPOSSIBLE POSSIBLE*

Calligraphy provided the catalyst for Steve Jobs to start thinking differently about the world and the role he would play in making it better. For Bill Strickland, a Pittsburgh, Pennsylvania, community leader and author, the catalyst was pottery. In 1965, Strickland was attending Oliver High School in the tough Manchester neighborhood of Pittsburgh. "Attending" is putting it kindly. Strickland was close to flunking out of school because he had missed so many classes. His life changed dramatically on a Wednesday afternoon when he walked by a classroom full of kilns, pots, and ceramics. The art teacher, Frank Ross, turned to the sixteen-year-old and asked, "How can I help you, son?" Little did Ross know that his question would launch the career of a man whose name would become synonymous with social innovation.

I asked Strickland how learning ceramics had been a turning point in his life. "I grew up in a tough black neighborhood in the inner city, and nobody ever made pottery. I had never seen it done before. It was magic," he said. "It told me that there was a whole world that I had not considered because it hadn't come across my field of vision. By meeting this man [Frank Ross] who introduced me to the experience, it set my life in motion and fueled my dreams. If it hadn't been for that pottery class, I'd be in jail or dead."[2]

Trusting Your Passion

Pottery literally saved Strickland's life. It also provided the foundation of an after-school arts program that Strickland started in 1968, the Manchester Craftsmen's Guild (MCG). Strickland ran the center—which introduced at-risk youths to the magic of pottery, photography, and painting—as he completed his undergraduate degree at the University of Pittsburgh.

After college, Strickland, a dean's list honor student, pursued an interest in flying. He took lessons and, seven years later, became a pilot for Braniff Airlines. He flew on weekends and returned to work at his center on Monday mornings. (Strickland likes to joke that he hasn't slept in thirty years.) Braniff fell on hard times (it would go out of business in 1982), and Strickland was laid off. He could have found another job as a pilot—a competing airline had offered him a position—but after thinking long and hard about it, Strickland realized that while he liked flying, it wasn't his calling, his destiny. He wanted to change the world. Strickland devoted himself full-time to his ventures, an after-school program, and a new adult-jobs training program. "I was teaching kids to throw pots and helping my neighbors get jobs," he said, "not because I needed to but because I *wanted* to. That made all the difference."

Strickland knows exactly what Steve Jobs meant when he said getting fired from Apple was the best thing that could have happened to him. According to Strickland, "Passion won't protect you against setbacks, but it will ensure that no failure is ever final." In Strickland's experience, setbacks become learning experiences, giving you the chance to refine your vision and to rethink your approach. Most important, Strickland says, setbacks remind you of how much your dreams mean to you.

Strickland is a "social innovator" whose name has been listed among the outstanding innovators in Pittsburgh history, including Andrew Carnegie, the steel magnate and philanthropist who developed an inexpensive and efficient way to produce steel; Henry Heinz, who, although best known for ketchup, developed steam-pressure cooking, railroad refrigeration cars, and vacuum canning techniques; Dr. Jonas Salk, who created the polio vaccine; and a young man named Chad Hurley, who developed a new way to distribute video over the Internet and called it YouTube. Strickland didn't invent a vaccine, a new technology, or breakthrough manufacturing techniques, but his theories on social change are extraordinary and impactful: "If you see people as assets and not liabilities, you can change the world in a profound way," he said.

"What role did passion play in the success of your social innovations?" I asked Strickland.

"Passion," he said, "is the emotional fuel that drives your vision. It's what you hold on to when your ideas are challenged and people turn you down, when you are rejected by 'experts' and the people closest to you. It's the fuel that keeps you going when there is no outside validation for your dream. I had a vision for creating a center that would alter the conversation about poor people. I wanted to redefine the way we think about poverty."

Strickland's organization, Manchester Bidwell, is not just a center. It's a cultural oasis. Twenty years after he started the center, Strickland had raised enough money to fulfill his dream of hiring an architect who had studied with Frank Lloyd Wright to build a new facility. The same architect designed the terminal at the Pittsburgh International Airport. Today Manchester Bidwell welcomes poor teenagers and people who are unemployed with beautiful art, custom furniture, gourmet kitchens, and a world-class, 350-seat concert hall that has hosted jazz greats such as Dizzy Gillespie, Herbie Hancock, and Wynton Marsalis.

Waterfalls also greet visitors. "If you want to involve yourself in the lives of people who have been given up on, you have to look like the solution and not the problem," Strickland says. "I think that welfare moms, poor kids, and ex-steelworkers deserve a fountain, and so I put a beautiful fountain in the courtyard. Water greets you as you enter. Water is life; water is human possibility. I created the kind of world that redeems the soul and gives people hope."

Strickland's contributions have not gone unrecognized. He has been invited to the White House, was awarded a Genius Grant by the MacArthur Foundation, and receives standing ovations wherever he speaks. Manchester Bidwell programs reach thousands of students and adults in the Pittsburgh area as well as nearly a dozen cities around the country that have affiliate centers based on the Manchester Bidwell philosophy, a philosophy that says everyone has a life that is worth something and can contribute to institutions that make up his or her community.

Strickland found this acclaim not because he set out to be an innovator but because he decided to pursue a calling that gave his life purpose. As a result, the institution he evolved is credited for creating a theory of social innovation that works: 80 percent of the more than three thousand schoolchildren who participate in the programs every year complete high school and attend college, while Manchester Bidwell places adults in many of Pittsburgh's largest companies, including the University of Pittsburgh, where Strickland serves as a trustee.

Strickland's nonprofit organization is now a required-reading case study in the entrepreneurship class at the Harvard Business School. Strickland says the bright young men and women at Harvard have given him their best shots, finding plenty of reasons why he should have failed. But they missed the magic ingredient to success. The new generation of entrepreneurs is learning a simple lesson in innovation that they will not find in PowerPoint presentations or spreadsheets, a lesson that both Strickland and Steve Jobs have been preaching for decades: follow your heart and don't settle for a path that is inconsistent with what you feel is your true destiny. "The fear of failure can stifle anyone's

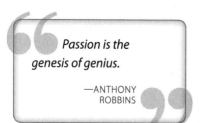

Passion is the genesis of genius.

—ANTHONY ROBBINS

dream of living an extraordinary life," says Strickland. "And the way you overcome that fear is by trusting your passion."

Failing 5,126 Times

Inventors are, by definition, failures. They fail far more often than they succeed. British inventor James Dyson was passionate about engineering, design, and vacuum cleaners. Yes, vacuums (there's a passion for everything). In 1978, he became frustrated with the performance of the vacuum cleaners on the market that lost suction as they picked up dirt. The problem was in the bag: it got clogged as it sucked up dirt and, as a result, would lose suction. Supported by his wife's salary as an art teacher, Dyson spent five years toiling on his idea, and on his 5,127th attempt, a working version of a dual-cyclone bagless vacuum cleaner emerged.

"I wanted to give up almost every day," Dyson said. "But one of the things I did when I was young was long distance running, from a mile up to ten miles. I was quite good at it, not because I was physically good, but because I had more determination. I learned that the moment you want to slow down is the moment you should accelerate. In long distance running, you go through a pain barrier. The same thing happens in research and development projects, or in starting any business. There's a terrible moment when failure is staring you in the face. And actually if you persevere a bit longer you'll start to climb out of it."[3]

Most people would have given up after the first few fits and starts, but Dyson plugged away. He reveled in failure, because that's what engineers do—they tinker, they test, they try out new ideas. They get a kick out of it. If you don't get a kick out of something, then do something else, because the odds of breakthrough success are against you. "I don't mind failure. I've always thought that schoolchildren should be marked by the number of failures they've had. The child who tries strange things and experiences lots of failures to get there is probably more creative," Dyson said.[4]

Dyson is so proud of his 5,126 failures that he memorialized his tribulations in a small brochure that comes with every vacuum cleaner his company sells—the Dyson Story. Although it took five years to build the product, that step was just the beginning. Dyson would face multiple rejections from established global companies such as Hoover, whose shortsighted executives saw only the immediate profits they were making from the sales of bags for vacuum cleaners. Hoover executives passed on Dyson's invention, even though they admitted that it worked nicely. Dyson has said that anger and frustration are prime motivators—as is necessity. Since no company would buy his invention, Dyson sold it directly to consumers, and not in the United Kingdom but Japan. The Japanese became enamored of the Dyson's styling and functionality. The Dyson did eventually become a hit in the inventor's home market and reached the rank of bestselling vacuum cleaner in the United Kingdom, outpacing the cleaners offered by manufacturers that had once rejected the idea. Hoover would later make a blunt admission: an executive said the company should have bought Dyson's idea and crushed it so it would never see the light of day. That way Hoover's dominance would remain intact. For many leaders, innovation—new ideas that improve people's lives—is not and will never be part of their company's DNA.

A *Forbes* reporter once asked Dyson why a lot of companies say they want to hire innovators but end up hiring "company men," people who had been doing the same function at other companies for years. According to Dyson:

> The trouble is you have human resource departments and headhunters, and you have to fill out forms, and then they try to recruit people that match what's said on the forms. I fight against it all the time, this idea that when you take someone on, you take someone on who's had experience in your field. There's a horrible expression, "hit the ground running." I hate that idea. In some cases, they might be perfect for you, but in most cases, the person's probably had the wrong sort of experience, and you've got to retrain them. So I much prefer to hire people

straight from university, or people who have been working in another field but did some interesting work. It's very difficult to get recruiters to think that way.[5]

"Surprise Me"

Dyson's observation mirrors the way Apple chose to recruit employees. Sharon Aby worked for Apple from 1983 to 1996, three of those years as a recruiter. In a personal interview she told me:

> We didn't want someone who desired to retire with a gold watch. We wanted entrepreneurs, demonstrated winners (even those who had just graduated but excelled in college), high-energy contributors who defined their previous role in terms of what they contributed and not what their titles were. We didn't hire from one industry. We had a collection of people who represented all walks of life. We believed that ingenuity came from everywhere. The main quality: expectation of excellence. We looked for people who were excited to create new things. As recruiters, we didn't settle. I fought with some managers who wanted to fill a role quickly to get a project moving, but if it took six months to find the best, they'd have to wait. We looked for people who had an energy for creating something new. Our motto was, "Surprise me."[6]

Steve Jobs, Bill Strickland, and James Dyson took different paths to successful innovations, but each individual story teaches the same lesson: Don't let your obsession die. Embrace it, revel in it, and use it to stand apart. Follow your heart and not the crowd. When you choose a college major solely to satisfy your parents, you raise the risk of becoming bored instead of energized by your classes. When you choose to open a business or franchise simply because your neighbor is doing well at it, you increase the likelihood of failure. And when you enter a career because your brother-in-law made a lot of money in it last year, you increase the odds of living an unsatisfied life. Above all, passion will keep you going when the inevitable hurdles and setbacks threaten to derail your dream.

Yum-O!

The Food Network star Rachael Ray has become a ubiquitous media presence with her fun, perky, and approachable personality. Ray was literally raised in a kitchen, because her family was in the restaurant business. The Ray family owned several restaurants in Cape Cod, Massachusetts. Ray began her cooking career in 1995 at the candy counter at a Macy's department store in New York City. She held several food-related positions before deciding she would rather live upstate than in the big city. Ray, who had a reputation as a tireless and passionate worker, became a food buyer for a gourmet food store in Albany.

Sometimes necessity is the mother of innovation—which was the case behind Ray's most popular idea—but when passion meets necessity, it's magic. Ray was selling more and more prepared dishes that she would assemble and cook herself. As the prepared foods became more popular, the store's fresh grocery sales began to decline. "So, I went around and asked all of my customers, 'Why do you not cook? Why are you not buying the groceries?' And everybody said the same thing: 'I have no time, and it's easier to cook the prepared meals.'"[7]

> *When your life is on course with its purpose, you are your most powerful.*
>
> —OPRAH

Ray's innovative idea was to offer classes called "30 Minute Meals." Ray figured that if people were willing to wait thirty minutes for a pizza delivery, they would be receptive to recipes that took them only thirty minutes to make. Ray hit a snag, though. No chef in the local area would teach the classes for little money, so she added another job to her position and taught the classes herself. A local television station offered her a cooking segment on the evening news, and she jumped at the chance, even though the station didn't pay her a dime other than a small stipend for ingredients. In fact, Ray lost money on the segments. Not getting paid didn't matter. Ray intuitively understood that following her passion would lead to better things—she wasn't sure where the path would lead, but she had faith that pursing her passion would make all the difference.

No amount of faith could have helped Ray predict what happened next. The local Albany show led to a segment on NBC's *Today* show. A call from the Food Network followed, and Ray signed on to host a show called "30 Minute Meals." Today Ray is the star of several shows on the channel, has sold millions of books, edits her own magazine, hosts a daytime talk show, and distributes a line of cooking ware. By the time you read this, it would not be surprising to learn that Ray has added yet another concept to her growing empire.

In 2008, Ray appeared at the Women's Conference in Long Beach, California. The conference is an annual event that Maria Shriver created to inspire women to live their best lives. It attracts hundreds of women, many of whom are entrepreneurs. During a panel discussion, actress Valerie Bertinelli asked Ray for the best piece of advice she could offer the women in the audience. Ray said, "I think that if you love what you do, the magic part happens organically. You go to work and you work harder than the next guy or the next lady because you love what you do. And, never waste your time on the things that you can't change or the opinions other people have of you."[8]

> *When you are inspired by some great purpose, some extraordinary project, all your thoughts break their bonds: your mind transcends limitations, your consciousness expands in every direction, and you find yourself in a new, great, and wonderful world. Dormant forces, faculties, and talents become alive, and you discover yourself to be a greater person by far than you ever dreamed yourself to be.*
>
> —PATANJALI

Starting a business is fraught with setbacks. But if you're following your inner voice—the thoughts that "won't leave you alone," to borrow from Strickland—failure is never final and, as Ray demonstrates, creative solutions are around the corner.

Homeless to Multimillionaire

Steve Jobs admits he was lucky to discover his passion at a young age. Most people are not as fortunate. They struggle with the question, "What am I passionate about?" Finding one's passion in business is not always easy. How do you know when you find it? For advice I turned to a man who had such a compelling rags-to-riches story that Hollywood turned it into a movie starring one of the world's most notable actors, Will Smith. Chris Gardner's book, *The Pursuit of Happyness*, inspired a movie with the same title. (*Happiness* is purposely spelled wrong in the title because it is the way it was spelled on the front of a dubious day-care center where Gardner dropped off his son while he struggled to find work.)

While pursuing an unpaid internship program at the brokerage firm Dean Witter Reynolds in 1981, Gardner spent a year on the streets with his two-year-old son. (In an interview for an article I wrote for *Bloomberg BusinessWeek* online, Gardner told me the movie producers cast a five-year-old boy in the role of Gardner's son so the two could have a dialogue, but in reality the boy was still in diapers.)[9] Gardner and his son sought shelter at night in the bathroom of a BART subway station in Oakland, California. Nobody at Gardner's workplace had a clue. Gardner eventually became a stockbroker. Two years later, he left for Bear Stearns, where he became a top earner. In 1987, he founded his own brokerage firm in Chicago, Gardner Rich. Today Gardner is a multimillionaire, a motivational speaker, a philanthropist, and an international businessman who launched a private equity fund that invests in South Africa. His partner in the fund is Nelson Mandela. Not bad for a guy who, six years before founding his own brokerage firm, was "fighting, scratching, and crawling my way out of the gutter with a baby on my back."[10]

"What's the one thing that changed your life?" I asked Gardner during an interview for the *BusinessWeek* profile.

"It's passion," he told me. "Passion is everything. In fact, you've got to be borderline fanatical about what you do."

Gardner's advice to entrepreneurs or career changers: "Be bold enough to find the one thing that you are passionate about. It might not be what you were trained to do. But be bold enough to do the one thing. Nobody needs to dig it but you."

"How do you know you found your passion?" I asked.

"Find something you love to do so much, you can't wait for the sun to rise to do it all over again."[11]

Think about that last quote. Are you doing something you love so much that you can't wait for the sun to rise to do it all over again? If not, what would Steve Jobs say? He would say, "Keep looking; don't settle."

Innovation requires creativity and energy. Donald Trump once said that without passion, you have no energy, and without energy, you have nothing. Loving what you do is the fuel that you need to keep working, keep striving, keep reaching for the life you imagine. Passion is not something you talk about; it's something you feel, and everyone can see it in you. When you're passionate about your work, you light up a room—it's in your eyes, your body language, your vocal inflection. It has the power to transform your world and, as a result, the worlds of the people you touch.

Finding Your Element

In his book *The Element*, Dr. Ken Robinson recounts a wonderful story about an eight-year-old girl, Gillian, who was having trouble in school: missing deadlines, testing poorly, and becoming easily distracted. This true story took place in the 1930s. School administers thought that Gillian had a problem and should be placed in a school for kids with learning disorders. Gillian's parents took her to the school psychologist, who questioned Gillian's mother for about twenty minutes, glancing at Gillian and making mental notes during the conversation. He then asked Gillian to remain in the office for a few minutes while he talked with her mother privately. Before he left the office, he turned on the radio. There was a window to the office, and he and Gillian's mother watched the little girl from the hallway. "Gillian was on her feet, moving around the room to the music. The two adults stood watching quietly for a few minutes, transfixed by the girl's grace. Anyone would have noticed there was something natural—even primal—about Gillian's movements. At last, the psychologist turned to Gillian's mother and said, 'You know, Mrs. Lynne, Gillian isn't sick. She's a dancer. Take her to a dance school.'"[12]

The little girl did attend dance school, the very next week. The little girl, Gillian Lynne, never lost her passion for dance. She entered the Royal Ballet School in London, met Andrew Lloyd Webber, and went on to create some of the most successful musical-theater productions in history, including *Cats* and *The Phantom of the Opera*. "Gillian wasn't a problem child. She didn't need to go away to a special school. She just needed to be who she really was," writes Robinson.[13]

Robinson and other scientists who study the field of human potential agree that the most successful among us are those who pursued their passions, regardless of the paycheck. "They pursued them because they couldn't imagine doing anything else with their lives," says Robinson. "Many people set aside their passions to pursue things they don't care about for the sake of financial security. The fact is, though, that the job you took because it 'pays the bills' could easily move offshore in the coming decade. If you have never learned to think creatively and to explore your true capacity, what will you do then?"[14] Robinson believes in order to compete in the global knowledge economy, where creativity and innovation will be rewarded, we have to think differently about how we approach education and our own careers and business choices.

No one person is good at everything, but every person is good at something. According to Robinson and other experts, the key to successful innovation is matching your passion with an aptitude—a core competency. Sometimes discovering your strengths requires a nudge in the right direction, a reminder to follow your innate ability. Take the case of one of my clients, SanDisk CEO Eli Harari.

SanDisk is one of the many technology companies I have had the good fortune to work with over the years. The company is the largest maker of flash memory cards that store pictures, video, and music on everything from digital cameras to smartphones. Cofounder Eli Harari is credited as the "father of flash." He good-naturedly likes to remind me that his innovation launched the digital camera revolution. Harari is a good example of passion meeting aptitude. Harari, an Israeli immigrant, came to America with $1,000 in his pocket, earned a Ph.D. in solid-state science from Princeton, where he studied physics and semiconductors, and traveled west to California to change the world. Since he had a passion for inventing things, he decided to channel his passion into building the next great . . . fishing rod. That's right, a rod and a reel. Not just any rod, mind you, but the ultimate retractable one. He decided to pursue this idea because he had read that America was home to twenty-six million fishermen. Harari, however, had never been fishing. After several failed attempts to invent a new fishing rod, Harari's focus on fishing wasn't flying with his wife. She set him straight. Their conversation went something like this:

"How many people on the earth know what you know about physics and semiconductors?" she asked.

"Maybe one hundred," Harari responded.

"Why don't you focus on your core competency?" she suggested.

She was right, Harari thought. Today SanDisk holds hundreds of patents that spin off hundreds of millions of dollars a year in royalties; it makes one of every two flash memory cards sold in the world and generates billions of dollars in annual revenue. Harari's passion for invention turned into innovations only when it was properly channeled to match his strengths.

Passion isn't enough, but when passion meets aptitude, it can indeed change the world. Steve Jobs married his passion for computers with his innate skill in electronics, design, and marketing—the ultimate combination of skills to translate the nascent personal computer market into tools for everyday people.

I Can Do It. I Understand It. I Like It.

James Patterson's first novel, released in 1976, sold about ten thousand copies. Today one out of seventeen hardcover books bought in the United States is a Patterson novel. Patterson, a former advertising executive, has transformed the author's role in the world of book publishing and introduced innovative ways of creating new titles, including the idea of using coauthors who specialize in a different series or genre. The *New York Times Magazine* observed that this type of collaboration might be seen as normal in advertising or other creative industries such as television, but bringing the approach to novels was novel at the time.

Patterson's passion for writing commercially appealing crime fiction kept him going in the face of numerous rejections; one after another after another publishing company turned down the manuscript for his first novel, *The Thomas Berryman Number*. After more than a dozen rejections, the novel was published, and Patterson, who wrote on a typewriter in his small New York City apartment, would go on to win a prestigious Edgar Award from the Mystery Writers of America. Millions of Patterson fans would never have the satisfaction of reading one of his thrillers had Patterson not followed his heart after graduating from Manhattan College in 1969. Patterson attended Vanderbilt University to pursue a career as a professor in English literature but dropped out after one year. "I had found two things that I loved, reading and writing. If I had become a college professor, I knew I was going to wind up killing them both off," Patterson said.[16]

> *I was lucky to get into computers when it was a very young and idealistic industry. There weren't many degrees offered in computer science, so people in computers were brilliant people from mathematics, physics, music, zoology, whatever. They loved it, and no one was really in it for the money.*[15]
>
> —STEVE JOBS

Patterson says he enjoyed reading commercially popular books such as *The Exorcist* and *The Day of the Jackal*. He reached the conclusion that "I can do this. I understand it, and I like it."[17] Steve Jobs went through a similar progression in his quest to commercialize computers. His confidence convinced him that he could do it. He understood electronics—not as well as Wozniak, who built the Apple I and Apple II, but close. (Jobs entered a science fair in junior high and built a silicon-controlled rectifier, a device to control alternating current.)[18] And above all, he liked it. Passion meets aptitude. The combination can, absolutely, change the world.

How Large Companies Can Encourage Garage Thinking

Jobs and Wozniak ultimately left their jobs to start Apple (Jobs left Atari, Wozniak left Hewlett-Packard). However, following your passion does not mean giving notice and setting up shop in your garage. A friend of mine is a multimillionaire and could easily live on a beach for the rest of his life. He continues to work every day at a Fortune 500 company in Silicon Valley because he is an engineer, loves his job, and would not dream of doing anything else. He is not interested in starting his own business because it would never provide the resources available to him in a firmly established company that leads the market. Another good friend is the top salesperson at her company and, again, has no intention of starting her own firm. She is passionate about sales provided she sells a product or service that she believes offers real value for her customers. You see, most people do not leave companies because they want to start a business in their garage. They leave because they are uninspired.

Many forward-thinking companies promote *intrapreneurship*, encouraging their employees to act like entrepreneurs, even in a larger corporate setting. These firms give employees the time to pursue their passions and encourage risk taking to create innovations. In fact, Steve Jobs discussed this concept as early as 1985. In an interview for *Newsweek*, Jobs said, "The Macintosh team was what is commonly known as intrapreneurship—only a few years before the term was coined—a group of people going, in essence, back to the garage, but in a large company."[19]

Google is one company that cultivates intrapreneurs. In a true workplace innovation, Google engineers are encouraged to devote 20 percent of their time—one day per week—to doing what they are really passionate about. Google believes in this concept so deeply that it is a selling point in the company's recruiting efforts. "Innovation Time Off" meets the engineers' need for meaning and self-fulfillment while encouraging the development of innovative products that will benefit the company. Gmail, Google News, Google Suggest, AdSense for Content, and Orkut are just some of the innovations that have been spawned during this creative time. Google executives credit the 20 percent time allotment for 50 percent of Google's new products.

Some companies do not have a system for intrapreneurship but welcome new ways of thinking about the traditional employee-employer relationship. When I worked as a vice president for Ketchum, a global public relations firm, the company recognized my passion for communications and storytelling, allowing me to carve out a unique role as a media-training, messaging, and presentation-skills coach for its largest clients. The company even allowed me to pursue my passion as an entrepreneur and worked with me to create a unique hybrid role in which I spent part of my time on Ketchum projects and the rest of my time building my brand as an author and speaker. Eventually I did leave Ketchum as my own company required more attention. Rather than seeing my departure as a loss, though, Ketchum contracted with me to provide services to its clients, both established clients who still wanted to work with me and new ones. The relationship has evolved to meet both of our needs—and to satisfy my passion.

Don't Waste Your Time Living Someone Else's Life

On a trip to New York City in 2009, I met with a young entrepreneur who wanted some help in crafting the message behind his start-up, an online competition community. I thought it was pretty bold that Craig Escobar was attempting to launch a new company in a recessionary environment, the worst economic period in America since the Great Depression. "I was a successful financial adviser, drove a brand-new Mercedes SL500, and managed a big team, for a twenty-three-year-old," Escobar told me.[20]

"A lot of people would love to be in your position. Why did you leave?" I asked.

Escobar opened his notebook and passed me a document that I immediately recognized—Steve Jobs's 2005 commencement address at Stanford University.

"I stayed with my career for a couple of years after I read this because everybody was proud of me and I was making good money," said Escobar, "but I didn't love what I did. The passion just wasn't there. When Steve Jobs got fired from Apple, he said the only thing that kept him going was that he loved what he did, and he advised all of us to find that one thing that we love to do. Don't settle. I was comfortable and 'successful,' but not fulfilled. Those words inspired me to find a path that would inspire me."

Escobar decided to combine three of his passions: entertainment, competition, and entrepreneurship. Escobar and his best friend, Clint, a musician, came up with an idea for a website that would allow musicians to compete online. "My stomach dropped when I found out that there were other companies doing something similar online," Escobar said. However, he remembered that Jobs didn't give up after being forced out of Apple. Indeed, Jobs continued to innovate, starting NeXT and Pixar. Escobar transformed his original idea from a music-only competition to a broader competition in which performers could compete in a range of categories, including music, comedy, and even business presentations.

Escobar's story is not unusual. I don't think Steve Jobs himself realized the impact his words would have on people around the world: men and women, leaders and managers, entrepreneurs and would-be entrepreneurs, who were reminded that the best ideas are created by those who are following their dreams. "Your time is limited, so don't waste it living someone else's life," Jobs said. "Stay hungry. Stay foolish."

iLessons

1 Do what you love. If you haven't found it yet, keep looking. Don't settle.

2 If you're an employee stuck in a job you hate, take steps today, even small ones, to find a company or position more compatible with your skills and your true calling. You will never be inspired enough to create exciting innovations if you are not passionate about your role.

3 If you manage a team of people in a large corporation, develop intrapreneurs, giving people the time, resources, and encouragement to follow their passions and develop new ideas and, above all, the confidence to risk failure.

Put a Dent in the Universe

We're gambling on our vision, and we would
rather do that than make "me-too" products.
For us, it's always the next dream.

—STEVE JOBS

CHAPTER 4

Inspire Evangelists

> **Imagination is the beginning of creation. You imagine what you desire; you will what you imagine; and at last you create what you will.**
>
> —GEORGE BERNARD SHAW

Apple successfully launched the personal computer revolution with the introduction of Apple II in June 1977. The Apple II, designed by Steve Wozniak, had a screen, a built-in keyboard, color graphics, sound, and a floppy disk drive. It also made "microcomputers" accessible and affordable and became one of the most successful personal computers of its time. It established Apple as a legitimate brand and paved the way for Apple's blockbuster IPO in 1980 and for the introduction of Macintosh in 1984.

At the time of the Apple II's launch, however, Apple was still small, occupying office space behind The Good Earth restaurant in Cupertino. As its name suggested, The Good Earth was an early entry in the healthful food category, well known in "the Valley" for its granola pancakes, vegetarian dishes, and whole-grain breads, which it served long before these items would be staples in casual restaurant chains around the country. The Good Earth was a favorite hangout for those early Apple employees, including cofounder Steve Jobs. The restaurant is long gone, and Apple has since moved to its global headquarters on One Infinite Loop, one mile away from its original space, but an extraordinary lunch meeting still burns brightly in the mind of Rob Campbell, CEO of Voalté, a company that builds wireless applications for the health care industry.

In 1977, Campbell—who would later develop PowerPoint—was a twenty-two-year-old programmer with a small software company in Denver. Campbell had created the first general accounting software program for the Apple II. He was excited about the emerging class of personal computers and began searching for a position at one of the companies at the forefront of the revolution. Steve Jobs had taken an interest in the young whiz kid and invited Campbell to meet with him in California.

Today anyone who got called by Steve Jobs personally would be on the next plane to the San Jose airport. In 1977, though, Jobs wasn't the legend that he is today, and Campbell did not know much about him, so he did his due diligence and, before meeting with Jobs, visited Apple competitors Tandy and Commodore. He first paid a visit to Tandy in Fort Worth, Texas.

"What is your vision for the personal computer?" Campbell asked Tandy executives.

"We think it could be the next big thing on everyone's wish list for the holiday season. It's the next CB radio!" they responded.[1]

Tandy owned Radio Shack, which it purchased in 1963. In the next twenty years, the number of Radio Shack outlets would grow to more than seven thousand around the world. The seventies were a big growth period for Radio Shack, largely because of the popularity of the CB (citizens band) radio in 1977. Tandy called CB the "survival tool for the energy crunch." Thanks to the success of the CB, Tandy had just come out of its strongest holiday season and was looking forward to the next year's hit. In the queue was the TRS-80 microcomputer. The first Radio Shack ads for the computer called it "affordable" at $600 ($2,000 in today's dollars) and targeted the computer for the school, home, office, and hobbyist markets.

CB radios were in full craze that year. Long-haul truckers had popularized the radios, which showed up frequently in popular culture, including movies such as *Smokey and the Bandit* and *The Gumball Rally* and songs such as C. W. McCall's "Convoy." The CB radio was one of the hottest fads of the seventies, and Tandy thought it had another fad on its hands with the new personal computer. Fads come and go, and Campbell wasn't inspired by the idea of participating in one.

Campbell followed his uninspiring meeting at Tandy with a visit to Commodore. Commodore made cash registers and had recently introduced its entry into the personal computer market in June 1977. The computer was called PET, short for Personal Electronic Transactor (not exactly an exciting name, but Commodore felt the acronym would make the technology warm and fuzzy). The PET was Commodore's first full-featured computer. At the time, Commodore's stock was trading at less than a dollar a share.

"What is your vision for the personal computer?" Campbell asked Commodore executives.

"We think it could help our stock rise above two dollars a share!" they said excitedly.

Stocks rise and fall, and Campbell wasn't inspired by the idea of helping a company raise its stock price.

"Next I met with Steve and Mike Markkula," Campbell told me. Markkula was twelve years older than Jobs and had built up some wealth after cashing in stock options from his previous employer, Intel. Markkula invested $250,000 in Apple, became part owner and employee number three, and acted as management mentor to the younger Jobs. Markkula also played a significant role in the technology advances of the Apple II. According to Steve Wozniak, it was Markkula who persuaded him to design a floppy disk drive for the computer, a feature that differentiated the Apple II from its competitors. Campbell sat down for lunch with Markkula and Jobs, a "long-haired kid in blue jeans."

"What is your vision for the personal computer?" Campbell asked the Apple executives.

Campbell says what happened next still gives him goose bumps, more than thirty years later.

"Steve Jobs was a magical storyteller. For the next hour, he talked about how personal computers were going to change the world. He painted a picture of how it would change everything about the way we worked, educated our children, and entertained ourselves. You couldn't help but to buy in."

Campbell did buy in and went to work for Apple.

"What is the one thing that set Steve Jobs apart from other leaders?" I asked Campbell.

"Steve has vision," he said. "He sees over the horizon."[2]

See Over the Horizon

Steve Jobs did not invent the personal computer, nor did he invent the MP3 player, yet he innovated around those devices with the introduction of the Mac and the iPod. Steve Jobs did not invent smartphones, nor did he invent the tablet computer, yet he innovated around those devices with the introduction of the iPhone and the iPad. Steve Jobs did not invent computer animation, nor was he the first to sell computers directly to consumers, yet he innovated around those ideas with the introduction of Pixar and Apple Stores. Although few large companies are as closely associated with their founder as Apple is, Jobs is not a one-man show. He knows what he doesn't know. Jobs "sees over the horizon" and hires people—the best in the business—who are inspired to make the dream a reality. Every innovation at Apple starts with a big, bold vision and a heavy dose of inspiration.

Innovation does not easily fit in a single package created, designed, and assembled by one individual. Rarely are new ideas commercialized without an inspired team of creative and passionate evangelists who turn those ideas into reality. Everyone knows Steve Jobs, but early in Apple's history, partners such as Steve Wozniak, Jeff Raskin, Mike Markkula, and Daniel Kottke shared Jobs's vision of putting computers into the hands of everyday people. Without them, there would be no Macintosh and no Apple. Today Jobs is surrounded by creative, bright individuals such as the brilliant designer Jonathan Ive, president Tim Cook, marketing vice president Phil Schiller, and many others. Remember, inventions or ideas become innovations when they are turned into useful products or

> " You can dream, create, design, and build the most wonderful place in the world, but it takes people to make the dream a reality.
>
> —WALT DISNEY

services that improve people's lives. No single idea that Jobs ever had would have stood a chance of becoming a successful innovation had he not been able to persuade others to join him on his journey. And nobody would have joined Jobs without having been inspired by his vision.

"Steve has a power of vision that is almost frightening," in the words of Trip Hawkins, former Apple vice president of strategy and marketing. "When Steve believes in something, the power of that vision can literally sweep aside any objections or problems. They just cease to exist."[3] If passion is the fuel that gives innovators the energy to pursue their dreams, vision provides the direction that inspires evangelists to join the innovator on the journey.

Educating the Consumer

Apple's Preliminary Confidential Offering Memorandum is a thirty-eight-page document that Apple used in 1977 to seek a private placement of funds to facilitate the company's growth. The document provides a fascinating glimpse into Apple's early history and reveals the vision behind the Apple II and the personal computer market. The memorandum acknowledged that the "average Joe" has very little concept of the "functions he can perform or the resultant benefits to be obtained from operating his own, personal, home computer."[4] It highlights the benefits the average person would enjoy should Apple become successful in building a computer for the mass market. Amazingly, most of Apple's predications turned out to be true. Here is how the Apple memorandum described the ways the personal computer would change the world:

- » Personal enjoyment
- » Increased variety of entertainment
- » Time, money saved
- » Better financial decisions
- » Increased leisure time
- » Security of personal information
- » Elimination of wasted paper, energy, and storage space

» Improved standard of living
» Increased learning efficiency
» Reduced pollution[5]

The document was drafted at a time when the personal computer was largely relegated to the hobbyist market, a small group of sophisticated technical wizards who were capable of designing, constructing, and programming their own equipment. According to the memorandum, "The major distinguishing characteristic of the true home computing market is the relative lack of technical, mathematical, or scientifically related interest of the user. In addition, due to the general lack of knowledge of the benefits offered by the computer, most potential customers do not have even the slightest desire to purchase one today. It will therefore be necessary to educate the market regarding the benefits derived from ownership. It is forecasted that indeed, by 1985, a household using a computer will have significant advantages over one that doesn't."[6] One could just imagine how a young Steve Jobs inspired Rob Campbell with such a vision.

A Vision That Launched the Computer Revolution

"I can tell you almost to the day when the computer revolution as I see it started, the revolution that today has changed the lives of everyone," writes Steve Wozniak in his biography, *iWoz*. "It happened at the very first meeting of a strange, geeky group of people called the Homebrew Computer Club in March 1975. This was a group of people fascinated with technology and the things it could be . . . After my first meeting, I started designing the computer that would later be known as the Apple I. It was that inspiring. Almost from the beginning, Homebrew had a goal: to bring computer technology within the range of the average person, to make it so people could afford to have a computer and do things with it."[7]

Wozniak did not attend those meetings alone. He took along his friend Steve Jobs. Jobs shared the Homebrew vision and made it Apple's mantra for the next three decades: to put computers into the hands of everyday people. The vision was simple, bold, and intoxicating. The "vision" was not posted in the hallways, but everyone knew it. In 1984, the vision would take center stage in Apple's marketing campaign for the Macintosh with the tagline "A computer for the rest of us." A bold vision inspires team members and turns them into evangelists for a project. And evangelists can, beyond doubt, change the world.

A vision is much different from a mission statement. A mission statement describes what you make; a vision is how you will make the world a better place. According to Jobs, there is no "system" of innovation at Apple. Instead, "You hire good people who will challenge each other every day to make the best products possible. That's why you don't see any big posters on the walls around here, stating our mission statement. Our corporate culture is simple."[8]

We Were Revolutionaries

When they cofounded Apple, Jobs was twenty-one and Wozniak was twenty-six. As Leander Kahney describes, "Wozniak was the hardware genius, the chip-head engineer, but Jobs understood the whole package. Thanks to Jobs's ideas about design and advertising, the Apple II became the first successful mass-market computer for ordinary consumers."[9] Kahney points out that when Jobs moved on to the Macintosh project, he had not invented the graphical user interface that is a feature of almost every computer today (including Windows machines), but he brought it to the masses. "This has been Jobs's stated goal from the very beginning: to create easy-to-use technology for the widest possible audience."[10]

As you piece together the puzzle of Jobs's success, a clearer picture begins to emerge. Yes, Jobs "sees beyond the horizon," but you could see to Pluto and still fail to create anything of value unless you can inspire others to follow your vision. Everyone (employees, customers, and investors) understands exactly what Apple stands for. People have known since the beginning, because Jobs's vision has never wavered. Thirty years after attending those Homebrew meetings with Wozniak, Jobs made it clear that his original vision continued to drive all of Apple's efforts. In a 2004 interview for

> *We started out to get a computer in the hands of everyday people, and we succeeded beyond our wildest dreams.*
>
> —STEVE JOBS

The Guardian, Jobs said, "There's a very strong DNA within Apple, and that's about taking state-of-the-art technology and making it easy for people."[11]

"Big companies like IBM and Digital Equipment didn't hear our social message," wrote Wozniak. "And they didn't have a clue how powerful a force this small computer vision could be. In this, we were revolutionaries."[12]

How Xerox Grabbed Defeat from the Jaws of Victory

In 1979, when Jobs was twenty-four, his vision led to a series of events that changed the way all of us use computers. "I visited Xerox PARC. It was a very important visit," Jobs said. "I remember being shown a rudimentary graphical user interface. It was incomplete, some of it wasn't even right, but the germ of the idea was there. Within ten minutes, it was so obvious that every computer would work this way someday. You knew it with every bone in your body. Now, you could argue about the number of years it would take, you could argue about who the winners and losers in terms of companies in the industry might be, but I don't think rational people could argue that every computer would work this way someday."[13]

Jobs returned to Apple like a man on fire, ignited with a new sense of purpose. He wanted his entire programming team to get a tour of PARC (Palo Alto Research Center). Based in Palo Alto, California, PARC was and continues to be a research and development arm for Xerox. PARC scientists developed the laser printer, the Ethernet, and many other innovations that would find their way into our world. In the late 1970s, PARC had developed a graphical user interface (GUI) that allowed people to interact with computers via icons on the screen instead of text-based commands. Once Jobs saw it, he knew it would help satisfy his vision to put computers into the hands of everyday people.

At least one PARC founder, Adele Goldberg, warned Xerox executives that they were about to give away the kitchen sink. Goldberg's superiors dismissed her concerns and instructed her to show Jobs and his team around. It would turn out to be one of the worst decisions in corporate history (unless your name is Apple). Jobs and his team were escorted on a tour of PARC. Among the innovations they saw was a pointing device called a mouse that could move a cursor around a screen that had graphical icons. PARC scientist Larry Tesler said, "After an hour looking at demos they [Apple programmers] understood our technology and what it meant more than any Xerox executive understood after years of showing it to them."[14] Tesler, spotting an opportunity to be part of history, soon joined Apple.

"Basically they were copier heads that just had no clue about a computer or what it could do," said Jobs. "And so they just grabbed defeat from the greatest victory in the computer industry. Xerox could have owned the entire computer industry today."[15] Xerox scientists missed the full implications of the technology under their very noses because it didn't fit into a bigger vision. Passion is meaningless without vision. Innovation demands both.

Jobs infused the Macintosh team with a vision and found the right people, the most brilliant engineers, to join him on the crusade. When the team strayed from the vision, he refocused their attention. In a 1996 PBS documentary, *Triumph of the Nerds*, Andy Hertzfeld, a member of the Macintosh design team, said "Steve was upset that the Mac took too long to boot up when you first turned it on, so he tried motivating Larry Kenyon [another Apple designer] by telling him, 'You know how many millions of people are going to buy this machine? It's going to be millions of people, and let's imagine that you can make it boot five seconds faster. That's five seconds times a million every day. That's fifty lifetimes. If you can shave five seconds off that, you're saving fifty lives.' And so it was a nice way of thinking about it, and we did get it to go faster."[16]

We Felt like David Fighting Goliath

Former Apple employee and Mac evangelist Guy Kawasaki said it took him twenty years to figure out the secret of innovation.

Innovation, he discovered, occurs when you decide to "make meaning." To make meaning implies that you want to make the world a better place. Kawasaki believes Apple and other great companies start with a noble purpose to make meaning and, as a result, make money. Apple changed the world because it started with the goal of making people more creative and more productive.

Passion and vision inspire people to build superior products, says Kawasaki. "The Macintosh Division shared a dream, the Macintosh Dream, of changing the world by bringing computers to more people so that they could improve their personal creativity and enrich their lives. We all thought we were going to change the world with our little computer, and we worked 90 hours a week to do it. We drank six-color Kool-Aid every day."[17] (Kawasaki's metaphor is a reference to the six-color Apple logo of the eighties.) Kawasaki says that working for Jobs was both terrifying and addictive. It was terrifying because Jobs would "crucify" a person if the work didn't meet his expectations, but "working for Steve was also ecstasy." He quips, "We would have worked in the Macintosh Division even if he'd given us Tang."[18] Kawasaki brings up an important point about vision, or "meaning." When people are inspired by a mission that is bigger than any one individual, they will work much, much harder than a group of individuals who are uninspired by their leader's vision.

> When people love their jobs for the work itself, they often feel committed to the organizations that make that work possible. Committed employees are likely to stay with an organization even when they are pursued by headhunters waving money.
>
> —HARVARD BUSINESS REVIEW

"We were out to change the world, and that was very intoxicating," said former Apple recruiter Sharon Aby. "You see, innovation cannot exist without a grand vision. Our vision was to change the world by putting computers into the hands of everyday people. We wanted to invent products that real people would actually use. We felt like David fighting Goliath. Everyone was aligned to the mission, and that empowered us to make decisions that were in the best interest of the company."[19]

The Epiphany That Gave Life to Buzz Lightyear

In 1986, Steve Jobs invested $5 million of his own money to purchase the Graphics Group from LucasFilm, a company made up of a team of talented computer animators. Less than ten years later, the company, renamed Pixar, made film history with *Toy Story*, the first computer-generated animated feature film. More movies followed, all hits: *A Bug's Life, Finding Nemo, Cars, Wall-E, Up*, and many others. By 2010, Pixar had won twenty-two Academy Awards and grossed more than $5.5 billion worldwide. Walt Disney, the company that started full-length movie animation, purchased Pixar in 2006, making Jobs Disney's largest shareholder.

As had happened seven years earlier during the visit to PARC, Steve Jobs had an epiphany moment, a vision of the future that burned so brightly that he was absolutely convinced of its outcome. This time it was another man's vision that inspired Jobs to become an evangelist and not the other way around. Jobs had paid a visit to Ed Catmull at the LucasFilm facility and was "blown away" by what he saw. Catmull was an innovator in the burgeoning field of high-tech computer graphics. Catmull's vision was to make the world's first computer-animated feature film. Jobs bought the division, which included computer technology and a core group of about forty-five highly talented LucasFilm animators. Ten years and $50 million later (most of it Jobs's money), Sheriff Woody, Buzz Lightyear, and a dozen other computer-generated characters would take over movie screens around the world. Pixar's first full-length movie, *Toy Story*, would gross more than $300 million worldwide and open the door for a new generation of marvelous and magical animated films.

Where Catmull had a vision of creating the first computer-generated feature film, Jobs had an even bolder vision for Pixar: "Over time we want Pixar to grow into a brand that embodies the same level of trust as the Disney brand," Jobs once said.[20] Once again, Jobs's vision came true. *Toy Story* is ranked ninety-ninth on the American Film Institute's list of the one hundred greatest American films of all time. The only other animated film making the list is Disney's *Snow White and the Seven Dwarfs*. Pixar would not exist today had it not been for the vision of two men: Catmull and Jobs. Vision drives innovation and keeps the energy level high when the inevitable setbacks occur. (Production on *Toy Story* was suspended for several months because executives at Disney wanted the script to be rewritten.) Successful innovation requires a team of people committed to the vision. "These are team sports," said Jobs. "You're trying to climb up a mountain bringing a lot of stuff. One person can't do it."[21]

We're Just Getting Started

On January 9, 2001, Steve Jobs spent eight minutes revealing a vision that would drive Apple (and computer) technology for the next decade. Not only did his vision turn out to be correct, but also Jobs was confident about it, and he very publicly revealed the vision for everyone to see. Jobs called his vision the "Digital Hub."

Many observers at the start of the new millennium believed the PC was dead or declining in value as independent digital devices were introduced for single tasks: cell phones, digital cameras, PDAs, MP3 players, DVD players, and the like. Some believed that these devices would eventually replace multiuse computers. Not Steve Jobs. Once again, he could see over the horizon.

"We're just getting started," Jobs said at the 2001 Macworld Expo. "I'd like to tell you where we're going. What's our vision? We think the PC is evolving just as it had from the time it was invented in 1975." Jobs followed that statement with a history lesson. He called the years from 1980 to 1994 the PC's "golden age of productivity" with the invention of the spreadsheet, word processors, and desktop publishing programs. In the mid-1990s, Jobs said, the Internet heralded the second golden age. "We think the PC is on the threshold of entering the third great age, the age of the digital lifestyle. We believe the Mac can become the digital hub of our emerging lifestyle, adding tremendous value to our other digital devices," Jobs predicted.[22]

Jobs's vision to turn the Mac into a digital hub inspired some of the most notable innovations of the computer age. As part of the

INSPIRE EVANGELISTS | **57**

strategy, Apple developed software to edit videos (iMovie), to organize photos (iPhoto), and to play music and videos (iTunes, iPod). The Digital Hub strategy would set Apple's course for the coming decade and reinvigorate an industry that had lost its mojo.

Microsoft's Missed Opportunity

Apple's new tablet, the iPad, was introduced in January 2010. When it went on sale in April, it shot out of the gate, selling one million units in twenty-eight days. Jobs was not the only visionary to see the need for a tablet computer. Another famous entrepreneur, Bill Gates, had this to say: "The PC took computing out of the back office and into everyone's office. The tablet takes cutting-edge PC technology and makes it available wherever you want it, which is why I'm already using a tablet as my everyday computer. It's a PC that is virtually without limits—and within five years I predict it will be the most popular form of PC sold in America."[23]

What's noteworthy here is that Gates made that forecast not in 2010 but on November 11, 2001! What happened? "Microsoft never developed a true system for innovation," claimed former Microsoft vice president Dick Brass. In a revealing opinion piece for the *New York Times* after Apple's introduction of the iPad, Brass made the case that Microsoft actually thwarted innovation. "Despite having one of the largest and best corporate laboratories in the world, and the luxury of not one but three chief technology officers, the company routinely manages to frustrate the efforts of its visionary thinkers."[24] As an example, Brass said it took a decade for a technology called ClearType (a method to improve the readability of text on a computer screen) to find its way out of the labs and on to Windows. He said it annoyed other Microsoft groups that felt "threatened by our success." As Brass tells it, he and his team were building the tablet PC in 2001, but the vice president in charge of Office at the time decided he didn't like the concept. The VP refused to modify Office applications to work properly on the tablet, essentially dooming the project. The tablet group at Microsoft was eliminated. It's a sad tale. Internecine warfare scuttled a project

> *Innovation has nothing to do with how many R&D dollars you have. When Apple came up with the Mac, IBM was spending at least one hundred times more on R&D. It's not about money. It's about the people you have, how you're led, and how much you get it.*
>
> —STEVE JOBS

that had cost hundreds of millions to develop and could have positioned Microsoft as one of the world's leading innovators in a new and exciting category of mobile computing.

To confirm Brass's argument, I checked with Tim Bajarin, a prominent analyst and Apple watcher. "The big difference is that everyone at Apple is on the same page, driven by Steve Jobs. That means every group and every project is in lockstep with Jobs's vision," Bajarin said. "Microsoft businesses are silos, and all of them are profit centers in their own right. In many cases, the right hand does not know what the left hand is doing. The tablet is a good example. It needed to be part of a grand mobile vision driven by a single group championing the future of mobile. Instead, Microsoft has had different groups managing different aspects of mobile (Zune, Windows Mobile, Tablet, and so on). As a result, they missed a golden opportunity to drive a total Windows mobile version of the tablet and innovate around it."[25]

The iPad story reinforces a key tenet of innovation: new ideas must fit into a broader vision articulated by a champion who keeps the organization focused on fulfilling the vision. Every organization, large and small, needs a "Steve Jobs"—a charismatic, visionary, and creative leader who has the influence to keep teams focused on the big picture.

Put a Dent in the Universe

"Steve had an incredible ability to rally people towards some common cause by painting an incredibly glorious cosmic objective," said former Apple marketing manager Trip Hawkins. "One of his favorite statements was 'Let's make a dent in the universe. We'll make it so important that it will make a dent in the universe.'"[26]

The question has been raised, how does one man such as Steve Jobs foster such a culture of enthusiasm that he creates a "reality distortion field," a phenomenon attributed to Jobs in which the leader convinces his team that anything is possible? In *The Journey Is the Reward*, an early biography of Steve Jobs, author Jeffrey Young attempts to answer the question, defining the exceptional skills that led to Jobs's success. Young concluded that Steve Jobs "had a salesman's belief in the product that he was producing, an evangelist's Bible-thumping passion, the zealot's singularity of purpose, and the poor kid's determination to make his business a success."[27]

At the end of his keynote presentation at the Macworld Expo in January 2007, Jobs left the audience with this thought: "There's an old Wayne Gretzky quote that I love. 'I skate to where the puck is going to be, not where it has been.' We've always tried to do that at Apple since the very beginning. And we always will."[28] Eleanor Roosevelt once said that the future belongs to those who believe in the beauty of their dreams. Steve Jobs always believed in the beauty of his dreams to change the world. Do you believe in yours?

iLessons

1 Never underestimate the power of a bold vision to move society forward.

2 Does your company or cause have a bold, specific, concise, and consistent vision that everyone on your team can internalize? If not, it's time you got one.

3 Do you know someone who has motivated others by communicating a big vision for his or her company or initiative? Pay attention to how such people incorporate that vision into their conversations.

CHAPTER 5

Think Differently About Your Vision

**Make no little plans; they have
no magic to stir men's blood.**

—DANIEL HUDSON BURNHAM, AMERICAN ARCHITECT

Nearly forty years after American astronaut Neil Armstrong stepped foot on the moon, he stepped out for dinner at an Italian restaurant in a small California town. A mutual friend had invited me to join in the meal with the American hero. Armstrong was the keynote speaker at a conference I attended earlier in the day. For three hours that evening, Armstrong regaled us with accounts about his trip to space, his first steps on the moon, and his life since returning to Earth. One thing that stuck in my mind during our conversation was the enormous number of small and large innovations—all mission critical—that were ultimately responsible for sending a man to the moon and returning him safely to Earth.

Armstrong was the most visible icon of NASA's Apollo space program. He was, after all, the first person to leave his footprint on the moon's surface, on July 20, 1969. But Armstrong had a lot of assistance—four hundred thousand helpers. It required the skills of four hundred thousand people to launch *Apollo 11*, land astronauts on the moon, and return them to Earth—four hundred thousand of the world's most brilliant rocket designers, engineers, technicians, scientists, inspectors, navigators, and even seamstresses who carefully stitched together the special space suits the men would need to survive the moon's extreme temperatures.

The moon landing would be viewed as a triumph of innovation and teamwork, yet the landing might never have happened—certainly not by the end of the 1960s—had it not been for one man's vision eight years earlier. On May 25, 1961, in a Joint Session of Congress, president John F. Kennedy set forth the vision confidently and unabashedly: "I believe this nation should commit itself to achieving the goal, before this decade is out, of landing a man on the moon and returning him safely to Earth. No single space project in this period will be more impressive to mankind."[1] At the time, few people knew exactly how a moon landing would be accomplished or whether it could even be done at all. Thousands of tasks, decisions, and problems had to be worked out. Rockets had not been built or designed, computers were not up to the task, and nobody knew how to keep astronauts alive in space. Kennedy's grand vision was short on details but bold enough to set forces in motion. By the tens of thousands, men and women who heard the call signed on to participate in an exciting and intoxicating goal, a purpose that would give their lives meaning and leave an indelible mark on humanity.

Big, bold visions have a way of inspiring teams. The people who worked on the Apollo program would need serious inspiration to face numerous setbacks, some quite tragic. On January 27, 1967, a spark lit an oxygen container on *Apollo 1*, and it burst into flames, killing three crewmen instantly. *Apollo 1* was destroyed before it even left the ground. The tragedy taught NASA some valuable lessons. Scientists redesigned the space capsule based on what they had learned. The goal was clear, and it so thoroughly captured the imaginations of thousands of scientists and engineers that they came up with solutions for every problem.

Kennedy adviser and speechwriter Ted Sorensen once said that man did not reach the moon because Kennedy wanted it done. Rather, people were intoxicated with the vision of space exploration. Kennedy gave it life and, by defining a specific goal and timetable, marshaled the collective innovative genius of thousands of the brightest minds. The moon program proved that anything is possible when a team of smart, dedicated people commit themselves to a common goal. For innovation to happen in any field, the person with the idea must inspire others to help transform the idea into a functional product, service, or initiative. One NASA engineer said that the vision of going to the moon took such hold of his imagination that he never wanted to fall asleep, because he could not wait to return to work the next morning. He had become a believer, an evangelist. Inspire evangelists and watch your ideas take off.

Steve Jobs's Moon Landing

There are striking similarities between Kennedy's race to the moon and Steve Jobs's race to put computers into the hands of everyday people. Both men gave stirring speeches that positioned the fulfillment of their visions as winning a battle between tyranny and freedom.

By the time Kennedy addressed Congress in 1961, the Soviet Union had already gone to space, successfully sending a man into orbit just one month earlier. Americans were worried. What would happen should a nuclear-powered communist country control the next frontier? It was against this backdrop that Kennedy said the following:

> If we are to win the battle that is now going on around the world between freedom and tyranny, the dramatic achievements in space in recent weeks should have made clear to us all, as did the *Sputnik* in 1957, the impact of this adventure on the minds of men everywhere . . . We are determined as a nation that freedom shall survive and succeed, and whatever the peril and setbacks, we have some very large advantages. The first is the simple fact that we are on the side of liberty—and since the beginning of history, and particularly since the end of the Second World War, liberty has been winning all over the globe. The second real asset is that we are not alone. We have friends

and allies all over the world who share our devotion to freedom, and our country is united in its commitment to freedom and is ready to do its duty.[2]

Kennedy was not selling a space program; Kennedy was selling freedom from oppression.

In 1983, Steve Jobs was not selling a computer; Jobs was selling freedom from an IBM-controlled universe. In the fall of that year, Jobs addressed an audience of Apple employees, mostly from the sales and marketing divisions. He talked about the upcoming introduction of Macintosh and unveiled the famous 1984 Macintosh advertisement for the first time. During this presentation, Jobs spent very little, if any, time on the Mac's features and benefits. Instead, he positioned the success of Macintosh as a race between tyranny and freedom, the "democratization of technology." Here are Jobs's exact words as he set the stage for the introduction of Macintosh:

It is 1958. IBM passes up the chance to buy a young, fledgling company that has invented a new technology called xerography. Two years later, Xerox is born, and IBM has been kicking themselves ever since. It is ten years later, the late sixties. Digital Equipment (DEC) and others invent the minicomputer. IBM dismisses the minicomputer as too small to do serious computing and therefore unimportant to their business. DEC grows to become a multihundred-million-dollar corporation before IBM finally enters the minicomputer market. It is now ten years later, the late seventies. In 1977, Apple, a young, fledgling company on the West Coast, invents the Apple II, the first personal computer as we know it today. IBM dismisses the personal computer as too small to do serious computing and unimportant to their business. The early eighties, 1981. Apple II has become the world's most popular computer, and Apple has grown to a $300 million company, becoming the fastest-growing corporation in American business history. With over fifty competitors, IBM enters the personal computer market in November 1981 with the IBM PC. It is now 1984. It appears IBM wants it all [Jobs's voice grows louder and more intense].

Apple is perceived to be the only hope to offer IBM a run for its money. Dealers initially welcoming IBM with open arms now fear an IBM-dominated and -controlled future. They are increasingly turning back to Apple as the only force that can ensure their future freedom. [applause] IBM wants it all and is aiming its guns on its last obstacle to industry control, Apple. Will Big Blue dominate the entire computer industry? [shouts of "No" from the audience] The entire information age? [shouts of "No" grow even louder] Was George Orwell right about 1984? [the audience shouts, "No, no" and erupts into manic applause][3]

The wild cheers Jobs received during that presentation tell you all you need to know about the power of vision. Nobody is inspired by a computer. Steve Jobs created fans by painting a vision of what computers could do. He turned fans into evangelists by painting a vision of Apple as the last company that could protect the masses from IBM's "domination." Vision inspires evangelists, and evangelists are key players in turning ideas into successful innovations.

> *When you're putting people on the moon, you're inspiring all of us to achieve the maximum of human potential, which is how our greatest problems will eventually be solved. Give yourself permission to dream. Fuel your kids' dreams, too.*
>
> —RANDY PAUSCH,
> *THE LAST LECTURE*

"Without the successful evangelism of third-party developers, Macintosh would have failed," said former Apple executive Guy Kawasaki.[4] He was referring to the fact that the original Macintosh shipped with very limited software. The computer industry believed only IBM PC clones would survive. Developers had to be inspired to write programs for the Mac. "In 1983 and 1984, Mike Boich and I sold the Macintosh dream to hundreds of software companies by appealing to their emotions—making history with Apple, wanting to change the world, or helping Apple succeed against IBM," Kawasaki wrote in *The Macintosh Way*.[5] The essence of evangelism, in Kawasaki's view, is to passionately show people how you're going to make history together. It has little to do with cash flow, profits, or marketing. You are selling a dream, not an object. "When you sell your product, people use it. When you evangelize people, they get infected, carry the torch for you, share your heartbeat, and defend you against your enemies. When you look in their eyes you see your logo."[6] The Macintosh way is not to sell; it's to evangelize. You cannot evangelize without a vision.

Meeting Impossible Deadlines

People want to feel something. They want to be moved and inspired. They want to believe in something bigger than they are—a noble purpose. Studies show that more than two-thirds of American workers are not "engaged" in their workplaces.[7] Successful leaders outline big, bold, and noble visions to cultivate cultures of innovation, unleashing the collective imagination of their teams. In the study of psychology, the Pygmalion effect refers to a phenomenon in which the greater the expectation that is placed on people, the better they perform. In other words, when challenged with a grand purpose, people will rise to meet the challenge. Researchers have found that great expectations act as a self-fulfilling prophecy. If a leader communicates a compelling vision and holds his or her team to high standards, subordinates will respond to meet those expectations.

Anything is possible when a team of committed individuals are inspired by a grand purpose. They will work harder, dream bigger, and find ways to make the impossible possible. On January 8, 1983, Steve Jobs held a conference call with the East Coast production team assembling the final pieces of the Macintosh for a road show during which Apple would introduce the new computer to dealers. Jobs was adamant that the software shipped with the Mac not be labeled "demo." It would send the wrong message, he advised. The deadline for disk duplication, January 16, was approaching, and the team members did not believe they would have the final "final" code in place. They wanted Jobs to let them off the hook and to ship demo software. Jeffrey Young, author of *Steve Jobs: The Journey Is the Reward*, picks up the story: "Steve wouldn't hear it. He didn't react with anger, as they were all expecting. He started telling them how great they were and how all of Apple was counting on them. Then he hung up before there was a chance to argue. Everyone in the conference room in Cupertino was stunned. They looked at one another. They were already exhausted, but Steve had done it again. They would make the deadline. He had challenged them to rise to the occasion, and he had chosen his people well. They wouldn't let him down."[8]

Few members of the Macintosh production team got any sleep that week, but with fifteen minutes to spare on Sunday morning, January 16, they delivered a final computer. "Some people aren't used to an environment where excellence is expected," Jobs once said. That's true. When excellence is expected, people will largely live up to the challenge. But Jobs left out one key point behind his success: teams will respond to challenge only if they believe in the grand purpose set forth by their leader. A weak vision leads to weak effort.

A Noble Purpose Sparks Innovation

Apple has thousands of inspired employees—evangelists—who, instead of saying, "We can't do that," say, "We may not know how we're going to do it, but we will figure it out." Steve Jobs has cultivated such an attitude from the beginning. According to Gary Hamel, author of *The Future of Management*, "A noble purpose inspires sacrifice, stimulates innovation and encourages perseverance. In doing so, it transforms great talent into exceptional accomplishment."[9]

In August 2005, one of the deadliest hurricanes in U.S. history, Hurricane Katrina, barreled down on Louisiana. Entergy, the power company that serves the region, scrambled to keep the lights on. One million customers had lost power, and fifteen hundred Entergy employees had lost their homes or had to be evacuated.

> *Here's what you find at a lot of companies. You know how you see a show car, and it's really cool, and then four years later you see the production car, and it sucks? And you go, what happened? They had it! They had it in the palm of their hands! They grabbed defeat from the jaws of victory! What happened was, the designers came up with this really great idea. Then they take it to the engineers, and the engineers go, "Nah, we can't do that. That's impossible." And so it gets a lot worse. Then they take it to the manufacturing people, and they go, "We can't build that!" And it gets a lot worse.*[10]
>
> —STEVE JOBS

Wayne Leonard, Entergy's CEO, told employees to deal with their own personal crises. Take as much time as you need before returning to work, he said. One day, one week, one month—no questions would be asked. Their jobs were guaranteed. What happened next was astonishing. Well, astonishing to anybody who does not understand the power of a noble purpose. Despite their own circumstances, just about every Entergy employee returned to work immediately. It wasn't unusual to find them working sixteen hours a day for seven straight days.

By the end of the first week, power was restored to more than half a million Entergy customers, a remarkable achievement by all accounts. None of the affected employees *had* to return to work. They *wanted* to. And they wanted to because Leonard had cultivated a culture of service, a workplace based on one simple vision: to leave the world a better place than how they found it. In other words, for Entergy employees, their work always represented more than a paycheck. "Our employees know that what they do makes a real difference in people's lives," Leonard told me. "We don't just provide electricity. We cool homes in the summer and warm them in the winter. We allow people to cook their food, clean the environment, and educate their children."[11] If Entergy's displaced employees had viewed their roles as "just another job," instead of providing hope to those who lost power, its customers might have remained in the dark a lot longer. In one of the most inspiring e-mails I've ever read, Leonard told his employees:

In every man and woman's life, there is a defining moment. It is a brief intersection of circumstances and choices that define a person for better or worse, a life of unfilled potential or a life that mattered, that made a difference. It is true of individuals and it is true of business. We have great passion for the difference we make in others' lives. We provide a commodity that sustains life. But, more importantly, we provide the most precious commodity of all—hope.[12]

Entergy provides electricity, but its employees believe in the company's bigger vision, which is to make a positive impact on people's lives. Apple makes computers, but its employees believe in the company's bigger vision, which is to make tools to improve people's lives. When exceptional leaders paint a compelling vision of the future, and when they expect excellence from their teams, it inspires people to achieve results they never thought possible.

"But I don't have a noble purpose," you may say to yourself. "I'm not sending people to the moon or building a computer that will change the world." Perhaps not, but most likely you do have ideas, products, or services that improve the lives of your customers and that, even in a small way, make the world a better place. You may not be exploring outer space, but you're making someone's life here on Earth a little better, and that's a noble goal.

Building a Vision One Scoop at a Time

Successful innovators find a noble purpose in just about anything, even ice cream. My daughters and I love Cold Stone Creamery ice cream. They know that a visit to Daddy's office usually means a walk across the street to the ice cream shop. Inside we are met by enthusiastic teenagers who scoop rich, delicious ice cream, slather it on cold granite, and mix in any ingredient my daughters choose, such as brownies, candy, or—my favorite—cookie dough. Toss a tip into the jar and they'll sing a song. Cold Stone Creamery offers more than ice cream; it offers an experience.

In 1999, Cold Stone Creamery was a small ice cream chain of seventy-four stores, primarily in Arizona. That's when former CEO Doug Ducey entered the picture. Ducey told me his "goal" was to expand to one thousand stores nationwide in the following five years. It would not be easy. Cold Stone Creamery was largely unknown and competing against established brands such as Baskin-Robbins and Dairy Queen. No employee is going to work hard, offer exceptional customer service, and come up with innovative ideas just because a company CEO wants to grow the number of stores.

Ducey knew he had to create an inspiring vision. He thought carefully about the company's strengths: it made high-quality ice cream and offered something unique—singing ice cream scoopers. Ducey unveiled a bold vision to his franchise owners in 1999: the world will know us as the ultimate ice cream experience. By fulfilling the vision, he contended, Cold Stone Creamery would become one of the bestselling ice cream brands in the country and reach its goal of one thousand stores by December 31, 2004.

"Experience" would differentiate Cold Stone Creamery from the other ice cream shops. Even though the chain was fairly small by national franchise standards, Ducey could see that fans of Cold Stone Creamery were developing an emotional connection to the brand. Of course, the ice cream—made fresh daily—played a part in establishing this devotion, but the emotional engagement came from what Ducey dubbed "the X-factor": the mix of entertainment and energy that has turned Cold Stone Creamery from just another ice cream shop into a destination. According to Ducey, "It was a grand vision that would require hard work—it would get us up early, keep us up late, and tap all our energies and skills."[13] It was a stretch goal but achievable, believable, and consistent with the company's core values.

Once Ducey announced it publicly, momentum was established. Over the next five years, the vision took on a life of its own, inspiring the entire Cold Stone Creamery team of employees and franchise owners to make it come true. Ducey did achieve his goal and announced the one-thousandth store opening at the annual franchise meeting in January 2005. Today Cold Stone Creamery has more than fourteen hundred locations around the country and continues to develop innovative ice cream creations. Meanwhile, its vision has not wavered. "The Ultimate Ice Cream Experience" continues to be the company's mantra.

Never Underestimate a Group of Desperate Moms

Chicago's East Lakeview neighborhood is a gentrified enclave on the city's North Side. New condos and high-rises stand next to historic buildings and churches. It's a bustling neighborhood of restaurants, bars, and bistros. A nice place to live but, until recently, not a nice place to send your kids to public school. Jacqueline Edelberg, the mother of a two-and-half-year-old girl, wanted to change it.

Although Edelberg, a Ph.D. from the University of Chicago and a Fulbright scholar, could afford to send her child to a private school, she was a product of Chicago public schools and believed in the mission of the public school system. The local school, Nettelhorst, was in terrible shape. It was undesirable by the neighborhood, the kids who were bussed there from overcrowded schools, or even their parents—and that was what the principal said about it. "Out of three hundred families in my neighborhood, only six sent their kids to Nettelhorst," Edelberg told me.[14]

In her first visit to the school in 2003, Edelberg and a friend met with the principal, who asked the ladies, "What would we have to do to get your kids to come here?" Stunned by the invitation, the two women returned the next day with a five-page wish list. "Well, let's get started. We have a busy year ahead of us," said the principal. And, with that message, the forces were set in motion to improve a dilapidated public school.

Edelberg could not do it alone and needed inspired evangelists to take up the cause. She designated her group of eight "mommy friends" who met regularly for playdates at the local park. While they sat around a sandbox, she articulated her vision: every kid deserves a great neighborhood public school. "Instead of talking about what's on sale at The Gap, let's fix this school so we can send our kids there," Edelberg challenged her friends.[15] The wheels began to turn. As the women talked, they discovered that each had a unique skill, valuable business experience they had attained before setting aside their careers to become stay-at-home moms. One had worked in the advertising department of a Fortune 500 company, while others had experience as lawyers or marketing professionals. Each had skills that could be leveraged. "Now, instead of creating ads for Twinkies, we could serve the far nobler purpose of revitalizing our local school," said Edelberg. The mothers treated the project as they would a business, dividing into teams and focusing on infrastructure improvements, marketing, public relations, and enrichment in the form of after-school programs.

Since the Chicago public school system had no resources to devote to the rehabilitation of the school, the mothers had to find innovative solutions. They decided to partner with individuals and companies. They asked local artists to paint—adopt a classroom. Today the school is filled with murals, sculptures, and vibrant colors. They asked ballet, karate, and music teachers to hold classes after school so six hundred students would not be thrown onto the street after the last bell. They asked local chefs to teach culinary classes in a newly designed kitchen classroom.

Nine months later, the mothers held their first open house. Three hundred families showed up, and seventy-eight signed up their kids on the spot. In the coming years, more families enrolled. Four years after the mothers shared their vision around a sandbox, test scores tripled and Nettelhorst third-graders ranked the highest in the city. Today test scores continue to rank among the highest in Chicago's public schools, and in the last two years, every seventh- and eighth-grader scored well enough to be considered for any of the highly selective magnet schools in the city. "The process of all these creative minds coming together to make this work created something that was much more than the sum of its parts. It happened far faster than we ever anticipated. It is now a model for other neighborhoods around Chicago," says Edelberg. "Schools have to radically change the way they do business if they want to be the heart of a community. It requires a new vision for what they provide, how they provide it, and what they offer."[16]

Never underestimate the power of vision to create change at any level. And never underestimate eight desperate moms who want the best for their kids.

Embrace Vision, Not Mission

A compelling vision is far different from a mission statement. Traditional mission statements are long, convoluted paragraphs, typically drawn up by committee, and destined to be tucked into a drawer somewhere and largely forgotten. Not one business professional I've ever met—not one—has ever been able to recite his or her company's mission word for word. If you cannot remember it, then why bother? Toss the mission statement. It's a waste of time. Make a vision instead; it's far more inspiring.

A vision is a picture of a better world that your product or service makes possible. Captivating visions inspire investors, employees, and customers—and best of all, they inspire those stakeholders to become evangelists for the organization. An inspiring vision meets three criteria. It's specific, concise, and consistent.

» **Specific.** The problem with most mission statements is that they're too ambiguous. How many times have you heard that a particular company's mission is to offer "best-of-breed, customer-centered solutions . . . blah, blah, blah"? They do not say anything meaningful. When Starbucks CEO Howard Schultz pitched investors on the original concept behind Starbucks, he painted the vision of "a third place between work and home." Now, that's specific. It's tangible. You can visualize it in your mind's eye.

» **Concise.** When the Google guys, Sergey Brin and Larry Page, walked into the offices of Sequoia Capital, executives asked the young college students for their vision. Brin and Page responded, "To provide access to the world's information in one click." That one sentence was so inspiring that investors at the Silicon Valley venture firm not only funded the company but also now require any entrepreneur who steps foot into the office to articulate the company's vision in ten words or fewer. One Sequoia investor told me, "If you can't describe what you do in ten words or fewer, I'm not buying, I'm not investing, I'm not interested. Period."

» **Consistent.** A vision is meaningless if it does not have the power to persuade, and it cannot persuade if nobody knows about it! Marc Benioff, CEO of cloud computing pioneer salesforce.com, once told me that he placed his company's vision—the end of software—on laminated cards so every employee could carry it at all times. He even had pins made with the word "Software" and a big red line through it. The vision was consistently delivered across all company channels—in presentations, on the website, in advertisements, and in all marketing material.

Now consider Steve Jobs's original vision for Apple: *A computer in the hands of everyday people.* It's concise: eight words and thirty-five characters, short enough to fit in a Twitter post. It's specific: putting a computer in the hands of everyday people. And it was consistent: Steve Jobs took every opportunity to communicate the vision, and he did so relentlessly. Think about the other visions discussed earlier. Kennedy's vision was to land a man on the moon and return him safely to Earth by the end of the decade. You can't get much more specific than that. Kennedy even set a timetable. Edelberg challenged her friends with the vision, "Every kid deserves a great neighborhood public school." The vision was specific and concise, fewer than ten words. Ducey's vision for Cold Stone was concise, specific, and consistent. "The world will know us as the ultimate ice cream experience": that sentence was posted everywhere, in every store, so employees always knew what they were striving for.

"Companies, as they grow to become multibillion-dollar entities, somehow lose their vision," Steve Jobs has said. "They insert lots of layers of middle management between the people running the company and the people doing the work. They no longer have an inherent feel or a passion about the products. The creative people, the ones who care passionately, have to persuade five layers of management to do what they know is the right thing. The great people leave, and you end up with mediocrity. The way we will not become a vanilla corporation is to put together small teams of

THINK DIFFERENTLY ABOUT YOUR VISION | **75**

great people and set them to build their dreams. We are artists, not engineers."[17]

Avoid becoming a "vanilla corporation." Think about the kind of company you would like to work for or the kind of cause you want to back. Do you want to work for a leader who is always reacting to the competition instead of keeping an eye on the future? Do you want to work for a leader who has you scrambling this way one day and that way the next, with no clear destination? Do you want to put your time into a cause with no distinct purpose? Of course you don't, and neither do the people you need to inspire. A culture of innovation cannot exist without vision—a picture of the world that is so inspiring that it elicits the best ideas from the best minds. Vision starts at the top. Vision begins with you.

A Vision for Your Personal Brand

All innovative companies have visionary leaders. Vision must be present for creativity to flourish. The same holds true for the most important brand of all: the brand of *you*. If you see yourself as a "brand," then you owe it to yourself to have a vision for what you hope to accomplish. A larger-than-life vision will get you up in the morning and get the creative juices flowing.

In 2003, I was assigned to cover the first one hundred days of the Arnold Schwarzenegger administration for Los Angeles–based CBS 2. The famous film actor and bodybuilder had been elected governor of California in a special recall election of then governor Gray Davis. For three months, I had a front-row seat to many of Governor Schwarzenegger's speeches. Some of these stuck strictly to policy themes, but many were intensely personal, especially when he spoke to youth groups. After listening to dozens of speeches, I realized that great ideas and great successes all begin with a passionate vision—and it's just as important for individuals as it is for corporations.

I never got tired of hearing Schwarzenegger's incredible story: the story of a young man in a small Austrian village who comes to the United States, wins Mr. Olympia (seven times), becomes a world-famous actor, marries a Kennedy, and is elected the thirty-eighth governor of California. On its face it's a story of the American dream. But none of it would have happened without vision. Schwarzenegger repeatedly said that his vision, when he was as young as ten, was to come to America to take advantage of all the opportunities the United States had to offer. Winning Mr. Olympia was a goal, a ticket to fulfilling his vision.

Schwarzenegger saw the vision in his mind's eye every day, through every grueling rep, through every setback. In his own mind he had already achieved success in America. Now he simply had to go through the motions. Schwarzenegger did not know exactly how he was going to achieve his vision, but he trusted that the right people and the right opportunities would come his way.

An inspiring vision is important if only to give you the confidence to keep going when everyone around you tells you why you will never succeed. Everyone thought Schwarzenegger was crazy—including his parents, friends, and later Hollywood agents who could never conceive of hiring a non-English-speaking, six-foot-two bodybuilder who wanted to become an actor. One man did. Director James Cameron, who knows something about a passionate commitment to his vision, cast Schwarzenegger in *The Terminator*. Cameron saw Schwarzenegger's thick accent as an asset. His line "I'll be back" became one of the most famous quotes in movie history precisely because it was spoken with a thick Austrian accent, by a robot! "Always trust yourself and in your vision, no matter what anyone else thinks," Schwarzenegger would say. And he would know: as an influential film star, and later as governor of California, Arnold has managed to spread his vision to others far and wide.

With the proliferation of the Internet, social networking tools, and "open-innovation" processes where ideas are encouraged from all members of an organization, ideas are everywhere and accessible to anyone. In other words, great ideas alone are less likely to differentiate your brand from the competition. The Italian management professor and innovation expert Roberto Verganti believes the next decade belongs not to those who generate ideas but to visionaries who will build arenas to unleash the power of ideas and transform those ideas into action. "To generate fresh ideas, we have been told to think outside the box and then jump back in; vision building destroys the box and builds a new one," according to Verganti. "I'm certainly not questioning the essential value of ideas. They will still ignite the innovation process. Tossing around a large number of ideas will still be important, especially for incremental improvements. It is not one or the other. It is a shift in the most rare and precious asset that will drive competitive advantage: visions."[18]

Steve Jobs does not believe in systems of innovation because, in his opinion, innovation occurs when you hire really smart people and inspire them to build great products. Sounds simple. But where does inspiration come from? People are inspired by a vision, a grand purpose, which gives their life meaning. And Jobs has always been a master at articulating a grand purpose. According to Jobs, "When I hire somebody really senior, competence is the ante. They have to be really smart. But the real issue for me is, are they going to fall in love with Apple? Because if they fall in love with Apple, everything else will take care of itself."[19] Make people fall in love with you, your company, or your service. Inspire them with a vision so compelling that they can't help but come along for the ride.

---

iLessons

1 Give yourself permission to dream big. Create a vision for your brand that inspires you to get up every morning. Develop a noble purpose that gives your life meaning. Chances are it will inspire your team as well.

2 Put your vision to the test. Make it bold, specific, concise, and consistent. Make sure your vision fits easily in a Twitter post of 140 characters or fewer.

3 See yourself having already accomplished your vision, regardless of how far it is in the future. Passion is the fuel that gives you energy to reach your dreams, but vision provides the road map.

Kick-Start
Your Brain

Creativity is just connecting things.

—STEVE JOBS

CHAPTER 6

Seek Out New Experiences

Part of what made the Macintosh great was that the people working on it were musicians, and poets, and artists, and zoologists, and historians who also happened to be the best computer scientists in the world.

—STEVE JOBS

The company name "Apple" fell from a tree, literally, dropping right into Steve Jobs's vision of what a computer should be—simple and approachable. When Jobs and Woz formed a partnership to build computers, the then twenty-one-year-old Jobs was still seeking spiritual enlightenment seven hundred miles from his parents' modest, single-story home in Los Altos, California. Although Jobs had dropped out of Reed College, in Portland, he returned to Oregon periodically to share ideas with like-minded people in a Zen-influenced commune called the All-One Farm where they grew—you guessed it—apples. Few people know exactly what happened there, and those who do know—such as Jobs—haven't said much. It's reasonable to assume that there was a whole lot of meditation happening, perhaps with the aid of some "herbs." It was the seventies, after all. Regardless of what might have happened on the apple farm, it's safe to say that the experience—outside the confines of engineering-driven Silicon

Valley—kick-started Steve's creative mind. On one trip, Jobs made a seemingly inconsequential observation, an innovation with a "small *i*." But his idea provides an A-level course in brand identity.

Jobs and Wozniak had decided to start their own company with $1,000 (the money needed to build ready-made printed circuit boards). Woz sold his beloved HP 65 calculator for $500, and Jobs sold his equally beloved VW van for a few hundred more. And with that, the two friends were in business. They just needed a name to make the partnership complete. As Woz tells the story, "I remember I was driving Steve back from the airport along Highway 85. Steve was coming back from a visit to Oregon to a place he called an 'apple orchard.' It was actually some kind of commune. Steve suggested a name—Apple Computer . . . We both tried to come up with technical-sounding names that were better, but we couldn't think of any good ones. Apple was so much better, better than any other name we could think of. So Apple it was. Apple it had to be."[1]

The story of Steve Jobs and the apple orchard gives us an early glimpse into how Jobs's mind works. Yes, there is only one Steve Jobs, just as there is only one person with your unique skills and experience. And no, not everyone can replicate Steve Jobs's success in the computer industry. But we all can learn to be far more creative than we are today, which directly leads to innovation and success. The question is, how? What can Steve Jobs teach us?

Creativity Is Connecting Things

Psychologists have spent years trying to discover the answer to the question, "What makes innovators different?" In one of the most thorough examinations of the subject, Harvard researchers spent six years and interviewed three thousand executives to find out. Their conclusions are interesting, but the investigators could have saved themselves a lot of time by simply asking Steve Jobs. According to the Harvard research, the number one skill that separates innovators from noncreative professionals is "associating": the ability to successfully connect seemingly unrelated questions, problems, or ideas from different fields. "The more diverse our experience and knowledge, the more connections the brain can make. Fresh inputs trigger new associations; for some, these lead to novel ideas."[2]

The three-year Harvard research project confirms what Jobs told a reporter fifteen years earlier: "Creativity is just connecting things." Here's what the researchers had to say:

> When you ask creative people how they did something they feel a little guilty because they didn't really do it; they just saw something. It seemed obvious to them after a while. That's because they were able to connect experiences they've had and synthesize new things. And the reason they were able to do that was that they've had more experiences or they had thought more about their experiences than other people. Unfortunately, that's too rare a commodity. A lot of people in our industry haven't had very diverse experiences. So they don't have enough dots to connect, and they end up with very linear solutions without a broad perspective on the problem. The broader one's understanding of the human experience, the better design we will have.[3]

Of course, we will never know if the neurons and synapses are firing any differently in Jobs's brain as opposed to the average human brain, but leading scientists who study the creative process do seem to agree that one reason behind Jobs's ability to generate idea after idea is that, as the Harvard researchers observe, "he has spent a lifetime exploring new and unrelated things—the art of calligraphy, meditation practices in an Indian ashram, the fine details of a Mercedes-Benz."[4]

The three business professors who conducted the research for "The Innovator's DNA," published in the December 2009 *Harvard Business Review*, offer an enticing comparison. First, imagine that you have an identical twin, they suggest. Now imagine that you both have the same brains and natural talents and that you both have been assigned the task of creating a new business venture. You have one week to do it. "During that week, you come up with ideas alone in your room. By contrast, your twin (1) talks with 10 people—including an engineer, a musician, a stay-at-home dad, and a designer—about the venture (2) visits three innovative start-ups to observe what they do (3) samples five 'new to the market' products (4) shows a prototype he's built to five people and (5) asks the question, 'What if I tried this?' . . . who do you bet will come up with the more innovative (and doable) idea?"[5] In this example, Steve Jobs could easily play the role of your twin. Jobs is more effective than most people at generating creative ideas because he is skilled at making associations, connecting seemingly unrelated things. Most important, he makes a conscious decision to do so. He doesn't always know where or how the dots will connect, but he has faith that they will.

Food Processors, Rice Cookers, and Computer Magnets

A Cuisinart food processor has little in common with a home computer. It's a consumer "appliance" that makes your life easier and is found in the home. Other than that, the two products serve completely different functions. If you think the way Steve Jobs does, however, you find inspiration everywhere, even on the shelf at Macy's.

If you see old photographs of the Apple I and Apple II computers, you notice that the two look nothing alike. The former was a fully assembled circuit board that contained about sixty chips. It went on sale in July 1976, three months after Jobs and Woz agreed to go into business together. The Apple I was sold as a kit, mostly to hobbyists, who added components to the circuit board to make a fully functioning computer. It would have exasperated and confused "everyday people." Apple introduced the Apple II one year later, and it was this computer—the Apple II— that put the company on the map and launched the long, amazing journey that would turn Jobs into a global icon. The Apple II was the most popular personal computer of its time: easy to use, with a color screen, an integrated keyboard, eight internal expansion slots, and a unique plastic case. The story of the case is a classic example of "association": a connection happened because Steve Jobs decided to look outside the computer industry for inspiration.

While Woz was improving the internal circuitry and design of what would become the Apple II, Jobs concentrated on the case, which, in his opinion, had to appeal to nonhobbyists looking for a complete, ready-to-use computer. Otherwise it would not have the mass-market appeal that would be required to make the product, and the company, successful. Jobs envisioned the computer in the home, perhaps the kitchen, where the entire family would enjoy using it. Clearly the Apple II had to have a far more approachable look and feel than any computer existing at the time. It would have to be more like a kitchen appliance and less like something found in a hobbyist's garage.

"It was clear to me that for every hardware hobbyist who wanted to assemble his own computer, there were a thousand people who couldn't do that but wanted to mess around with the programming . . . just like I did when I was 10. My dream for the Apple II was to sell the first real packaged computer . . . I got a bug up my rear that I wanted the computer in a plastic case," Jobs said.[6] Although an industrial designer, Jerry Manock, was hired to design the computer, he took his instructions from Steve Jobs, who found his inspiration not in an electronics store—but at Macy's. "He found it in the kitchen section of Macy's while looking at Cuisinart food processors," writes Leander Kahney, author of *Inside Steve's Brain*. "Here was what the Apple II needed: a nice molded plastic case with smooth edges, muted colors, and a lightly textured surface."[7] The molded case—an innovation in computer design—was the spark that Apple II needed to make it one of the most popular personal computers ever manufactured. It also turned Jobs and Woz into millionaires many times over. Woz invented the Apple II, but Jobs's creative thinking turned it into an appliance that everyday people would use and enjoy.

In one of the most misinterpreted quotes of Steve Jobs's career, he said, "Good artists copy, great artists steal."[8] Some critics have cited that quote to support their opinion that Steve Jobs does not have original ideas. But if you read the entire quote, which rarely appears in print, you will realize that Jobs was talking about finding inspiration *outside* of the computer industry—in other words, connecting seemingly unrelated things. The entire quote reads: "It comes down to trying to expose yourself to the best things that humans have done and then try to bring those things in to what you're doing. Picasso had a saying. He said, 'Good artists copy, great artists steal.' We've always been shameless about stealing great ideas. Part of what made the Macintosh great was that the people working on it were musicians, and poets, and artists, and zoologists, and historians who also happened to be the best computer scientists in the world." When one sees the quote in its entirety, it becomes clear that Jobs is not talking about stealing as much as he's reinforcing the notion of association, having diverse experiences that kick-start the creative process.

Steve Jobs makes so many associations that Apple continues to innovate in every aspect of its computer designs, right down to the power cord. The AC adapter that plugs an Apple laptop into a wall socket is called MagSafe; it's a magnet that connects the computer to the power cord. Many computer users either have experienced or fear the experience of getting a foot caught in the power cord and watching helplessly as the computer topples with a bang to the floor. MagSafe is intended to prevent that dreaded scenario by easily and safely disconnecting the computer from the cord. Apple "stole" the idea from the Japanese. More specifically, Apple made an "association" between two basically unrelated things, rice cookers and computers.

> " *The reason Apple is able to create products like the iPad is because we always try to be at the intersection of technology and liberal arts, to be able to get the best of both.*
>
> —STEVE JOBS "

For years, Japanese rice cookers had been built with magnetic latches for the sole reason of preventing a spill. When a computer falls to the floor, you might lose a replaceable object; if a boiling rice cooker falls to the floor, especially if a child is responsible for tripping on the power cord, the consequences could be irreparable tragedy. When MagSafe was introduced in 2006 for Apple MacBooks, message boards lit up with enthusiastic customers who thought it was one of the coolest, most innovative concepts to come along in a long time. Others dismissed it as an "old" idea, pointing to Japanese rice cookers and deep fryers at Wal-Mart that had the same feature.

It wasn't a new idea. Innovation occurred because Apple made an association that none of its competitors had considered.

How Steve Jobs "Sees" Things Differently

This notion of making creative associations through seeking out new experiences is worth exploring more closely, as it plays a significant role in the way Steve Jobs has generated one innovative product after another, and another, and another. Jobs is a classic iconoclast, one who aggressively seeks out, attacks, and overthrows conventional ideas. And iconoclasts, especially the successful ones, have an "affinity for new experiences," according to esteemed Emory University neuroscientist Gregory Berns.

In his insightful book *Iconoclast: A Neuroscientist Reveals How to Think Differently*, Berns could have been writing about Jobs when he said, "To see things differently than other people, the most effective solution is to bombard the brain with things it has never encountered before. Novelty releases the perceptual process from the shackles of past experiences and forces the brain to make new judgments."[9]

Berns declares that the skills of the iconoclast are attainable if we understand how iconoclasts supercharge their brains to make new connections. That's good news for Steve Jobs admirers who want to learn how he thinks.

Jobs doesn't see things differently from the rest of us. Jobs *perceives* things differently. Vision is not the same as perception; perception separates the innovator from the imitator. Vision is the process by which photons of light hit the photoreceptive cells of the eye's retina and get transmitted as neural impulses to different parts of the brain. Perception, as Berns points out, "is the much more complex process by which the brain *interprets* these signals."[10] Dozens of individuals saw the graphical user interface at the Xerox

PARC facility in Palo Alto, but it was Jobs who *perceived* it differently. He had an epiphany, a massive jolt of creativity.

Epiphanies rarely occur in familiar surroundings, according to Berns. This makes sense, especially if you recall the story of Steve Jobs and the apple orchard. His brainstorm was to link two words that don't look as if they belong together—*apple* and *computer*. The epiphany occurred several hundred miles away from Jobs's "work" environment, which at the time was still his parents' garage! Some skeptics said the company needed a more technical, formal-sounding name. Otherwise it would never be taken seriously, they claimed. Those skeptics, of course, did not *perceive* things the way Jobs did. The whole point was to soften up the image of computers to make them more appealing to average people. What could be simpler and more approachable than an apple? "It seems almost obvious that breakthroughs in perception do not come from simply staring at an object and thinking harder about it," says Berns. "Breakthroughs come from a perceptual system that is confronted with something that it doesn't know how to interpret. Unfamiliarity forces the brain to discard its usual categories of perception and create new ones."[11]

The key to "thinking differently" is to perceive things differently, through the lenses of a trailblazer. And to see things through these lenses, you must force your brain to make connections it otherwise would have missed. It sounds difficult, but there are simple ways to get the creative juices flowing. First, though, you must understand why it's difficult.

Your brain is the ultimate green technology; to keep you alive, it's always looking for ways to conserve energy. The phrase "creatures of habit" rings true because our brains operate under what psychologists call repetition suppression. Simply put, when your brain is confronted by the same visual stimulus repeatedly, the neural responses are reduced. Your brain is doing what it has evolved to do, which is to run the systems in your body as efficiently as possible. In order for our imaginations to operate at peak levels, however, those neurons have to fire at maximum output. Scientists such as Berns who have studied innovation, creativity, and brain behavior say the answer is to "bombard the brain with new experiences."[12]

When Steve Jobs studied calligraphy, it was such a novel experience that it ignited his creativity. When Jobs spent time meditating in an apple orchard, he experienced something new, and it led to some creative insights. When Jobs visited India in the 1970s, he experienced something radically different from his life in a California suburb. And when Jobs hired musicians, artists, poets, and historians, he was exposing himself to new experiences and novel ways of looking at a problem. Some of Jobs's most creative insights are the direct result of seeking out novel experiences either in physical locations or among the people with whom he chose to associate.

> *I wish him [Bill Gates] the best, I really do. I just think he and Microsoft are a bit narrow. He'd be a broader guy if he had dropped acid once or gone off to an ashram when he was younger.*[13]
>
> —STEVE JOBS

The Crankless Volkswagen

Steve Jobs sought out novel experiences both physically and intellectually. A physical change in location certainly fulfills the recommendation of psychologists to seek novel experiences, but often a successful brainstorm can be accomplished by approaching a problem in a novel way. Steve Jobs uses analogies and metaphors to initiate the creative process and to think differently about customers' problems.

An analogy shows a similarity between two different things. Using analogies is an effective technique in developing message platforms because it helps listeners understand new concepts. By comparing an idea with which your audience is unfamiliar to something they know something about, you increase the likelihood that they will buy into the concept. Jobs uses frequent analogies in his presentations when he introduces pioneering products. He also seems to use analogies when he's thinking about potential solutions to a problem. Seeing something novel in a familiar light allows him to make creative connections. Let's take the example of the crankless Volkswagen.

IBM released its first personal computer in the summer of 1981. By November of that year, Jobs had refined the plan behind the computer that would become the Macintosh. Most important for his team, the plan described what made the Macintosh different from new products offered by competitors such as IBM. The business plan, written by Steve Jobs himself, has rarely been quoted in popular books or publications, yet it provides a fascinating glimpse into one of the most creative minds of our time. Here is how Jobs described the Macintosh:

> Since 1979 Apple has invested millions of dollars and thousands of man-hours in the development of a consistent user interface that will take the crank out of the personal computer . . . The philosophy behind the Macintosh is very simple: in order for a personal computer to become a truly mass-market commodity, it will have to be functional, inexpensive, very friendly, and easy to use. Macintosh represents a significant step in the evolution of the mass-market personal computer. Macintosh is Apple's crankless Volkswagen, affordable to the quality conscious.[14]

The power of Steve's vision and his analogy ignited a wave of enthusiasm throughout Apple in the early 1980s. We've discussed the importance of vision to spark innovation, but the most creative visions require creative thinking, and creative thinking is the result of novel experiences and novel ways of looking at common problems.

The Telephone of the Computer Industry

Steve Jobs, the innovator, also found a useful analogy in the work of another brilliant innovator: the inventor of the telephone, Alexander Graham Bell. "We want to make a product like the first telephone. We want to make mass-market appliances," said Jobs.

"This is what the Macintosh is all about. It's the first telephone of our industry."[15]

Jobs saw Bell's invention as analogous to the Macintosh because in 1844, prior to the telephone, people were predicting that a telegraph machine would be on every desk in America. Jobs held that it never would have worked, because the majority of people would never have learned to use it. The sequence of Morse code dots and dashes was simply too daunting for most people. They could learn it, but few would want to. Jobs challenged the Macintosh team to make the first "telephone of the computer industry," a computer easy enough for the average person to learn how to use.

The telephone analogy also helped Jobs come up with a vision for what the Macintosh would look like. He was always a big thinker, with a knack for the inspiring analogy, as author Jeffrey Young relates: "As he thought about the machine, meditated on it, and considered his options, he spent hours staring at telephones on desks and in houses. The more he stared, the more he was struck by one thing: Many telephones sat on top of the telephone directory and that seemed to be the maximum space that a computer should take up on a desk."[16]

Young described what happened next. Jobs entered a design meeting with a phone book tucked under his arm. He threw it on the table and mandated that the Macintosh's footprint be no bigger than a telephone book. Keep in mind that a computer that fit on a telephone book would have to be three times smaller than any computer then on the market. *Three times smaller.* The designers were shocked at the request, and some were outspoken in their skepticism. Then again, as we discussed in the previous principle, a big, bold, and inspiring vision has a way of sparking creativity. Sure enough, the team responded and figured out how to build the computer vertically instead of horizontally. According to Young, "The vertical orientation reinforced the idea, for all who worked on the machine, that they were breaking new ground with the Mac, that they were producing a revolutionary little computer like none other that had ever been built. It was not so much revolutionary as innovative. The magic of the Mac was in the packaging, the mix of features. That mixing and matching, the shuffling and recycling of old ideas into a new package, was always Steve's strong suit."[17]

Does Steve Jobs see things differently? Yes. Is this skill unique to Jobs? No. You can learn to be more creative as long as you keep in mind that your brain will fight you every step of the way. By pursuing new experiences and thinking differently about common problems, you are asking your brain to expend energy when its natural role is to conserve as much as energy as possible. It's not easy, but by forcing yourself out of your comfort zone—physically and mentally—you will kick-start the firing of synapses, improving the odds of generating remarkable new ideas that have the potential of transforming your business and your life. Don't be surprised to discover novel approaches to common problems as you broaden your understanding of the human experience.

iLessons

1 Use analogies or metaphors to think about a problem. By finding the similarities between two things that are unalike, your brain makes new and sometimes profound connections.

2 Leave your comfort zone from time to time. Doing so is critical for the creative process to thrive.

3 Don't live in fear of the new. Embrace change. Embrace diversity of opinion and experience.

CHAPTER 7

Think Differently About How You Think

Imagination is more important than knowledge.

—ALBERT EINSTEIN

One of the most innovative periods in history traces its origin to Florence, Italy. The Renaissance started in the fourteenth century and spread across Europe for the next four hundred years. An explosion of ideas characterized the period. Painters, sculptors, thinkers, and inventors flourished. Geniuses such as Leonardo da Vinci and Michelangelo contributed to the significant cultural, scientific, and artistic advances of the era and came to define the term Renaissance man.

Scholars debate how the Renaissance started and why it began in Florence. Some have suggested that it was the result of luck and timing—a bunch of great thinkers were all born at the same time, and they all lived in Tuscany. Highly improbable. The more popular theory is referred to as the "Medici effect," suggesting that the role played by Lorenzo de' Medici and his wealthy family had much, if not everything, to do with setting the foundation for the greatest cultural movement in Earth's history.

Historians credit the Medici family for acting as a catalyst for innovation because the Medicis made a conscious effort to bring people together from vastly different fields and disciplines—architects, scientists, sculptors, poets, and painters. In many instances, these talents were rolled up into one person. For example, Leonardo da Vinci was a scientist, mathematician, inventor, painter, sculptor, engineer, and writer. He was a true "Renaissance man" and was widely admired for being so diverse. Thinkers of the time such as Leonardo had three principal traits in common: insatiable curiosity, a desire to challenge the status quo, and the knowledge that creative inspiration comes from seeking out new experiences. Does this list sound familiar? It should. These qualities are very much like the traits that drove the breakthrough success of another entrepreneur, Steve Jobs. Whether it's taking a calligraphy course, visiting an ashram, using a telephone as inspiration for a computer, or partnering with gifted designers outside the world of computers, Steve Jobs understands that "creativity is connecting things." Divergent experiences allow him to make connections others would typically miss. In "The Innovator's DNA," Harvard researchers conclude, "The world's most innovative companies prosper by capitalizing on the divergent associations of their founders, executives and employees."[1]

> *Contrary to conventional wisdom, innovation isn't about a genetic endowment magically given to some and not others; it's a set of skills that can be developed with practice. If you want to be one of the really successful people that make a mark in business, you want to be the person that comes up with the idea, not just the person who carries out others' ideas.*[2]
>
> —DR. JEFFREY DYER, BRIGHAM YOUNG UNIVERSITY

Act Different to Think Different

Apple's mantra, "Think Different," sounds simple, but researchers who study innovation have discovered that to think differently, you have to *act* differently. "Most executives view creativity and innovation as a 'black box' or something that other people are good at, but they don't know how to do it themselves," according to Jeffrey Dyer, a Brigham Young University management professor.[3] Dyer, along with two other researchers, surveyed three thousand executives and managers for "The Innovator's DNA." Regarding how respondents generated creative ideas, the article stated, "In almost every case they could describe engaging in a behavior before having the idea. Something they had watched, someone they had talked to, some sort of experiment they had conducted, or some question they had asked, was the trigger for the idea."[4] Acting differently prods the brain to make new, creative connections. Although Dyer and his colleagues did not speak directly to Steve Jobs, the study's conclusions fit what we know about Jobs and how he generates creative ideas. In fact, they echo some of Jobs's own words on the topic of innovation and the creative process.

The Innovator's DNA

Dyer and his fellow researchers, Hal B. Gregersen and Clayton M. Christensen, identified five skills that separate true innovators from the rest of us. We've already discussed "association," seeking out diverse experiences. Here is a short summary of the other four skills that can help you jump-start your own creative process.

QUESTIONING

Innovators get a kick out of questioning the status quo. Researchers found that successful innovators spend a tremendous amount of time thinking about how to change the world. More specifically, when they brainstorm, they ask questions such as, "If we did this, what would happen?" Many entrepreneurs could remember the specific questions they asked themselves when they had their most exciting breakthrough. For example, Michael Dell, who spoke to the researchers, said his idea for creating Dell Computer sprang up after he asked himself, "Why does a computer cost five times as much as the sum of its parts?"

To ask effective questions, researchers suggest that you pose queries in terms of "Why," "Why not," and "What if." They found that most managers are dedicated to improving the status quo a little, not blowing it up entirely. Questions that begin with "How" are more likely to lead to small improvements. The "Why" and "What if" questions lead to more explosive answers.

Apple's iPad might never have been created had it not been for Steve Jobs's asking effective questions. If he had asked his team, "How can we build a better e-book reader for the iPhone?" a new device would never have entered the conversation. Instead, he asked, "*Why* isn't there a middle category of device, in between a laptop and a smartphone? *What if* we built one?" The "What if" question sparked a discussion: a middle category would have to be far better than either a smartphone or laptop for doing some key tasks such as browsing the Web, enjoying and sharing photographs, and reading e-books. The questions led to the creation of Apple's most innovative device since the iPhone, a product that has the potential to revolutionize the worlds of publishing, entertainment, and media.

In a 1996 *Wired* interview, Steve Jobs said, "There's a phrase in Buddhism, a 'beginner's mind.' It's wonderful to have a beginner's mind."[5] Jobs was talking about a concept in Zen Buddhism called *shoshin*. It means having an attitude of openness, an eagerness to learn, and a lack of preconceptions. Zen teachers say that having a beginner's mind suggests facing life the way a small child does, full of curiosity, wonder, and amazement. It's easier to challenge the status quo because you are free to ask questions in the form of "Why . . .?" and "What if . . .?" It's a mind open to all possibilities.

EXPERIMENTING

Successful innovators engage in "active" experimentation, whether it's intellectual exploration, physical tinkering, or seeking out new surroundings. Steve Jobs is an experimenter, physically and spiritually. He's a physical experimenter because he likes to take apart devices to see how they work. He's just as focused on the inside of a device as he is on how it looks. At the same time, Jobs is also a spiritual experimenter. For example, Jobs took an interest in Zen Buddhism during the eighteen months he spent "dropping in" at Reed College. He said he was attracted to Zen because "it placed value on experience versus intellectual understanding." He explained, "I saw a lot of people contemplating things but it didn't seem to lead too many places. I got very interested in people who had discovered something more significant than an intellectual, abstract understanding."[6]

It's not widely known, but Jobs's spiritual experiments are actually the inspiration behind several early Apple innovations. For example, Jobs became convinced that the Apple II should not have a fan to cool the power supply. He thought consumers would find a quiet computer more attractive. "This conviction grew from his meditation interests, because the noisy fans that all the other computers included were intrusive and distracted from the pure elegance of the machine."[7] A fanless computer required a power supply that did not generate the intense heat characteristic of computers of the time. According to some authors who wrote about Apple's early history, Wozniak was not interested in power supplies, nor were many young engineers at the time, who considered power supplies a stodgy branch of electronics that didn't need to be fiddled with. Jobs "saw" things differently. Jobs's vision, based on his intellectual experimentation, challenged the status quo. He hired an engineer, Rod Holt, who designed an innovative power supply for the computer, one that substantially reduced the size of the Apple II and—yes—eliminated the necessity for a fan.

The only way to come up with something new—something world-changing—is to think outside of the constraints everyone else has. You have to think outside of the artificial limits every-one else has already set.[8]

—STEVE WOZNIAK

NETWORKING

Most people think of "networking" as handing out business cards at a chamber of commerce mixer. Researchers found that innovators do network, but not in the traditional sense. Instead, they surround themselves with interesting people who expand their domain of knowledge. For example, Michael Lazaridis, the founder of Research in Motion, told researchers his inspiration for the BlackBerry occurred at a conference. Likewise, David Neeleman came up with formative ideas for JetBlue at conferences he had attended. Innovators the likes of Lazaridis and Neeleman purposely sought out new experiences and new people, knowing that fresh ideas would jump-start their own creative processes. This is classic Renaissance thinking. Steve Jobs does not attend many conferences, but he connects with others outside of technology to widen his perspective. For example, walk into any Apple Store and you will find products designed by Jobs's friend Philippe Starck, a contemporary designer more widely known for hotel lobbies, or for tape dispensers and baby monitors sold at Target, than he is for computers.

> *Sometimes a simple change of environment is enough to jog the perceptual system out of familiar categories. This may be one reason why restaurants figure so prominently as sites of perceptual breakthroughs. A more drastic change of environment—traveling to another country, for example—is even more effective. When confronted with places never seen before, the brain must create new categories. It is in this process that the brain jumbles around old ideas with new images to create new syntheses.[9]*
>
> —GREGORY BERNS, *ICONOCLAST*

The more people you network with outside your field, the more "connections" you'll make that could lead to breakthrough ideas. For instance, Marc Benioff told me that his idea for creating salesforce.com evangelists came from his relationship with rap star MC Hammer. The rapper told Benioff about a hip-hop concept called "street teams," local networks of fans that back a particular artist. Benioff applied the idea to his start-up and created a "City Tour" program, in which he would meet with local users to extend the salesforce.com message, ignite passion for the product, and bring customers together who would evangelize for the company. Benioff's "genius" was in his ability to seize on a concept that was conventional in one community—the hip-hop scene—and apply it in an unconventional way to a new community, a technical one.

OBSERVING

Innovators watch people carefully, especially the behavior of potential customers. It's during these times of observation that successful innovators seem to discover their chief breakthroughs. The researchers recount the stories of Intuit founder Scott Cook, who came up with Quicken after watching his wife struggle in frustration to keep track of her finances, and of Pierre Omidyar, who launched eBay in 1996 after linking three unconnected dots: "a fascination with creating more-efficient markets . . . his fiancée's desire to locate hard-to-find Pez dispensers and the ineffectiveness of local classified ads in locating such items."[10]

Innovative companies such as Intel have long known about the power of observation. Intel hires thousands of engineers to build next-generation microprocessors for computers, cars, netbooks, GPS devices, and a wide variety of other electronic applications that touch your life every day. Engineers are only part of the story. While those engineers are designing the next generation of technologies, another group of employees often can be found thousands of miles away, visiting small villages in India, living with a family in Malaysia, or watching students in another locale use computers in a classroom. They are anthropologists, and their job is to help Intel see the world through customers' eyes.

The anthropologists, or ethnographers, convey what they learn to engineers, who, in turn, build technology compatible with the everyday lives of average people. For example, there are significant differences between America and Asia regarding the size and configuration of people's homes, and since Intel is very interested in the future of electronics in the home, these differences influence computer and technology design for different global markets.

Anthropologists discovered that dust and a lack of electricity were problems in remote Indian villages, so Intel designed computer technology for laptops that incorporated longer battery life and dust-resistant casings. Anthropologists also learned that many families liked to share photos and videos from their laptop computers, but connecting to a television screen was too complicated for most people, so viewers settled for huddling around a small laptop screen. Based on this information, engineers created Intel Wireless Display technology to wirelessly send laptop information to a television screen. In this way Intel has systematized "getting out of the office."

Remember that the brain's role is to conserve energy. Observations jump-start the creative process and force your mind to make connections it otherwise would have avoided. Intel has learned that making effective observations requires meeting people in their surroundings, not one's own.

Adriana Herrera is a principal for ERA Communications, a public relations firm with offices located in Hawaii and San Diego. Prior to working in public relations, Herrera had experience in industrial and organizational psychology, during which she studied creative thinking. Her firm is dedicated to nurturing a culture of creativity. One element of that creative culture is meeting clients in atypical surroundings. Since creativity rarely happens in a gray meeting room, ERA client meetings are held outdoors—walking, hiking, and even surfing (this is Hawaii, after all). Brainstorm meetings take place in public gardens, along public beaches, or on the waves as participants paddle surfboards. "My educational background in psychology taught me that when we do something physical, the synapses are firing, and the blood is flowing to the brain," says Herrera.[11]

Herrera's firm was handed the task of promoting a San Diego conference aimed at reducing waste. When Herrera scheduled a meeting with the San Diego Environmental Services information officer, she suggested that instead of meeting in his office or at a coffee shop, they meet at a landfill to "talk trash." The experience gave Herrera ideas to help her effectively communicate the purpose of the San Diego Zero Waste Business Conference.

> The human brain is intensely interactive. You use multiple parts of it in every task you perform. It is in fact in the dynamic use of the brain—finding new connections between things—that true breakthroughs occur. Albert Einstein, for instance, took great advantage of the dynamics of intelligence. Einstein's prowess as a scientist and mathematician is legend. However, Einstein was a student of all forms of expression, believing that he could put anything that challenged the mind to use in a variety of ways. For instance, he interviewed poets to learn more about the role of intuition and imagination . . . his success came not from the brute strength of his mental processing power but from his imagination and creativity.[12]
>
> —KEN ROBINSON, *THE ELEMENT*

Companies that are successful at blazing new trails—whether it's a new way of delivering software (salesforce.com), designing microprocessors (Intel), creating public relations campaigns (ERA Communications), or introducing new computing, music, and entertainment devices (Apple)—are typically led by people who understand that the brain needs some help to get the creative juices flowing. These leaders seek out new experiences to make clever associations, connecting seemingly unrelated ideas to gain new knowledge.

Seeking out new experiences can help you unleash the creative process. For this approach to work, though, you must trust that breaking out of your familiar physical or mental routine will lead to unfamiliar breakthroughs, not now, perhaps, but someday. Routine is the enemy of growth, progress, and innovation, but it takes confidence to believe that breaking free of routine will clear new, creative pathways in your brain. Creativity doesn't always happen on your schedule. Something you saw on that exotic trip to a foreign country two years ago may spark an idea today that you can apply to your business. Attending the conference that had nothing to do with your field may turn out one day to give you the brainstorm you need to take your company to the next level. Observing your customer in her environment or scheduling a meeting outdoors may eventually translate to a successful new idea. And taking that offbeat class—as with Jobs and the calligraphy class—may lead to a new way of looking at the world, only *years later*. "You can't connect the dots looking forward; you can only connect them looking backwards," Steve Jobs said in his Stanford commencement speech. "So you have to trust that the dots will somehow connect in your future. You have to trust in something—your gut, destiny, life, karma, whatever. This approach has never let me down, and it has made all the difference in my life."

iLessons

1 Spend fifteen minutes a day asking questions that challenge the status quo. Instead of asking "How," use questions that begin with "Why" and "What if."

2 Seek out new experiences. If you typically read nonfiction texts, read a fiction book. If you usually choose business publications from the magazine stand, visit another category once in a while, such as home and gardening or arts and antiques. Attend conferences outside of your industry. Volunteer for local events that have nothing to do with your job. Take every opportunity to travel. Researchers have documented that the more countries a person has lived in, the more likely the person is to leverage that experience to create innovative ideas, processes, or methods.

3 Hire outside of conventional norms. Recall what Steve Jobs said about the people who designed and marketed the original Macintosh. The team was successful because it included musicians, artists, poets, and scientists. Organizational psychologists and innovative design firms have discovered that the most creative teams are diverse, composed of people with vastly different, but complementary, talents, skills, and experiences.

Sell Dreams, Not Products

We, too, are going to think differently and
serve the people who have been buying
our products since the beginning. Because
a lot of times people think they're crazy,
but in that craziness we see genius.

—STEVE JOBS

CHAPTER 8

See Genius in Their Craziness

The people who are crazy enough to think they can change the world are the ones who do.

—APPLE AD

The Macworld Expo on August 7, 1997, could have been Apple's final act. Jobs had been away from the company he'd founded for eleven years, and the company was turning out lackluster products under a string of CEOs. Chief executives John Sculley, Michael Spindler, and Gil Amelio all had advanced degrees in business, engineering, or physics. They were smart guys, except for one fatal flaw: they all failed to understand Apple's core customer. As a result, Apple sales had plummeted, from $11 billion in 1995 to about $7 billion. Apple was losing money and employees. Many Apple veterans were disillusioned and resigned their posts. Some left involuntarily when Gil Amelio laid off thousands in 1996. Apple was close to bankruptcy. The company that sparked a computer revolution was in real danger of flaming out.

At that Macworld Expo in Boston, Steve Jobs—whom Amelio had brought back as an Apple "adviser"—took the stage to thunderous applause, making several announcements, including Amelio's resignation and the appointment of a new board of directors. Jobs would keep his role as CEO at Pixar but would take over Apple in the "interim." The real headline, however, had little to do with who was not there and instead focused on who *was* there, at least via satellite. Jobs announced a $150 million investment from Apple's nemesis, Microsoft. Bill Gates appeared on a giant video screen. He was greeted with mild applause and a smattering of boos. Jobs quickly came to Gates's defense and made it clear that the two companies had to work together for the best interest of the industry—and for Apple's survival. The event was also notable for the fact that no new products were introduced. So, the press understandably focused on the return of Steve Jobs and the "Microsoft deal." Looking back, the keynote presentation gave us a glimpse into the innovation strategy that would lead to Apple's resurgence: Jobs knew his customers better than anyone at the company. He understood their needs, hopes, and dreams. Above all, he embraced their craziness.

Our Customers Are Out to Change the World

In the weeks prior to the Boston speech, Jobs had asked one hundred people at Apple this question: Who is the largest education company in the world? Only two people answered correctly: Apple. The company was, hands down, the largest supplier of products to the education community. Apple accounted for a full 65 percent of all computers used by teachers. According to Jobs, if people within the company did not know—or appreciate—their core customer, then it would be impossible to create new products to meet customers' needs.

In addition to the education market, Apple was the dominant computing tool among creative professionals in the publishing and design fields. Jobs cited the fact that even though Apple's market share was 7 percent, Apple accounted for 80 percent of all computers used in advertising, graphic design, prepress, and printing. Sixty-four percent of all Internet sites were also created using Macs. The "creative types" were clearly an important customer for Apple, a customer base the company could leverage as it was nursed back to health. Jobs believed Apple had neglected this core customer base of creative professionals. "For example, 10 to 15 percent of Mac sales can be traced directly back to people using Adobe Photoshop as their power app," Jobs told the audience. "When was the last time you saw Adobe and Apple comarketing Photoshop? When is the last time Apple went to Adobe and asked, 'How can we make a computer that runs Photoshop faster?' We will focus much more on these things."[1]

Prior to Jobs's keynote, an issue of *Wired* magazine carried a cover photo of an Apple logo sprouting thorns. The headline read: "Pray." Another publication proclaimed, "Apple has become irrelevant."[2] Where many people saw a dying company, Jobs saw a company that was extremely relevant, because he knew his customers and the role Apple played in their lives. Apple was executing brilliantly, Jobs asserted. It was just executing on the wrong things and not meeting the needs of its twenty-five million core customers.

Jobs closed his presentation in Boston with an observation that foreshadowed one of the most influential ad campaigns in corporate history and set the tone for an Apple resurgence. Jobs paused, lowered his voice, and slowed his tempo. He spent the next two minutes describing Apple's core customer—the customer's skills, needs, and dreams:

> Lastly, I want to talk a little about Apple the brand and what it means to a lot of us . . . I think you still have to think differently to buy an Apple computer. I think the people who do buy them do think differently. They are the creative spirits in this world. They are people who are not out to get a job done; they are out to change the world. And they are out to change the world using whatever great tools they can get. And we make tools for those kinds of people. Hopefully, what you've seen here today are some beginning steps that give you some confidence that we, too, are going to think differently and serve the people who have been buying our products since the beginning. Because a lot of times people think they're crazy, but in that craziness we see genius, and those are the people we're making tools for.[3]

Here's to the Crazy Ones

One month after the Boston Macworld Expo, Apple launched the "Think Different" ad campaign, widely credited for restoring Apple's image after the debacle of the previous years. The campaign, created by TBWA/Chiat/Day, launched in September 1997. It received critical acclaim, developed a large cult following, and remained the centerpiece of Apple's advertising efforts until 2002, an eternity for a corporate image campaign. In the prior eleven years, without Steve Jobs at the helm, the company had lost its status as a trailblazer. It took thirty seconds to restore the image. The television ad was ultimately successful because it reminded Apple employees who their customers were, and, for customers, it reinforced the idea that they were doing business with a brand that understood their hopes and dreams.

The television ads that composed the "Think Different" campaign were called "Crazy Ones." It was one of the most innovative advertising campaigns of all time. In the television spot, a black-and-white montage of heroes, thinkers, inventors, and rebels filled the screen: Albert Einstein smoking a pipe, Bob Dylan playing a harmonica, Martin Luther King Jr. delivering the "I have a dream" speech, Richard Branson shaking a bottle of champagne, Martha Graham dancing, and Picasso painting. As the inspiring images filled the screen, actor Richard Dreyfuss read a free-verse poem that, while not written by Steve Jobs, reflected his belief in the spirit of discovery:

> Here's to the crazy ones. The misfits. The rebels. The trouble-makers. The round pegs in the square holes. The ones who see things differently. They're not fond of rules. And they have no respect for the status quo. You can quote them, disagree with them, glorify or vilify them. About the only thing you can't do is ignore them. Because they change things. They push the human race forward. And while some may see them as the crazy ones, we see genius. Because the people who are crazy enough to think they can change the world are the ones who do.[4]

Reading the text doesn't have the same impact as listening to Dreyfuss recite it, which you can do on YouTube (you tube.com/watch?v=XUfH-BEBMoY). You really should watch it to appreciate how an accomplished actor can make the words on a page come alive. Steve Jobs said the ad campaign was intended to remind Apple employees who their heroes are. It also reminded customers to believe in themselves, their hopes, their dreams. The commercial ends with a little girl opening her eyes as if she is seeing the possibilities ahead of her. The implied message was that people who use Apple computers could also see the possibilities that others did not. They were the "creative spirits" in the world, the square pegs in the round holes. Apple was speaking directly to them.

The ad campaign, along with the presentation by Jobs that preceded it, reveals a fundamental difference between radical innovators and mediocre copycats: the former believe in their customers' dreams and their ability to change the world; the latter see their customers as dollar signs and nothing more.

> *The whole purpose of the "Think Different" campaign was that people had forgotten about what Apple stood for, including the employees. We thought long and hard about how you tell somebody what you stand for, what your values are, and it occurred to us that if you don't know somebody very well, you can ask them, "Who are your heroes?" You can learn a lot about people by hearing who their heroes are. So we said, "Okay, we'll tell them who our heroes are."*[5]
>
> —STEVE JOBS

Customers Aren't "Eyeballs"

From 1995 to 2000, during the height of the dot-com boom, companies were spawned that offered little or no value proposition. They were in the business of chasing "eyeballs." Entrepreneurs, investors, and analysts were largely united in the belief that once enough eye-balls had landed on a site, these young companies would succeed in "monetizing" them. We all know what happened. Some people who arrived early for the digital gold rush got rich; most went bust. I was hosting a financial show at the time on a national television network called TechTV, now G4 (my colleagues included technology author Leo Laporte, *PC* magazine columnist John Dvorak, and Internet entrepreneur and Digg founder Kevin Rose). It was an ideal platform from which to view what became known as "irrational exuberance." I recall meeting the poster boys for the dot-com bubble, Stephan Paternot and Todd Krizelman. They became known as the Bubble Boys and not in a good way.

The two friends started TheGlobe.com. It went public in November 1998 and posted one of the biggest single-day gains in IPO history. To this day I can't tell you exactly how TheGlobe.com would improve anyone's life or, frankly, what it did. As it turned out, neither could the founders at the time. It was some kind of free-chat, free-messaging site—a "portal," for lack of a better word. It didn't matter to the founders. The boys spent money like crazy, made a big show of their success, and lost everything one year later when TheGlobe.com fell to Earth. The share price dropped from a high of $97 to about a dime. In hindsight, its demise should have been easy to predict. A CNN video crew filmed Paternot in a New York club dancing with his model girlfriend. "Got the girl. Got the money. Now I'm ready to live a disgusting frivolous life," he said.[6] Needless to say, these guys never shared the Steve Jobs ethos. While the Bubble Boys were busy playing the role of tycoons, Jobs was building real products to help real customers achieve real goals. In Apple's world, unlike the Bubble Boys', customers aren't "eyeballs." They are men and women, young and old, professionals and amateurs, who have one thing in common: they dream of a better life. Apple has created world-changing products precisely because they help their customers fulfill their world-changing dreams.

Walk into most any nightclub on any given night and you're likely to see the DJ playing music off a Mac. Some use PCs, but Mac notebooks seem to be the DJ tool of choice. Now, I'm not exactly a club hopper, so I assumed that DJs are hip and, well, Macs are cool. However, when I asked one DJ at a Las Vegas nightclub why he used a Mac, the first thing out of his mouth had nothing to do with being hip. "It doesn't crash. I can't risk losing my gig at the Venetian because my computer froze," he said.

This DJ was not using a Mac to look cool. He was using it because it was reliable. His dream was to become a successful DJ who would be hired for the best nightclubs in Vegas, New York, and London. He's a devoted Apple evangelist because the company's products help him achieve his dream. If the Mac's aesthetic design makes him look hip, that's frosting. His overriding concern is that the dreaded "blue screen of death" would surely end his dreams, no matter how trendy he looked.

We Figure Out What We Want

Steve Jobs knows his customers so well that he can build great products without focus groups. He sees no need for them. Nor does Jobs conduct a lot of market research or hire consultants. "The only consultants I've ever hired in my 10 years is one firm to analyze Gateway's retail strategy so I would not make some of the same mistakes [when launching Apple's retail stores] they made. But we never hire consultants per se. We just want to make great products," Jobs once said.[7]

This is not to say that Apple does not listen to its customers; it most certainly does, and the result is a constant stream of updates, colors, features, and functionality. But remember, there's innovation with a small *i* and innovation with a big *I*. There may be "no *I* in *team*," as the saying goes, but there is a great big *I* in *Innovation*, and when it comes to breakthrough success at Apple, Steve Jobs is not hesitant to ask himself, "What would *I* want?" It turns out that Jobs and the people who work at Apple are the company's best focus group. Asked why Apple doesn't do focus groups, Jobs responded:

> It's not about pop culture and it's not about fooling people, and it's not about convincing people that they want something they don't. *We figure out what we want.* And I think we're pretty good at having the right discipline to think through whether a lot of other people are going to want it, too. That's what we get paid

to do. So you can't go out and ask people, you know, what's the next big thing? There's a great quote by Henry Ford, right? He said, "If I'd have asked my customers what they wanted, they would have told me 'A faster horse.'"[8]

"Steve Jobs avoids most focus groups like the plague," wrote tech analyst Rob Enderle. "It comes down to the very real fact that most customers don't know what they want in a new product." Enderle suspects that had Apple resorted to focus groups in developing the iPad, the product would have been closer to what the Microsoft tablet was a decade earlier. It would have been more expensive, heavier, and more capable—a laptop without the keyboard. Instead, Apple introduced a device that was thin, light, and simple to use. According to Enderle, Apple will sell millions of more units than it would have if the company had asked customers what they wanted. "Most vendors shotgun out products that have been focus-group tested in the hope that volume and choice will effectively cover their potential audience and capture the customer," Enderle states. "Apple, on the other hand, builds few products and uses marketing to drive customers to its offerings."[9]

Jobs said it's hard to design by focus groups because most of the time people don't know what they want until you show it to them. So, how do Apple employees solve this dilemma of not knowing whether a product will fly with their customers before they build it? It's simple, really. They turn to the ultimate focus group, the group with the most demanding criteria: themselves. *We figure out what we want.* Apple's DNA is a consumer company, and it's the consumer that Jobs and his team think about obsessively. If something appeals to Jobs and his team, it will probably appeal to vast numbers of people outside of Apple, enough to make the product highly popular and richly profitable.

Technology Epiphanies

Innovation "consultants" enjoy rattling off buzzwords such as *user-centric innovation, mass collaboration,* and *crowdsourcing.* All of these terms are jargon for the key idea that one should pay close attention to customers and involve customers directly in the development and deployment of new products or services. You never hear Steve Jobs use these coinages, but you often hear them from innovation "experts." That tells me these experts don't quite get it. Steve Jobs isn't impressed with jargon. He's impressed by creating something so simple, approachable, and aesthetically pleasing that it helps Apple's customers improve their lives.

Apple listens to its customers every day. However, the real secret behind Apple's innovations, the innovation with a capital *I*, comes not from listening to users but from introducing its customers to a completely new way of thinking about solutions for their problems. This is what Jobs means when he says Apple doesn't do focus groups. In no way is he recommending that you stop listening to your customers. He's advocating that you get closer than ever to your customers. So close, in fact, that you tell them what they need well before they realize it themselves.

Italian management professor Robert Verganti makes a persuasive argument that companies that create radical innovations put forth a vision, or what he calls a *proposal*, telling us what we will love. "Insights do not move from users to Apple but the other way around. More than Apple listening to us, it's us who listen to Apple," Verganti says.[10] Listening to your customers is acceptable for driving incremental innovation, but it hardly generates breakthroughs, says Verganti. A better description for what Apple delivers is what Verganti calls a "technology epiphany," a vision of what the customer will want in the future. In this way Apple changes the way you see the world. According to Verganti, Apple is not driven by a "user-centered" approach to innovation as much as it is driven by something far more meaningful, and that is customer value. "If you focus on being proud of what kind of products you offer to consumers, then eventually your company will be successful and shareholder value will come. Many CEOs and frontline managers are so focused on shareholder value they forget about the consumer value, which is ultimately what makes a company profitable."[11] Apple is a supremely profitable company because it focuses on the needs of its core customers. Steve Jobs began revealing technology epiphanies with the introduction of the Apple II and continues to do so today, most notably in the areas of music, telecommunications, and mobile computing.

THE RECIPE FOR DIGITAL MUSIC

Apple did not introduce the iPod in 2001 to start a revolution; it introduced the iPod to solve its customers' pain. The digital music players of the time that were based on small memory chips could store only a few dozen songs, not much better than a portable CD player. A few products based on a new, 2.5-inch Fujitsu hard drive could hold potentially thousands of songs but had a fundamental flaw: excruciatingly slow speeds from the computer to the player. Apple had the solution: FireWire.

On October 23, 2001, Steve Jobs introduced the first iPod: "1,000 songs in your pocket." He described it as a quantum leap in listening to music, because listeners could carry their entire music libraries in their pockets. In his presentation, Jobs spent several minutes on FireWire, demonstrating exactly how the iPod would solve the problem of painfully slow transfers. Apple developed FireWire in the 1990s as a method of delivering information very quickly between digital devices. By incorporating the technology into its new music player, Apple solved a problem that music fans had complained about. Here's how Jobs revealed the solution:

> Apple invented FireWire, and we ship FireWire on every computer we make. It's built into iPod. It's the first and only music player with FireWire. Why? Because it's fast. You can download an entire CD onto an iPod in five to ten seconds. Let's take a look at how it compares to USB. Five to ten seconds to load an entire CD with FireWire. On a USB, you're talking five minutes. Let's talk about one thousand songs. On iPod with FireWire it is under ten minutes, on a USB player it is five hours. Can you imagine? You get to watch it for five hours as it loads the songs. Under ten minutes with iPod. It's thirty times faster than any other MP3 player.[12]

Of course, there were other notable aspects of the iPod. It had a scroll wheel for easy navigation, ten hours of battery life, a small form factor (the size of a deck of cards), and Apple's classic ease-of-use design elements. In short, the iPod was a much better digital music player. But it was *not* a radical innovation. The "technology epiphany" occurred two years later with the launch of the iTunes Music Store.

On April 28, 2003, Steve Jobs redefined what it meant to acquire and enjoy music. In Verganti's words, Jobs made a proposal to his customers—one that no focus group would have offered: in return for paying for music, only ninety-nine cents a song, customers would enjoy a more satisfying music experience. If he had simply listened to his customers, none would have told Jobs that they wanted to pay for music. Jobs had to change the way his customers thought about their experience. He did so by starting with a history lesson. "We all know that in 1999, there was this phenomenon called Napster. It was shut down in 2001, but it demonstrated some things for us. It demonstrated that the Internet was made for music delivery. Its offspring, Kazaa, is alive and well today. There's a good side and a bad side to this. The good side is, it offers users near instant gratification, at least compared to going down to the record store. The downside is, it's stealing. So, from a user's point of view, let's look at the good side and the downside."[13]

Jobs then rattled off a list of benefits offered by the status quo:

» A vast selection of music, better than any record store on the planet
» Unlimited CD burning
» Store music on an unlimited number of MP3 players
» It's free!

"What's wrong with this?" Jobs asked. He answered his own question with a discussion of the "dark side" of the status quo:

» Very unreliable downloads
» Very unreliable quality ("A lot of these songs are encoded by seven-year-olds, and they don't do a great job.")
» There are no previews ("You can spend a lot of time downloading a song to find out it's not the one you wanted.")
» No album cover-art
» It's stealing[14]

"Most people don't focus on these things," Jobs said. "They focus on the good things. Well, why has this proliferated? Because there is no legal alternative that's worth beans." Following that prologue, Jobs introduced the iTunes Music Store, "Music downloads done right."

Jobs described how Apple negotiated landmark deals with the major record labels. The original iTunes Store was launched with two hundred thousand tracks, and with those came the rights to own your music on an unlimited number of iPods. Jobs knew some consumers might consider even ninety-nine cents per song as too expensive, especially when they could get music for free. So, he addressed this issue:

> How much is ninety-nine cents? How many of you had a Starbucks latte this morning? That's three bucks. You could have bought three songs. And think about how many lattes are being sold around the world today. Now let's look at the downsides again. What does it mean to have unreliable downloads or unreliable encoding? Here is a typical scenario. You go to Kazaa to find one song. You never find one song; you find fifty to sixty of them. And you've got to pick which one of those is going to give you a reliable download. You often pick wrong. The download is as slow as molasses and craps out halfway through. You try again and get the same result. After a few times, you finally download the song, only to find the last four seconds is cut off, or it has a glitch in the middle, or it was encoded by someone who didn't know what they were doing and it sounds bad. You try again and again, and after fifteen minutes you finally succeed in getting a clean version of the song you want. What that means is you'll spend an hour to get four songs that you can get at under four bucks from Apple. That means you're working for under minimum wage! In addition, you are stealing.[15]

The iTunes Music Store is an example of a technology epiphany. "The iPod is not simply a portable music player. The entire system that Apple created—the iPod, the iTunes software application, the iTunes Store, the business model for selling music—offers a seamless experience . . . Thus the iPod's success is not only due, as many claim, to its sleek style and unique functionalities such as its user interface and the number of songs it can carry. The main reason for its success comes from the meaning people associate with the iPod's immaterial components," says Verganti.[16]

Apple's fortunes took off after the radical innovation of the iTunes Music Store and not from its introduction of the iPod. The iPod was an impressive, but incremental, form of innovation. The Music Store sparked a revolution. Verganti reminds us that Apple introduced the iPod in 2001 and the iTunes Store in 2003; iTunes support for Windows arrived one year later. Verganti points out that demand for the iPod started to soar in 2004, when sales were eight times as high as the cumulative sales of the first two years. Today the iTunes Store accounts for more than 70 percent of all legal online digital music sales worldwide, making Apple the world's largest music retailer. As of this writing, ten billion songs have been downloaded. The iTunes catalog has grown to more than twelve million songs, fifty-five thousand TV shows, and eighty-five hundred movies.

How did Apple become the world's most successful music company? Did it invent music players? No. Did it create music content? No. Was Apple the first company to make digital music available for downloading? No. But Apple did do something no other company had done: it radically improved the customer experience.

Whereas the iPod was a classic example of user-centered design (you have a problem, we have a solution), the iTunes Store was an example of radical innovation, which, as Verganti observes, "seldom emerges by chasing users."[17] Instead, Apple made a *proposal* to its customers. If you're willing to pay a small amount for your music, here is what we will provide in return: fast, easy, reliable downloads, a vast library of content, and good karma!

APPLE REVOLUTIONIZES THE PHONE

The iPod transformed Apple and the entire music industry. In 2007, the iPhone transformed Apple once again—and revolutionized the entire telecommunications industry. *Time* magazine heralded the iPhone as the best invention of 2007, for several reasons:

» **It's pretty.** (Jobs believes good design is as important as good technology.)

» **It's touchy-feely.** Just as Apple pioneered the graphical user interface with Macintosh, it knew what to do with multitouch technology, giving users the illusion of manipulating data with their hands.

» **It will make other phones better.**

» **It's not a phone; it's a platform.** This turned out to be true as thousands of third-party developers created "apps" that make our lives easier.[18]

What's interesting to note is that none of the reasons that impressed *Time*'s reporters would have come up in focus groups had Apple asked customers what they wanted in a smartphone experience. Imagine if Apple had asked members of a focus group if they would consider doing without a stylus. *No stylus? What would you want us to use? How would we navigate the screen? With our fingers? That's absurd. Please make a phone with a retractable keyboard and we'll be happy.* Customers don't innovate; they iterate. So, Apple had to make a proposal, a vision of how the phone could change your life. In his own words, here is how Steve Jobs proposed his vision in January 2007:

> The most advanced phones are called "smartphones," so they say. They typically combine a phone plus e-mail plus a baby Internet. The problem is they are not so smart and they are not so easy to use. . . . They're really complicated. . . . What we want is to make a leapfrog product that is way smarter than any mobile device has ever been and supereasy to use. This is what iPhone is. . . .[19]

Steve Jobs and the iPhone team relied on their instincts. They were their own best customers. "We all had cell phones. We just hated them, they were so awful to use. The software was terrible. The hardware wasn't very good. We talked to our friends, and they all hated their cell phones, too. Everybody seemed to hate their phones," Steve Jobs told a *Fortune* magazine reporter. He continued:

> It was a great challenge. Let's make a great phone that we fall in love with. And we've got the technology. We've got the miniaturization from the iPod. We've got the sophisticated operating

system from Mac. Nobody had ever thought about putting operating systems as sophisticated as OS X inside a phone, so that was a real question. We had a big debate inside the company whether we could do that or not. And that was one where I had to adjudicate it and say, "We're going to do it." The smartest software guys were saying they can do it, so let's give them a shot. And they did.[20]

By challenging the status quo and making a proposal for what a phone could be, Steve Jobs not only created a better phone but also created an entire "ecosystem," a vibrant network of developers who built applications (140,000 apps and growing) that few people realized they would come to enjoy and rely on every day.

Former Mac evangelist and Alltop founder Guy Kawasaki once said that the purpose of innovation is not to build cool products and cool technologies; the purpose of innovation is happy people. In other words, use all the digital tools at your disposal to create new products and services (computers, websites, smartphones, advanced diagnostic equipment, etc.), but always keep in mind that the goal is the same: putting a smile on someone's face. Maintain a commitment to excellence and an insatiable desire to upend the status quo.

FILLING A GAP CUSTOMERS DIDN'T KNOW THEY HAD

On Saturday, April 3, 2010, thousands of people stood in long lines outside Apple Stores across America. (See Figure 8.1.) Many had been in line all night to be one of the first to buy a new iPad. Among the early fans: Apple cofounder Steve Wozniak, who drove up on his Segway scooter to a mall store in San Jose. He arrived at six o'clock Friday evening. Yes, the night *before* the store's opening. (Steve Jobs himself took a more leisurely trip into an Apple Store near his house in Palo Alto around noon on Saturday.) Woz left the store with two new iPads for his wife's parents. "They're not ready for the complicated computer world," he told *PCWorld*. "They have these old computers. But the iPad simplifies things. It's like a restart. We all say we want things to be simpler. All of a sudden we have this simple thing."[21]

FIGURE 8.1 "Early" adopters hurry up and wait for opportunity to purchase a new iPad. Bobby Bank/Getty Image News

You'd think that if your son-in-law pioneered the personal computer, you might be comfortable with computers or at least take some lessons from him. Wozniak's comments to *PCWorld* reinforce the fact that, for many people, computers are all-in-all too complicated. Wozniak suggested that the iPad would appeal to those who find traditional computers daunting. He was right. Three hundred thousand iPads were sold on the first day. It's too early to tell just how popular the iPad will ultimately be, but what is clear is that Jobs had transformed computing yet again, making products that people actually like to use.

It's safe to say that the iPad wasn't the result of a focus group. How could it be? It's hard to believe that traditional computer users would have expressed the following preferences: *I'd like a computer that's bigger than a smartphone but not quite as large as a laptop. Make sure it can't place phone calls, and don't load it up with all the features of a full-featured computer. Please don't include a mouse, and, while you're at it, leave out the keyboard as well; I'd like to navigate the new device with my fingers.* Apple's customers did not ask for the iPad, but they got it anyway, and once they did, they realized they couldn't live without it.

Newsweek's Dan Lyons originally deemed the iPad to be a product that he wouldn't fall in love with. He assumed it would simply be a bigger version of Apple's iPod Touch, a device that includes all the iPhone's applications but without the phone features. "Then I got a chance to use an iPad, and it hit me: I want one. Right away I could see how I'd use it. I'd keep it in the living room to check e-mail and browse the Web. I'd take it to the kitchen and read *The New York Times* while I eat breakfast. I'd bring it with me on a plane to watch movies and read books," Lyons wrote. "That may not be life-changing, but is it worth 500 bucks? Yup. Done. Sold."[22]

Let's go invent tomorrow instead of wondering about what happened yesterday.

—STEVE JOBS, AT D: ALL THINGS DIGITAL

Gizmodo's Jesus Diaz suggested that iPad is the future of computing, because it requires no training whatsoever. "Normal people don't like today's computers," he wrote. "Most loathe them because they can't fully understand their absurd complexity . . . Just like the iPhone changed the idea of what a phone should be without anyone truly realizing it, Apple's new computer will completely and permanently change our idea of what a computer is and how it should behave."[23]

The iPad fills a gap, one that most of us didn't know existed. That is, until Steve Jobs revealed it:

Most of us use laptops and a smartphone. A question has arisen, is there room for a third category of device in the middle? Something in between a laptop and a smartphone? We've pondered this question for years. The bar is pretty high. In order to create a new category of devices, those devices are going to have to be far better at doing some key tasks, better than the laptop and better than a smartphone. What kinds of tasks? Things like browsing the Web. That's a pretty tall order. Doing e-mail. Enjoying and sharing photographs. Watching videos. Enjoying your music collection. Playing games. Reading e-books. If there's going to be a third category of device, it's going to have to be better at these kinds of tasks than either a laptop or smartphone; otherwise it has no reason for being.[24]

Jobs then outlined a list of benefits that customers would find once they used the new device. In Jobs's words, these are the benefits consumers would enjoy with the iPad experience:

» Best browsing experience you've ever had
» It's a dream to type on
» Wonderful way to share your photos
» Awesome way to enjoy your music collection
» Amazing to watch TV shows and movies on
» More intimate than a laptop, more capable than a smartphone[25]

Apple customers did not ask for a tablet computer, but once Apple proposed the technology epiphany, its customers fell in love with it.

What Jobs and Streisand Have in Common

Some observers suggest that most companies will never be able to innovate the way Apple does. It's certainly possible to adopt the principles that drive Steve Jobs, but the simple truth is that most leaders don't have the stomach to follow through. Apple introduces amazing products because a commitment to excellence runs deeply within its DNA. "Some people aren't used to an environment where excellence is expected," Steve Jobs told *BusinessWeek* in 1988. Jobs made the remark in response to a claim by an ex-employee who said Jobs drove his employees too hard. Jobs didn't seem fazed. "Part of my responsibility is to be a yardstick of quality," he said.[26]

Jobs's habit of keeping a close eye on every aspect of product design might have lost him a few employees, but it has won him legions of devoted customers. Jobs is relentlessly focused on the customer and his or her experience with the product and the company. He will not tolerate anything that doesn't meet his exacting standards. If he pisses off a few people in the process, so be it. "Steve Jobs did call people 'bozos,'" said former Apple employee

Sharon Aby, "but so did a lot of other employees. A bozo was somebody who tried to push through something that wasn't in the best interest of the customer. We had higher standards than anyone else." Aby says that Jobs brought the same commitment to excellence that Barbra Streisand brings to her music. Streisand would drive recording engineers crazy because she insisted on recording her songs over and over until it sounded just right. The producers and engineers would say they couldn't hear a difference, but after dozens of takes they had to admit that the song was indeed better. "Steve Jobs can hear things others can't," says Aby, "and in the end, he made it better."[27]

So, why can't most companies innovate the way Apple does? Because they lack two things: Jobs's commitment to excellence and Jobs's commitment to the customer experience. "He would scrutinize everything, down to the pixel level," according to former Apple manager Cordell Ratzlaff in a *Wired* magazine interview.[28] No detail is too small. When Jobs announced Mac OS X in January 2000, he said one of the design goals for the new user interface, Aqua, was to make the screen look so good that you'd want to lick it. It was the first Mac OS to include the red, yellow, and green buttons, which Jobs had spent months making sure were just right. He wanted the buttons to mirror the effect of a traffic signal (red means close, yellow minimizes the image, and green maximizes). Jobs obsessed over exactly how the buttons looked, their fit and finish, and how they behaved when a cursor rolled over them.

> We don't do focus groups. They just ensure that you don't offend anyone, and produce bland, inoffensive products.
>
> —JONATHAN IVE, APPLE VP

"Jobs shuns laborious studies of users locked in a conference room," writes Leander Kahney. "He plays with the new technology himself, noting his own reactions to it, which is given as feedback to his engineers. If something is too hard to use, Jobs gives instructions for it to be simplified . . . if it works for him, it'll work for Apple's customers."[29]

Steve Jobs creates innovative products that continue to astonish his customers because he knows them really, really well. He empathizes with them. In many ways, he knows them better than they know themselves. He sees their genius, and they are the people he makes tools for.

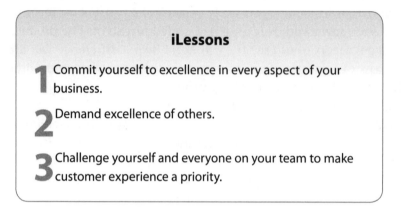

iLessons

1 Commit yourself to excellence in every aspect of your business.

2 Demand excellence of others.

3 Challenge yourself and everyone on your team to make customer experience a priority.

CHAPTER 9

Think Differently About Your Customers

Nobody cares about your products (except you).

—DAVID MEERMAN SCOTT, MARKETING STRATEGIST

Adrian Salamunovic and Nazim Ahmed found millions of dollars buried in their DNA. The two friends and entrepreneurs started a company from scratch and built it into a multimillion-dollar business in five short years, thanks to ideas they adopted from Apple and something we're all born with—DNA. Their company, DNA 11, turns DNA into art. It's as simple as that. They send customers a kit with a special cheek swab to collect the DNA. The customer returns the sample, and the company turns the DNA into art that the customer can hang on the wall.

In 2005, Salamunovic was a full-time Internet consultant, and Ahmed was working in sales for a biotech company. One day over a glass of wine, Ahmed showed his friend some images of DNA. "The abstract part of my brain thought it looked like a Mark Rothko painting," Salamunovic told me.[1] Rothko was a Russian-born abstract expressionist painter who made his career in New York after his parents immigrated to America. Salamunovic wanted one for himself because he thought it would look cool on his wall. He considered that other people might also want DNA "art" for themselves. It struck me that the DNA 11 story is not unlike the Apple founding: Two friends, working full-time jobs, are looking to make their own impact in the world. One is more scientifically minded than the other but cannot commercialize the product without his friend's marketing insight. The marketing guy is able to make unique connections because his diverse experiences and interests kick-start the creative side of his brain. The two friends don't do any market research or listen to focus groups. Instead, they create something they would enjoy themselves.

Salamunovic and Ahmed poured their combined savings, all $2,000 of it, into starting their own company in Ahmed's six-hundred-square-foot apartment. Here is where the Apple ethos kicks in. Most of their start-up capital went to a professional photographer who captured portraits for the website. Salamunovic's vision was to create the "Apple of the art world," so before he does anything, he asks himself, "What would Steve do?" And Jobs would not use stock photography. The two founders also asked themselves, "How would Apple design the product? How many products would Apple offer? How would Apple create the customer experience?" Every aspect of DNA 11's customer experience is modeled after

> We're drowning in a sea of technological crap, because every product that is released to the market is a result of multiple compromises based on decisions by the product manager, the engineering manager, the marketing manager, the sales manager and everyone else who has skin in the game as they prepare the offering to meet what they think are the target customer's needs. The reason Jobs and [Jonathan] Ive [Apple design guru] get it right is because they design sexy products with elegant and simple interfaces—for themselves. Then they count on their hip gaggle of early adopters to see it the same way. Once the snowball starts rolling, it's all momentum from there.[2]
>
> —ALAIN BREILLATT, DIRECTOR OF PRODUCT MANAGEMENT, NIELSEN COMPANY

Apple. By asking themselves these questions, the two entrepreneurs generated $1 million in sales in their first year.

Steve Jobs doesn't use focus groups, and neither does DNA 11. If the two entrepreneurs had convened a group of friends or outsiders as an informal focus group, DNA 11 would never have been born. Think about it. If Salamunovic had asked a group of people what they wanted in an art piece for their homes, nobody would have said, "Take my DNA and turn it into an art piece I can hang on the wall." Customers didn't know they wanted it, but once they saw it, they fell in love with the idea. Today DNA 11 designs and ships art pieces to customers in fifty countries.

Transformational breakthroughs are rarely the result of focus groups. Customers didn't ask for the iTunes Store, but today they can't live without it. Customers didn't ask for the iPhone, but today millions of people can't live without it. Customers didn't ask for the iPad, but many have found that it's a product they couldn't imagine living without.

Successful innovators such as Steve Jobs may not use focus groups, but they keep their ears to the ground to improve their products, selection, and buying experience. DNA 11 is a prime example. People love their pets, and because Salamunovic always pays attention to his customers, he began noticing that more and more people were asking for DNA of pets to be made into art. This was not something that Salamunovic had envisioned when he started DNA 11, but he responded to his customers' requests. Adding this service satisfied a "need" on the part of his current customers and also communicated a new offering to other customers who might never have thought about it. DNA 11 now fields hundreds of requests for "Pet Portraits," a popular niche for the thriving company. Salamunovic also learned that the $1,200 price tag for the most expensive DNA portrait was out of reach for a lot of their prospective customers, so he asked himself, "What would Steve do?" The answer: Steve would offer a lower-priced option, "the equivalent of the iPod Shuffle," Salamunovic reasoned. Today DNA 11 provides options for several price points, beginning with "DNA Mini Portraits."

DNA 11 did not become successful because of market research or focus groups. It became successful because it helped its customers fulfill their dreams (in this case, the desire for more personalized, unique art). What dreams do your customers have? Sell dreams, not products.

Father of the $5 Footlong

Stuart Frankel is an entrepreneur who owned two Subway franchises in Miami. Frankel's innovative idea sparked a fast-food revolution. It was a simple idea that grew out of an understanding of his customers—not asking them, but *knowing* them. South Miami was in a recession, and many of Frankel's customers were facing financial hardships. Frankel came up with an idea to bolster sales, especially during slow periods of the week. He would sell the twelve-inch sandwiches for $5. No market research went behind the $5 price. Frankel just liked simple, round numbers, and it appeared cheap enough for his financially strapped customers.

Frankel's customers loved the idea. Soon the lines went out the door. This simple, innovative idea was responsible for reviving the Subway chain nationwide, generating an estimated $3.8 billion in annual sales. Today Subway is among the top ten fast-food brands in the United States, largely because of the success of the $5 footlong campaign. But it almost didn't happen.

"Frankel, along with two other local managers in economically ravaged South Florida, ceaselessly championed the idea to Subway's corporate leadership and faced widespread skepticism," according to *BusinessWeek*. [3] It took more than a year for the idea to finally appeal to the head honchos at corporate, who decided to test-drive the idea in select cities before rolling it out nationwide. Why did it take so long to catch on? Because the corporate suits weren't thinking the way Apple thinks at the time. Frankel's idea was not created according to Subway's preconceived notion of innovation—market research and focus groups that could back up the validity of the idea. After all, how could a franchise owner know more than the M.B.A.s at corporate headquarters? "It violated all our normal processes," said Subway's marketing chief. Thankfully for Subway, "corporate" soon came around and saw the appeal of Frankel's idea.

The campaign launched on March 23, 2008. Franchise owners reported a 25 percent sales jump in the first two weeks. Copycats soon followed. Boston Market, Domino's, KFC, and T.G.I. Friday's all began offering $5 menu items. Five dollars was the magic number. No focus group came up with it. Frankel did because he *knew* his customers and understood the struggles they faced to make ends meet. Frankel's idea did not fulfill a "need." Nobody needs a Subway sandwich. What people craved was a simple desire to make their daily lives a little better: a good meal at a great price. They were looking for value, and Frankel delivered it. For most companies it probably would not be wise to give up your marketing research entirely, but every once in a while, violate your "process." You'll be glad you did, and your customers will love you.

Building Self-Esteem One Board Game at a Time

During a vacation in the Hamptons, Richard Tait and his wife, Karen, were playing their favorite board game, Pictionary, with some friends. Karen and Richard were unbeaten. They dusted their opponents at Pictionary. Their friends wanted revenge, so they challenged Tait and his wife to a game of Scrabble. Despite the fact that Scrabble was not Tait's best game and that his friends were "demons" at it, Tait blamed himself for the defeat that ensued. The loss did not lead to an "aha" moment as much as it left Tait with a feeling of looking like an idiot in front of his family and friends. The epiphany hit him on the plane ride home to Seattle: *What if a game existed that had something for all players, where everyone had a chance to shine, to show off a special talent and be celebrated for that skill?* To fulfill Tait's vision, the game would have to include performance challenges, data and trivia challenges, language and word puzzles, and creative activities. Tait pulled out the airplane napkin under his drink and sketched the idea on the back of it. On that flight, Cranium was born.

Tait had such a strong belief in the power of his vision that he left Microsoft to start the company. When Tait's father asked his son, "What am I going to tell my friends?" Tait's response—as recounted on a CNBC show—was, "Tell them I'm following my heart; I'm going to change the world." Cranium became one of the fastest-selling board games in history, received the prestigious "Game of the Year" designation at New York's Toy Fair, and was sold to Hasbro for nearly $80 million a short ten years after it started as an idea on the back of a napkin.

Cranium succeeded in a crowded toy category because its founder was not out to sell products; he was determined to fulfill dreams. Richard Tait, a former client of mine, told me that he never intended to build a board game. Rather, he was determined to build self-esteem, to bring out the best in people. When I consulted for Cranium on its messaging platform, we had decided that "Everyone Shines" should be the company's tagline. It seemed to summarize everything the company stood for. I was happy to see that Hasbro retained the mantra. Cranium's founder never asked potential customers what they wanted in a new toy or game. Tait built a game that he would enjoy playing. He also knew that family and friends craved more togetherness time and that everyone wants to "shine" in one way or another. So, he fulfilled dreams. He created toys, games, and books that brought people together and revealed their unique, often hidden, talents. Cranium unleashed inner artists, singers, spellers, and geniuses. When you fulfill dreams, success is inevitable.

What Business Are You In?

If you want to create truly innovative products or services, ask yourself, "What business am I really in?" The correct answer is not always the obvious one. When I interviewed Starbucks founder Howard Schultz for one of my previous books, *10 Simple Secrets of the World's Greatest Business Communicators*, I was astonished that he rarely mentioned the word *coffee* in our conversation. "We're not in the coffee business. It is what we sell as a product, but it's not what we stand for," Schultz explained.[4]

Starbucks is in the business of selling dreams, not coffee. It sells dreams to customers who desire a "third place" between work and home. It sells dreams to employees who crave a workplace that treats them with dignity and respect. Starbucks is not in the coffee business, and that's why it's successful. Cranium is not in the game business; it's in the business of selling self-esteem. Apple is not in the computer business; it's in the business of unleashing your personal creativity. Distinguishing between products and dreams is fundamental to creating innovative products and services that change the world.

Feel Their Pain

Your customers don't care about you. It sounds harsh, but it's true. They don't care about the success of your company. They don't care about your product or service. They care about themselves, their dreams, their goals. Now, they will care much more if you help them reach their goals, and to do that, you must understand their goals, as well as their needs and deepest desires.

Social media expert David Meerman Scott recommends the creation of a buyer persona: "Buyer personas are one of the most fundamental aspects of great marketing. A buyer persona represents a distinct group of potential customers, an archetypal person whom you want your marketing to reach. Targeting your work to buyer personas prevents you from sitting on your butt in your comfortable office just making stuff up about your products, which is the cause of most ineffective marketing."[5]

According to Meerman Scott, a buyer persona must be customized to your target customers. A university administrator might visualize a student or parent, a politician would keep a typical voter in mind, while a nonprofit director would see a donor. "By truly understanding the market problems that your products and services solve for your buyer personas, you transform your marketing from mere product-specific, egocentric gobbledygook that only you understand and care about into valuable information people are eager to consume and that they use to make the choice to do business with your organization," says Meerman Scott.[6]

How well do you know your customers? Create a buyer persona so specific and vivid that you can literally "feel their pain." Once you do, you'll be closer to capturing the Apple ethos.

Tell More Stories

As Steve Jobs did at the end of his presentation in 1997, you'll want to find ways to remind your employees about who your customers are. One effective means is through the sharing of stories.

Cranium's Richard Tait told me he read customer e-mails every night before he went to bed, about one hundred per day. Each night, he would forward several stories to his employees so they would have them in their in-boxes the next morning. For example, "The woman who wrote me at 11:30 one night—she has four kids of her own and three foster children. Instead of kicking her feet up at the end of a long day and enjoying a glass of wine, she's writing to tell me about the sense of togetherness our games bring to her family; a family previously fragmented and separated by age, ethnicities, and backgrounds. This woman is writing at 11:30 at night to thank me for creating these products. When is the last time you wrote to a company, thanking them for creating a product? I don't know about you, but I've never done it in my life. One of our core values as a company is to delight our customers at every turn. Those moments of delight inspire me every day and I use it as fuel to inspire my team."[7]

Tait took the storytelling a step further. He would post stories around the office environment. E-mails, letters, and photographs were framed or laminated and placed everywhere—in the hallway, on countertops in the kitchen, and in the lobby. Stories helped Cranium employees see the difference they were making in people's lives. The stories also inspired employees to develop creative ideas of their own, which evolved into new games, books, and toys that delighted their customers.

Every member of your team is looking to be a part of something special. As we've discussed, innovation rarely happens as a result of one person's idea. It takes a team to commercialize that idea, and those players need continuous inspiration to overcome the hurdles that will inevitably arise on the journey. Stories are powerful motivators. Tell more of them.

The first three principles set the stage for innovation to happen—passion, vision, and kick-starting the creative process. However, innovation is more than an idea. Innovation occurs when an idea is turned into an actual product, service, company, initiative, or action that moves society forward. Getting to know your customers—really *knowing* them, including their hopes, dreams, and goals—will make you more likely to turn your ideas into successful products. And for that to happen, you must see genius in their craziness.

iLessons

1 When it comes to your customer, it's not about you; it's about them. Your customers don't care about you; they care about their dreams. They are asking themselves, "How will this product or service make my life better?" Help them fulfill their dreams and watch your sales soar.

2 Be your own focus group. No outside focus group will give you the green light to develop breakthrough innovation.

3 Listening to your customer is not as valuable as *knowing* your customer. Maintain a "pixel-level" obsession with every aspect of the customer experience.

Say No to 1,000 Things

**I'm as proud of what we don't do
as I am of what we do.**

—STEVE JOBS

CHAPTER 10

Simplicity Is the Ultimate Sophistication

The way we approach design is by trying to achieve the most with the very least. We are absolutely consumed by trying to develop a solution that is very simple, because as physical beings we understand clarity.

—JONATHAN IVE, APPLE DESIGN GURU

A simple two-by-two printed table tells you everything you need to know about how Steve Jobs creates innovative products that people love. In a 1998 Macworld presentation in New York, Jobs acknowledged that Apple had been in a death spiral one year earlier and was taking the first steps to nurse itself back to health. The prescription called for a reduction in the number of products Apple offered. Jobs outlined the strategy as follows:

> When we got to the company a year ago, there were fifteen product platforms and a zillion variants of each one. [slide shows a dizzying display of product platforms with numbers such as 1,400, 2,400, and 3,400] I couldn't figure this out myself. After

three weeks, I said, "How are we going to recommend these products to others when we don't even know what products to recommend to our friends?" So, we went back to business school 101 and asked, "What do people want?" Well, they want two kinds of products: consumer and professional. In each of those two categories we need desktop and portable models. If we had four great products, that's all we need. As a matter of fact, if we only had four, we could put the A-team on every single one of them. And if we only had four, we could turn them all every nine months instead of every eighteen months. And if we only had four, we could be working on the next generation of each one as we're introducing the first generation. That's what we decided to do, to focus on four great products.[1]

Figure 10.1 replicates the two-by-two slide that Jobs displayed in his presentation. He later filled in the four cells with Power Mac G3 (desktop pro), PowerBook G3 (portable pro), iMac (desktop consumer), and a question mark in the cell for the portable consumer product, which he promised would be introduced the following year (Apple introduced the clamshell iBook in 1999). By the end of 1998, Steve Jobs had cut Apple's total product offerings from 350 to 10, a significant reduction by anyone's standards.

Simplifying Apple's product line ultimately helped to resuscitate the company, leading to one of the most successful financial decades of any company in U.S. business history. By simplifying everything—product offerings to product design—Apple leapfrogged its

FIGURE 10.1 1998 Macworld Presentation Slide: Product Table[2]

	CONSUMER	PRO
DESKTOP		
PORTABLE		

competition, creating easy-to-use products that stunned reviewers and brought joy to millions of customers around the world.

Focus on What's Important

In Apple's world, *simplicity* and *focus* are one and the same. In 2004, *BusinessWeek* carried a cover story titled "The Seed of Apple's Innovation."

"How do you systemize innovation?" the reporter asked Steve Jobs.

"The system is that there is no system. That doesn't mean we don't have process. Apple is a very disciplined company, and we have great processes. But that's not what it's about," said Jobs. As the response continues, we learn that he sees his role as keeping his team focused on what counts—the most important tasks and products.

> Process makes you more efficient. But innovation comes from people meeting up in the hallways or calling each other at 10:30 at night with a new idea, or because they realized something that shoots holes in how we've being thinking about a problem. It's ad hoc meetings of six people called by someone who thinks he has figured out the coolest new thing ever and who wants to know what other people think of his idea. And it comes from saying no to 1,000 things to make sure we don't get on the wrong track or try to do too much. We're always thinking about new markets we could enter, but it's only by saying no that you can concentrate on the things that are really important. [3]

Jobs says "no" to a lot of things, even if it angers some customers and partners. In April 2010, Jobs posted a memo on the Apple website defending his decision to say no to flash-on iPods, iPhones, and iPads. He said that alternative products offer the best opportunity to create stable, advanced, and innovative mobile computer platforms. Jobs relentlessly focuses on the customer experience, and he says no to anything he believes will compromise an elegant experience. This principle is most evident in design.

His Name Is Ive—Jonathan Ive

To understand the role that focus plays in Apple's innovations, we need to spend some time talking about a man who shares Steve Jobs's design philosophy, an executive who has overseen most of Apple's breakthrough designs since Steve Jobs returned in 1996.

Jonathan Ive's official title at Apple is Senior Vice President, Industrial Design. His unofficial title is Apple's design guru, and he's responsible for so many design innovations at Apple that his ideas alone could be the subject of a book. Ive performs the role that Steve Wozniak played in Apple's early history. He brings Jobs's vision to life.

When Jobs returned to Apple in the late 1990s after an eleven-year absence from the company, Ive was already there. Jobs recognized his talents and elevated the London-born Ive to oversee Apple's industrial design. Jobs saw something he liked in Ive: a passion for simplicity, aesthetically pleasing design ideas, and a relentless work ethic. (Ive often put in seventy-hour workweeks.)

Ive had dreamed of working at Apple from the time he first encountered a Mac. As Ive tells the story, he disliked reading instruction manuals, and the Mac was the first computer he could use immediately without the manuals he so detested. "I remember the first time I saw an Apple product. I remember it clearly. When I saw this product, I got a very clear sense of the people who designed and made it," said Ive.[4]

It was a profound moment for Ive, a "wow" moment that changed his life. Millions of people who now enjoy Apple's products for their brilliantly elegant design owe their experience to Ive's reaction.

Ive finds inspiration all around him, even in a flower garden. He once said the iMac 2002 and its unique swivel display attached to a stainless steel neck was inspired by a sunflower. Inspiration is everywhere, but Ive's ideas result in new products only when they meet two criteria: simplicity and accessibility. In Ive's opinion, the problem with most products is that the companies that build the products do not really care about the customer experience. When you care, he says, products become much more than a collection of parts. Every detail is refined, and, most important, if something does not need to be there, it's eliminated.

A Quarter-Pound Breakthrough

In October 2008, Apple introduced its next-generation MacBook laptop computer. Steve Jobs invited Jonathan Ive onstage to explain the new process of building portable computers, a process that allowed Apple to offer notebooks that were lighter and sturdier. What followed was a short course in Apple's design philosophy and the power of focus.

Ive told the audience that Apple's new "aluminum unibody enclosure" eliminated 60 percent of the computer's major structural parts. Reducing the number of parts naturally made the computer thinner. Contrary to what you'd expect, eliminating parts also made it more rigid and robust—the computer was stronger. "It's a breakthrough in how we design and build notebooks," Ive said.[5]

Prior to 2008, MacBooks were assembled from multiple parts. Ive pointed out that the process allowed Apple to build best-in-class computers in terms of size and weight, but the company was looking for a new way to build notebooks. It found the answer by process of elimination. "Rather than start with a thin piece of aluminum and add multiple parts of internal structure, we discovered that if we started with a thick piece of aluminum and actually removed material to create mechanical features in the structure, we could make a much lighter and, importantly, much stronger part," Ive said. "We started with a single slab of high-grade aluminum that weighed over 2.5 pounds. We end with a remarkably precise part that weighs one-quarter of a pound. It's light and very strong."[6]

Get Design Out of the Way

Apple refines every detail in the ultimate quest to reduce—or elim-inate—complexity. If something does not have to be there, it isn't. "A lot of what we seem to be doing in a product like the iPhone is getting design out of the way. It feels almost inevitable, almost underdesigned, and it feels almost like, of course it is that way. Why would it be any other way?"[7]

Discussing the design of the ultrathin MacBook Air, Ive said, "It's really important in a product to have a sense of the hierarchy, what's important and what's not important, by removing those things that are vying for your attention. For example, an indicator has a value when it's indicating something, but if it's not indicat-ing something, it shouldn't be there [the MacBook's sleep indicator light goes away when the laptop is in use]. We spend so much more time to make it less conspicuous and less obvious . . . it's quite obsessive, isn't it?"[8] Yes, Ive does sound obsessive, especially when he is fixated on something as obscure as an indicator light. It's an obsession that few companies have, and Apple's customers are the ones who benefit.

During an interview for the British newspaper *The Observer*, Ive showed the reporter a notebook in which he'd sketched every pos-sible knob, lever, and button that could have been installed on the first iPod. His notes also displayed what the design team finally agreed on, the scroll wheel, which gave the iPod its innovative look and functionality. "Everything on an Apple product is similarly considered, explored, improved, and designed to be as easy and as uncluttered as possible," wrote reporter Sheryl Garratt.[9]

According to Garratt, the iPod represented a major breakthrough in innovation, because it changed an entire product category. "The others were fiddly, trivial-looking plastic things cluttered with but-tons and dials, appealing mainly to gadget-obsessed geeks with the time to figure out how to work them. By contrast, the iPod was a sleek digital jukebox that fitted snugly in the palm of your hand; it could hold one thousand songs—to begin with—and allowed you access to them in just a couple of clicks of its elegant navigation wheel. If you cared anything at all about music, as soon as you held it and understood how easy it was to use, you wanted one. It changed everything."[10]

In a *New York Times Magazine* article published two years after the iPod was introduced, journalist Rob Walker asked Ive a series of questions about the iPod's design. At one point Ive's voice trailed off from the discussion. He paused and said, "It's almost easier to talk about it as what it's not."[11]

Ive explained that Jobs's vision was to build a "focused" device. "It was about not trying to do too much with the device—which would have been its complication and, therefore, its demise. The enabling features aren't obvious and evident, because the key was getting rid of stuff," Ive told Walker. "What's interesting is that out of that simplicity, and almost that unashamed sense of simplicity, and expressing it, came a very different product. But difference wasn't the goal. It's actually very easy to create a different thing. What was exciting is starting to realize that its difference was really a consequence of this quest to make it a very simple thing."[12] Apple was not ahead of its time in creating a device to play downloadable music. But it was way, way ahead of its competitors in building a device that was so simple, uncluttered, and focused that it was a joy to use.

> *Plug it in. Whirrrrrr. Done.*
>
> —STEVE JOBS, ON THE IPOD'S SIMPLICITY

Ive's design for the iPod focused the consumer's attention on the purpose for which the device was made: listening to music. Anything that detracted from the goal of enjoying music had no place in the final product. Too many buttons most certainly would have distracted from the product's principal focus. Even the color of the original iPod was chosen to minimize distraction: white. Introducing a simple, minimalist design in a shockingly neutral color made it unmistakable and, ultimately, remarkable.

In Steven Levy's 2006 book, *The Perfect Thing: How the iPod Shuffles Commerce, Culture, and Coolness*, Ive said that consumers are surrounded by products clamoring for their attention. Designers add more and more features (clutter) in the misguided attempt to stand out. More features make products forgettable. It sounds counterintuitive, but eliminating clutter actually makes a product stand out. The product is more elegant. And elegance is seductive. Great designers such as Ive engage our imaginations by *leaving out the right things*. According to Ive:

> Music was much more important than design. Our goal was to get design out of the way. We wanted to create a very, very new object. But think of how many hundreds of thousands of objects of this sort there have been in the last twenty years! This was a fairly ambitious challenge—not to create another trivial digital small object. The goal wasn't to try to make it immediately and instantly recognizable at twenty feet. But it is. It is, because of the consequence of the more important goal—just to try to design a product that was efficient, elegant and simple. What it really was about, in some sense, was getting design out of the way.[13]

"Simplicity is the ultimate sophistication," Steve Jobs told Levy in discussing the iPod's design.[14] Jobs was careful to add, however, that simplicity means much more than just removing things. Simplicity is focusing on the essential meaning of the product. According to Jobs:

> When you start looking at a problem and it seems really simple with all these simple solutions, you don't really understand the complexity of the problem. And your solutions are way too oversimplified and they don't work. Then you get into the problem and see that it's really complicated. And you come up with all these convoluted solutions. That's sort of the middle and that's where most people stop, and the solutions tend to work for a while. But the really great person will keep on going and find, sort of, the key, underlying principle of the problem. And come up with a beautiful elegant solution that works.[15]

Most companies take the "middle" ground as Jobs described. They find a confusing solution for a complex problem. The truly great companies focus on the one thing the product is made for and design a simple, elegant solution to perform that one task.

A Leapfrog Product

On January 9, 2007, Steve Jobs announced the most innovative mobile phone on the planet: the iPhone, a device that redefined what a mobile phone could do. Its minimalism stunned the industry and consumers. As smartphone manufacturers kept adding more and more buttons and features, Apple went in the opposite direction—producing a phone that was more capable than its competitors with less clutter (one button and a large screen). Nobody had seen such simplicity in the smartphone category. Many reviews of the iPhone contained one of two words, often both: *simple* and *uncluttered*. In the following years, competitors played catch-up with their own touch screens, but the adjectives *simple* and *uncluttered* were rarely employed to describe their user interfaces. Some were "cluttered" or, at best, "relatively" simple to use, but few could replicate the iPhone's simplicity.

When it comes to simple, uncluttered interfaces, Apple gets it. Competitors try to match Apple's simplicity, but they often fall short. To Steve Jobs, design isn't just about how things look; design is how things work. The experience must be simple, elegant, and easy. "Great design means that one look and the end user reacts by knowing what to do with a knob or a button, without as much as even thinking about it," wrote technology analyst Om Malik. "I think this is what Apple's competitors fail to understand. Many confuse features—aka feeds and speeds—with what really connects with customers: user experiences."[16]

Prior to revealing the new iPhone in his keynote presentation, Steve Jobs took a few minutes to explain why Apple was getting into the phone business and how the Apple design philosophy had resulted in a phone that was more capable and more elegant than those of its competitors:

The most advanced phones are called smartphones. They typically combine a phone, e-mail, and a baby Internet. The problem
is they are not so smart and they are not so easy to use. Regular
cell phones are not so smart, and they're not so easy to use.
Smartphones are definitely a little smarter, but they're actually
harder to use. They're really complicated. Just for the basic stuff,
people have a hard time figuring out how to use them. What we
want to do is make a leapfrog product that is way smarter than
any mobile device has ever been and supereasy to use. This is
what iPhone is.[17]

Making a product that was "supereasy to use" meant that Apple
had to completely redesign the way a customer interacted with the
phone.

We're going to start with a revolutionary user interface. Why?
Here are four smartphones, the usual suspects. [slide shows
photos of Motorola Q, BlackBerry, Palm Treo, and Nokia E62]
What's wrong with their user interfaces? The problem with them
is in the bottom forty. They all have keyboards that are there
whether or not you need them to be there. And they all have
these control buttons that are fixed in plastic and are the same
for every application. Well, every application wants a slightly
different user interface, a slightly optimized set of buttons just
for it. What we're going to do is get rid of all these buttons and
just make a giant screen.[18]

Matthew May, author of *In Pursuit of Elegance*, says the best ideas
have something missing, and what's missing often leads to a more
elegant solution. May does not believe that everything simple is
elegant, but, he says, everything elegant is simple. The iPhone is
no exception. "By all accounts, the iPhone was a thing of beauty, a
piece of art, and irresistibly seductive," writes May. "But while the
iPhone dazzled the audience, it was what they didn't see that took
them by surprise, and even shocked them . . . Mr. Jobs had removed
the one physical feature that every phone in the world shared—the
keypad. In fact, there was no thumbwheel, no stylus, no buttons
to punch, dial, click, or scroll, except a single home button. Even

by Apple design standards, long known to honor clean and aesthetically pleasing lines, the iPhone had the sparest design ever conceived."[19]

In its quarterly earnings report for the period January through March 2010, Apple reported that the iPhone accounted for more than $5.5 billion of its quarterly revenues. Five billion! The total number of iPhones sold since 2007 had reached fifty-one million. Simplicity sells.

Even if you own no Apple products and are perfectly content with non-Apple devices, it would be hard to make the argument that any Apple product—iMac, MacBook, iPod, iPhone, iPad—is a confusing mess. Just the opposite. Complexity is diminished to make the products as simple and as easy to use as possible.

Apple Breaks the Law of Software Upgrades

Released on August 28, 2009, Mac OS X Snow Leopard is the seventh major version of Apple's Unix-based operating system. *New York Times* computer columnist David Pogue calls it a strange beast, for a couple of reasons:

> The first has to do with the Law of Software Upgrades, which has been in place since the dawn of personal computing. And that law says: "If you don't add new features every year, nobody will upgrade, and you won't make money." And so, to keep you upgrading, the world's software companies pile on more frequent features with every new version of their wares. Unfortunately this can't continue forever. Sooner or later, you wind up with a bloated, complex, incoherent mess of a program. The shocker of Snow Leopard, though, is that upping the feature count wasn't the point. In fact, Steve Jobs said, "We're hitting the Pause on new features." Instead, the point of Snow Leopard was the refinement of the perfectly good operating system that Apple already had in the previous version, Mac OS X Leopard (10.5).[20]

The refinements resulted in a better computer experience in a "ton" of ways, according to Pogue. Those refinements include a faster, stabler, and better-organized system. Refinement also led to an operating system that was smaller than the previous Mac OS X version. Snow Leopard freed up six gigabytes of hard drive space. Once again Apple had proved that eliminating complexity could result in a more robust system.

So Simple That a Two-Year-Old Can Use It

When you can make a gadget so elegant that adults love it and so simple that a child can use it, you know you're onto something. Apple is one of the few companies that can proudly claim that accomplishment. Shortly after the iPad was released in April 2010, blogger Todd Lappin handed the device to his two-and-a-half-year-old daughter and posted the video on YouTube. What happened next turned into a viral sensation and offered a lesson in innovative product design.

> In my experience, users react positively when things are clear and understandable... what bothers me today is the arbitrariness and thoughtlessness with which many things are produced and brought to market, not only in the sector of consumer goods, but also in architecture and advertising. We have too many unnecessary things everywhere.[21]
>
> DIETER RAMS, INDUSTRIAL DESIGNER

Within seconds, the little girl took right to it. Since using our fingers to manipulate things is a natural inclination, the child started scrolling through the icons on the tablet, clicked the movie icon, and even enlarged the screen. Lappin acknowledged that his daughter liked to play with her daddy's iPhone, so she had some experience with a touch screen, but given that this was her first encounter with a new product, her ability to navigate the device was astonishing.

"The elegance of the iPad lies in the fact that a 2.5-year-old can use it seamlessly, even without knowing how to read. The touch-interface is as natural to her as a simple hand gesture, and the navigation model is pared back to eliminate complexity," Lappin observed. "In theory, Apple could also give users access to the more complex, higher-level functionality that some power-users crave. But if nothing else, Apple's rise over the last few years—first with the iPod, and then with the iPhone— shows that selling simplicity is a powerful way to woo mass-market consumers."[22]

Within twenty-four hours of Lappin's uploading the video of his daughter using the iPad, the clip had been viewed more than 180,000 times. The video received nearly a million views within a month.

In a review for the *Chicago Sun-Times*, Andy Ihnatko noted that the design for the iPad was different from that of other tablet computers on the market. The others had a list of features a mile long. It's easy to add features, Ihnatko maintained, but adding more functions would also have added to system instability and customer confusion. Again, Apple went in the opposite direction, eliminating features and functions to make a product that is simple and elegant. "What happens when computer designers let go of every instinct that's hardwired into their DNA, and start practically from scratch? They create the iPad," wrote Ihnatko.[23]

In less than one month—twenty-eight days—Apple had sold one million iPads. Its simple, elegant, and easy-to-use interface proved irresistible to adults and two-and-a-half-year-olds alike.

Make It Dead Simple

Former Apple marketing executive Steve Chazin says Apple's magic comes from focus, which he defines this way: finding the one thing the company can do better than anyone else. "The iPod made getting music in your pocket dead simple. The iMac made getting on the Internet dead simple. The iPhone made putting the Internet, your phone, movies, and music in your pocket, dead simple," according to Chazin.[24]

Chazin noted that Apple never invented something completely new. It did not invent the personal computer, the MP3 player, downloadable music, the mobile phone, or the tablet computer. All the same, innovation is not limited to building something that nobody has ever seen. Instead, Apple does one thing very well: making complex things simple and elegant. That's what makes Apple the world's most innovative company.

When asked about Apple's secret to innovation, Apple's chief operating officer, Tim Cook, gave credit to Steve Jobs and his relentless commitment to focusing on what matters. In a wide-ranging discussion at a Goldman Sachs Technology Conference in February 2010, Cook described Apple's guiding philosophy:

> We are the most focused company that I know of or have read of or have any knowledge of. We say no to good ideas every day. We say no to great ideas in order to keep the amount of things we focus on very small in number, so that we can put enormous energy behind the ones we do choose. The table each of you are sitting at today, you could probably put every product on it that Apple makes, yet Apple's revenue last year was $40 billion. I think any other company that could say that is an oil company. That's not just saying yes to the right products, it's saying no to many products that are good ideas, but just not nearly as good as the other ones.[25]

In another fascinating insight, Cook equated hubris with complexity. He said that successful companies become arrogant when their sole goal is to get bigger. "I can tell you the management team at Apple would never let that happen. That's not what we're about," said Cook.

A Website That Speaks Volumes with Few Words

Apple's laserlike focus on simplicity extends to its website. When the iPad went on sale, it was the only featured product on the

Apple home page. The photo alone took up three-quarters of the screen along with the caption: "iPad is here." This is a consistent Apple technique on its website—removing products from the home page to make room for the new. See for yourself. Around the time that Apple releases a new product, visit apple.com; you'll note that everything is cleared to put the spotlight—the focus—on what's new. It's one of the cleanest, simplest, and most elegant sites of any major company. It's clean because of what Apple chooses to remove, not what it adds.

On March 18, 2010, Jerome York, a longtime Apple board director, passed away. On that day, Apple removed all of its product images from its home page and replaced them with a photo of York alongside a short message: "It is with deep sadness we announce the loss of a member of our corporate family and dear friend, Jerry York. Jerry courageously joined Apple's Board of Directors in 1997, when many doubted the company's future, and contributed his extraordinary character, business expertise, and leadership to help guide Apple for over a decade . . ."

> *Think digital, act analog. Use every digital tool at your disposal to create great products and services. But never lose sight of the fact that the purpose of innovation is not cool products and cool technologies but happy people. Happy people is a decidedly analog goal.*
>
> —GUY KAWASAKI

I recall being momentarily surprised to see the change in Apple's site, as I'm sure customers were as well. Although the static navigation buttons on the top of the site remained in place, the memorial was the only thing that appeared on the home page. First, it showed class. Second, it once again showed the power of focus and simplicity. Apple did not *add* the news to the home page or to its news section, as the majority of companies would have done. It *removed* items. The abstract impressionist painter Hans Hofmann once said, "The ability to simplify means to eliminate the unnecessary so that the necessary may speak." By eliminating distractions, clutter, and the unnecessary, Apple allows the necessary to speak—in its products and on its website.

Get Rid of the Crappy Stuff

On April 21, 2010, *Fast Company* magazine sponsored a conference called Innovation Uncensored. Nike president and CEO Mark Parker was one of the featured speakers. Parker told the story of what transpired when, shortly after he became CEO, he got a call from Steve Jobs.

"Do you have any advice?" Parker asked Jobs.

"Well, just one thing," said Jobs. "Nike makes some of the best products in the world. Products that you lust after. Absolutely beautiful, stunning products. But you also make a lot of crap. Just get rid of the crappy stuff and focus on the good stuff."

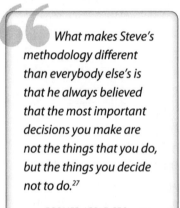

> *What makes Steve's methodology different than everybody else's is that he always believed that the most important decisions you make are not the things that you do, but the things you decide not to do.*[27]
>
> —FORMER APPLE CEO JOHN SCULLEY

Parker told his audience, "I expected a little pause and a laugh. There was a pause but no laugh. He was absolutely right. We have to edit."[26]

Parker used the word *edit* not in a design sense but in the context of making business decisions. Focus leads to great designs. It also leads to good business decisions. Tim Cook once commented that a traditional management philosophy taught in business schools is to reduce risk by diversifying your product offerings. Apple, he said, represents the anti–business school philosophy. Apple's approach is to put its resources behind a few products and commit to making those products exceptionally well.

"Apple is a $30 billion company yet we've got less than 30 major products. I don't know if that's ever been done before," Steve Jobs told *Fortune* magazine in 2008. He added:

Certainly the great consumer electronics companies of the past had thousands of products. We tend to focus much more. People think focus means saying yes to the thing you've got to focus on. But that's not what it means at all. It means saying no to the hundred other good ideas that there are. You have to pick carefully. I'm actually as proud of many of the things we haven't done as the things we have done. The clearest example was when we were pressured for years to do a PDA, and I realized one day that 90% of the people who use a PDA only take information out of it on the road. They don't put information into it. Pretty soon cell phones are going to do that, so the PDA market's going to get reduced to a fraction of its current size, and it won't really be sustainable. So we decided not to get into it. If we had gotten into it, we wouldn't have had the resources to do the iPod. We probably wouldn't have seen it coming.[28]

Early in Apple's history, lead investor Mike Markkula sent a memo to Apple's employees that outlined his marketing strategy. In that memo he talked about the importance of focus. Markkula wrote, "To do a good job of those things that we decide to do, we must eliminate all the unimportant opportunities, select from the remainder only those that we have the resources to do well, and concentrate our efforts on them.[29]

In product design and business strategy, subtraction often adds value. "Whether we're talking about a product, a performance, a market, or an organization, our addiction to addition results in inconsistency, overload, or waste, and sometimes all three," writes Matthew May.[30] Aviator Antoine de Saint-Exupéry could have been summing up the Apple philosophy when he said, "A designer knows he has achieved perfection not when there is nothing more to add, but when there is nothing left to take away."

Let's get back to the question asked earlier in the book: can any company innovate the way Apple does? Again, the answer is no. Anyone can learn the principles that drive Apple's innovation, but innovation takes courage, and few people have it. It takes courage to reduce the number of products a company offers from 350 to 10, as Jobs did in 1998. It takes courage to remove a keyboard from the face of a smartphone and replace those buttons with a giant screen, as Jobs did with the iPhone. It takes courage to eliminate code from an operating system to make it more stable and reliable, as Apple did with Snow Leopard. It takes courage to eliminate all of the words on a PowerPoint slide except one, as Steve Jobs often does in a presentation. It takes courage to feature just one product on the home page of a website. It takes courage to launch fewer new products in a year than your competitors launch in a month. It takes courage to adopt unpopular stands, such as saying Adobe flash is unfit for the modern mobile era, as Jobs did in April of 2010. And it takes courage to make a product so simple that a child can use it.

Do you have the guts to keep things simple? Steve Jobs does, and it's been crucial to his success.

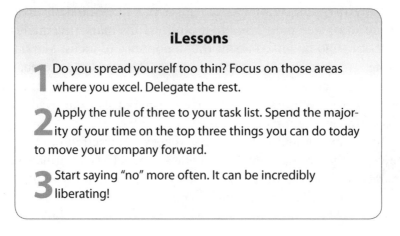

iLessons

1 Do you spread yourself too thin? Focus on those areas where you excel. Delegate the rest.

2 Apply the rule of three to your task list. Spend the majority of your time on the top three things you can do today to move your company forward.

3 Start saying "no" more often. It can be incredibly liberating!

CHAPTER 11

Think Differently About Design

A great piece of art is composed not just of what is in the final piece, but equally important, what is not.

—JIM COLLINS

t takes courage to be innovative, especially if you decide to eliminate clutter in favor of a focused, simple, and elegant design. In 2007, the designers at Pure Digital were courageous enough to come up with an innovative idea that would ultimately reinvigorate the stagnating video camcorder category. They set out to build the world's simplest video camera. The Flip camcorder instantly became the bestselling camcorder on Amazon.com. Three years later, it retains the top spot. In fact, as of this writing, Flip camcorders make up six of the top ten bestselling digital video cameras (the black model took the number one spot, followed by the white one). Just three years after its debut, a product some people dismissed as "a toy" because of its simplicity now commands 36 percent of all camcorders sold at retail![1]

Skeptics said the Flip would never be successful. It was too simple, they said. The Flip's designers knew better. They had surrounded themselves with Apple products for inspiration and internalized the Apple ethos—build a product that is supereasy to use. The Flip's success has been nothing short of phenomenal. The camcorder category had been stagnant for several years before Flip was introduced. Few companies were innovating in the space. The Flip changed everything. From 2008 to 2009, the video camcorder market grew by 35 percent. Flip products represented 90 percent of the growth! How did the Flip's critics get it so wrong? They weren't thinking the way Steve Jobs thinks.

The Magic of the Flip

In 2009, Cisco Systems purchased the creator of the Flip, Pure Digital. I wrote a story about the company for BusinessWeek.com, gaining access to the development team behind the product. I learned that most consumer electronics are built by engineers for engineers. The result is feature creep—adding more bells and whistles than most users will ever want or use. Flip designers went in the opposite direction. The Flip was driven by a philosophy that said every consumer touch point—the package, the product, and the website—must be simple, elegant, and focused. The following sections outline four Apple-like design principles that helped the Flip win the hearts and minds of consumers.

OBEY THE THIRTY-SECOND RULE

Flip designers had a test: whenever they created a prototype and handed it to someone, that person had to be able to turn it on and play with it within thirty seconds. Just as Apple's Jonathan Ive dislikes instruction manuals, so do the designers behind the Flip. Their customers would have to understand the product—and be able to use it within thirty seconds—without the aid of a manual.

The thirty-second rule governed many of the Flip's design decisions. Eschewing the addition of lots of features, designers limited the Flip to four buttons: on/off, record, playback, and delete. To maintain the simplicity of the user experience, everything required to use the device is built in (including a pop-out USB arm to connect the device to a computer). It allows the camera to ship with no installation CD and no cables. Everything the user needs is contained in the camera. According to Simon Fleming-Wood, senior director of marketing for Cisco Consumer Products, "Our competitors continue to cram features into their products. There is a temptation for us to play that game, but we will not. Our focus is on the user experience while the traditional players who come from the digital camera market see the world in terms of pixels and features. I'm glad they see the world that way because it misses the magic of Flip."[2]

OFFER SIMPLE PACKAGING AND INSTRUCTIONS

The Flip's box is distinguishable by what it eliminates. Flip designers resist the temptation to include all the specs on the package. "We want people to forget about the technology and enjoy the experience," Fleming-Wood told me. When you open the package, you see that the Flip does away with a thick user manual. Traditional user manuals are overwhelming, especially given that the vast majority of purchasers do not use many of the more advanced features on camcorders and still cameras. The Flip's designers had serious reservations about shipping the product with any guide, small or large. They had seriously considered shipping a consumer electronics device with no instruction manual. Ultimately they decided to include a short "quick-start" guide that would give their customers a sense of comfort, even though the goal was to design a product that required no manual. Above all, every design element had to be approachable and unintimidating.

You should not be surprised to learn that the Flip designers were inspired by Apple packaging. The boxes that contain Apple products are innovative because of their simplicity, style, and ease of use. Apple's commitment to de-cluttering the user experience extends to its packaging. Take a look at the MacBook Pro as an example. The box is not cluttered with photos and features; the front shows a side view of the metallic laptop on a stark white background with two words, MacBook Pro. Open the box and instead of being bombarded with components and accessories, you see only the top of the notebook, with the iconic Apple logo. (The logo itself is innovative. Jobs wanted a multicolored Apple with a bite taken out of it, to humanize the computer company. The six-color logo lasted until the late 1990s when Apple replaced it with a more modern, all-white, stylized logo.) The next layer reveals a black folder containing the instruction guide. The third layer has two simple compartments, which house the power adapter and the AC power cord. Everything about the package is designed so that the customer can set up the product and start using it right away. All Apple products are similarly packaged. Open an iPhone box and the first and only thing you see is the phone's screen. Peel back the next layer to expose the user guide. The third layer reveals three small compartments that contain the headphone, the USB sync cable, and a small AC adapter.

Building these boxes is not easy, nor inexpensive. Clearly Apple is committed to creating a simple user experience, down to the packaging level. In early 2010, I took a tour of a container plant in Modesto, California, to prepare for a speech to manufacturing executives. This particular company designs and manufactures boxes to carry products in the pharmaceuticals, food, and technology industries. The plant managers told me that Apple was their most demanding client. Nothing is taken for granted. The customer must have a pleasurable experience while unpacking an Apple product. That means the box colors, look, texture, handles, material, and compartments must provide a simple, satisfying experience at every step of the unpacking process.

Opening an Apple product is so thrilling for some people that they feel compelled to unpack "on camera" and upload the video to YouTube. There are literally thousands of links showing customers unpacking MacBooks, iPods, iPhones, and iPads. They can hardly contain their excitement. Yes, this YouTube trend is a bit odd, but that's what you can expect when people fall in love with every aspect of your product.

BUILD A SIMPLE WEBSITE

As opposed to being overwhelmed by products, visitors to the Flip website are presented with two types of cameras: the Ultra and the Mino. Complementing the simple home page, tabs are limited to products, where to buy, buzz, and support. In keeping with the Flip's simple communication principles, the information a consumer is searching for should be easily accessed within thirty seconds of the visitor's entering the site.

Here again, Flip designers might have learned something from Apple. Apple's design aesthetic reaches every customer touch point—from the product to the packaging to the site. In June 2010, Apple unveiled the next-generation iPhone: the iPhone 4. Visitors to the Apple home page were greeted with a photo of the new device along with a headline, "iPhone 4. This changes everything. Again." The Apple website reflects the simplicity of the product packaging. On first glance, the customer sees the featured product. The layers come next. For example, click the image of the iPhone and the site takes you to a more detailed product page, but it's a page that is still relatively simple. The subpage highlights four features of the new phone: videocalling, high-resolution display, multitasking capabilities, and HD video recording. Instead of filling up the entire page with product information, the site supports each feature with one short paragraph. If you want to learn more about any feature, click a related link that reveals more detailed information. The point is to eliminate clutter from each of the pages. Most designers try to cram everything onto one page, typically the home page. A confused customer is a lost customer. Apple doesn't lose too many customers.

DELIVER A SIMPLE PRESENTATION

When Fleming-Wood pitched retailers to persuade them to stock the new camera in 2007, he spent 50 percent of his pitch on one very simple slide. He asked them to "reimagine" the category. The slide contains photos of two camcorders: a traditional video camera and the Flip. Under the traditional camcorder are the words "Use this for special occasions." Under the Flip are the words "Use this for everything else." The slide frames the Flip philosophy and shows how the founders outlined their vision for the category. Flip, they said, would revolutionize the category just as point-and-shoot cameras democratized a still-camera market that was dominated by more advanced, SLR cameras. The design philosophy that drove the making of the video camera found its way into the design of the presentation. Introducing too much data on a slide would have been akin to adding too many features to the camera. The focus was on the big picture.

The famous French designer Philippe Starck, who designs some products for Apple, once said that "beautiful" and "trendy" are overrated; designers should instead aspire to be "good." With the Flip, we can understand what Starck means. The founders never set out to create a "beautiful" but unapproachable device. They didn't set out to create a device with "trendy" new features that increased complexity. They set out to build a good product that was approachable and fun. For these entrepreneurs, good trumped trendy as a design principle. As a result, they created one of the trendiest innovations the category has seen in years.

Robot, Fetch My Toothpaste

If you buy clothes, shoes, or office supplies online from retailers such as The Gap, Zappos, or Staples, your immediate experience typically ends at the site or on the phone with a customer service rep. In a day or two, your items arrive at your front door. Largely hidden from view is the complex series of events that your order ignites behind the scenes, in warehouse distribution centers around the country. If you paid a visit to one of these fulfillment centers, you would come upon thousands of mobile orange robots scurrying about, lifting various trays, cases, and consumer items and delivering those products to the humans who do the final packing before shipping it out their door to yours. Those robots are the brainchild of Mick Mountz, founder and CEO of Kiva Systems, a former Apple employee whom I interviewed for this book. Mountz learned a lot from Steve Jobs about reducing complexity, lessons that helped Mountz build an army of innovative robots that have revolutionized America's distribution centers.

As with Jobs, Mountz did not conduct traditional focus groups to start his company. Also as with Jobs, he knew his customers so well that he understood their pain. He *empathized*. During the dot-com boom, Mountz had worked at online grocer Webvan, where he encountered a business problem called "pick, pack, and ship." It was terribly unproductive for individuals on a distribution floor to receive an order for a green toothbrush, a blue toothbrush, and toothpaste and then to physically walk or move to a section of the warehouse, retrieve the items, and pack them. Mountz had a vision to make the warehouse distribution process easier and more productive.

As you know from principle two, a vision sets innovation in motion. Mountz's vision was not to build robots. Robots, as it turned out, were the best technology solution to solve a problem that retailers were experiencing in their fulfillment centers. Mountz asked the question, "What if the products could talk, walk, and jump into the box themselves?" It would solve the "pick, pack, and ship" problem that plagued major retailers. The answer led to the development of Kiva's unique robots.

"What did you learn from Apple?" I asked Mountz.

"Our approach was Apple-like in its simplicity," Mountz said. "If a retailer came to Kiva, we wanted to offer the complete solution. We would do the design, conduct the simulation, build the software, test, install, and make it all work together and then turn over the keys. As an operator, you wouldn't have to worry about material handling. You can turn your attention back to your customers and do what you do best: order fulfillment. This is very powerful for our customers like Staples, Walgreens, Gap, and Zappos. They no longer have to concern themselves with material handling. They can go back to being order fulfillment experts and get 'Mrs. Smith's' green sweater out the door."[3]

Under the hood, the Kiva system is enormously complex. Here again, Mountz learned from Apple that it is critical to hide the complexity from the customer. "When you buy an iPod, you're buying it because you want to listen to music," Mountz told me. "You don't want to be an expert in ripping MP3s or understanding file formats. You want to plug it in and see it work. That's our mantra at Kiva."

Ask yourself, *How can I make my customer's life easier, simpler, and better?* Innovative companies build products or offer services that allow the customer to focus on what the customer does best. Let's take the example of Kiva and one of its customers, Staples. Staples is in the business of shipping office supplies. It is not in the business of materials handling, nor does it want to be. Kiva's proposition to Staples was straightforward: let us deal with your materials handling, and you can turn your attention to shipping high-quality products to your customers. "At Apple we were enamored with technology and innovation, but not for technology's sake. We would apply computer graphics to make it more intuitive to do your job. It was all about simplifying your life," says Mountz.

Mountz also learned another lesson from Apple: design is how things work, not just how things look. Kiva's goal is to design simple, easy-to-use products. Creating simple products means reducing complexity by eliminating features or buttons that distract from the products' core task. The Kiva robots must be approachable to factory workers and plant managers. If the robots looked intimidating, it would be more difficult for the system to gain widespread adoption on the warehouse floors. According to Mountz, "When we designed the robots, we wanted them to look fun, friendly, approachable, and easy to use. Unlike a lot of complex technologies, our robots have only two buttons: on and off. We put the buttons on each side so that no matter which side you approach the robot from, you can touch the buttons without having to reach far. We made these robots so approachable that workers think of them as personal helpers. Some even have names for the robots!"

Many entrepreneurs who start successful businesses from scratch are committed to designing simple and elegant products that solve real-world problems. Mountz never intended to build robots. He intended to make businesses more productive. Robots turned out to be the solution. Today Kiva systems make workers up to four times more productive. Given that success rate, it's likely that one of Mountz's orange robots will be handling your next online purchase.

So Simple That You Don't Need a Manual

Innovation expert Robert Verganti says that sometimes when a product is overburdened by functionalities, it is a sign that the company leaders did not have a clear idea about what they wanted to achieve. They either failed to have a firm grasp of what the product should be or invited too many people to contribute to the end result, which also fosters confusion. "They follow democratic processes too closely, and sometimes this eventually puts aside any kind of focused functionality because different engineers and designers want different and sometimes incompatible things in the product," says Verganti.[4] According to Verganti, trying to make everyone happy adds to complexity, and the ultimate outcome is disappointment.

In the fall of 2009, I met with a team of Sonos executives who were about to launch a product that hid the complexity from a very complex technology. They did so successfully by focusing on the one thing their customers wanted from the product: delivery of music without wires.

The Sonos ZonePlayer S5 debuted in October 2009 and received rave reviews from reporters and consumers. It was the first all-in-one wireless music system that consumers could control from the Internet or iPhones. It seemed destined to be well received. The quality of the speakers was excellent, and—more important—it was a cinch to set up. Practically anyone could install it and have it working in five minutes. A review by Arik Hesseldahl summed it up: "Don't worry about consulting a manual. You'll never find yourself fiddling with obscure settings on your router. You may, however, find yourself listening to a lot more music."[5] Hesseldahl pointed out that competing products also had great sound but were "tricky" to set up and hard to navigate.

When I asked the Sonos team for the secret behind designing an innovative and successful product, their response was very Apple-like and went something like this: "We don't start with the technology. We start with people and their aspirations. We learn how people would like to experience music in their homes and design a system around it." In other words, Sonos designers did not start out with the goal of building an advanced wireless system; the system was the result of asking the question, *How do people want to enjoy music in their homes?* The question led to in-home visits, extensive research, and years of prototyping to get it just right. The result is what the designers called innovative simplicity: a customer can say, "I can use it and enjoy it," because it's not intimidating.

The system had to be very, very easy to set up. Everyone in the home had to be able to use it, even those who did not consider themselves to be tech savvy. Among the design goals was that customers had to fall in love with it within five minutes.

The Zen of Sushi

Restaurant-goers in New York, Milan, Tokyo, and Beverly Hills pay a small fortune for sushi made in the "Nobu style." Japanese master chef Nobuyuki Matsuhisa (Nobu) is considered an innovative culinary entrepreneur for blending traditional Japanese dishes with Peruvian ingredients. His masterpieces are known for freshness, high-quality ingredients, and a presentation that is deceptively simple. Nobu's ingredients are hard to find and even harder to prepare, but the complexity is hidden from the consumer. Actor Robert De Niro was so impressed with Nobu's creations when he visited a restaurant in Los Angeles that he funded an expansion of the restaurant in New York. Today Nobu owns more than a dozen restaurants around the world and is regarded by many as the world's greatest sushi chef.

Nobu's creations are innovative and imaginative. One unique combination is black cod with miso; another is octopus with yuzu juice and rocoto chili paste. Despite the exotic fare, the theme that runs across Nobu's culinary innovations is simplicity—simple techniques and a simple presentation to bring out the flavors.

Just as Jonathan Ive decided that the stark white color of the iPod would make the product stand out, Nobu sees a white dish as his canvas, allowing the food to grab your attention. Anything that distracts from the presentation or the experience of the unique flavor combinations must be eliminated. Nobu's recipes are a study in elimination. What he leaves out is just as important as the ingredients he keeps.

Nobu shares Steve Jobs's philosophy: do what you love. He has said that the most important ingredient for success is not technical expertise but passion, and not just for chefs but also for anyone who wants to succeed in a given field. It took all his passion to keep him in the restaurant business after his first restaurant, which was in Anchorage, Alaska, burned down just two months after it had opened. It was not insured, and Nobu had borrowed heavily to finance it. He was shaken and depressed, but determined that nothing would stop him from following the passion that had been in his heart from the age of thirteen: to create unforgettable sushi dishes.

Nobu also shares Jobs's commitment to excellence. Nothing is taken for granted. Order the scallop and cucumber dish and you will find fifteen thin cucumber slices carefully arranged in a circle on a stark white plate. Exactly seven pieces of scallops will surround the cucumber, and one small piece of cilantro will be carefully placed on each scallop section. Finally, one dab (not two) of rocoto chili paste will be placed in the middle of the cilantro. The menu is consistently simple. Anything that detracts from the focus of the main ingredient is edited out.

The Japanese see sushi presentation as a work of art. There are many different styles, but the overriding rule that governs all preparation is simplicity. The ingredients must speak for themselves. Too many rolls or too much garnish detracts from the focus of the flavors. Simple elegance. Innovation isn't always about adding things. It's asking yourself, what can I take away?

Saying No to 1,000 Nameplates

My previous book, *The Presentation Secrets of Steve Jobs*, opened up a dialogue between me and Ford CEO Alan Mulally, who told me he had read the book cover to cover. I started to follow Mulally's career at the American automaker much more closely. The first thing that struck me was his relentless optimism and positive energy. Mulally's e-mails, media interviews, and public presentations all reflect his unshakable commitment to building the best cars in the world. The second thing that impressed me was Mulally's strategy to accomplish his goal. His mantra: "Improve Focus. Simplify Operations."

Mulally was named president and CEO of Ford on September 5, 2006. The Ford family had tapped Mulally, a former Boeing aircraft executive, to bring a fresh perspective to the iconic American brand. Ford needed a serious injection of new blood. Just as Apple was close to death before Jobs's return in 1996, Ford was also knocking on death's door before Mulally's entrance. In 2006, it had lost $12.6 billion and its stock price had plunged below $2, a result of years of declining market share.

From the previous chapter, you may remember the first steps that Steve Jobs took to resurrect Apple: eliminating products to focus on what the company did best. Mulally, too, wasted no time in shedding brands. Jaguar was the first to go. Land Rover, Aston Martin, and Volvo soon followed. Ford cut the number of its platforms—chassis—from more than twenty to eight. It reduced its nameplates worldwide from ninety-seven to twenty-five. Each model represented hundreds of millions of dollars in engineering costs, and since Ford could not sell enough of each model, the move saved the company billions of dollars. In addition to saving money, it allowed the company to put its A-team on each of the products left. By simplifying operations, Mulally focused Ford's attention. The effort worked. Ford was the only U.S. car company that did not take a government bailout. It posted a $2.7 billion profit in 2009 and saw its stock price soar sixfold. Also, in a statistic you won't see in the headlines, Ford's internal surveys found that 87 percent of its employees believe the company is on the right track. By saying no, Ford said yes to success.

What's Minimal Is Not Simple

Don't confuse simplicity with minimalism. A "minimalist" design is a broad concept that people apply to all sorts of subjects—from presentations, to stage productions, to store interiors. Stroll into a Michael Kors boutique to shop for $500 handbags and you will find a lot of empty space, large tables, and a few handbags. That's minimalism. Visit the Google website and you will find one search box and a lot of white space. That's minimalism. Watch a Steve Jobs presentation and you will see many slides with no words, just photographs.

When it comes to innovation, less does really seem to be more. Yes, the simplest designs are minimal, but minimal designs are not always simple. *Focus* should be the goal, not minimalism. A beautifully designed website is elegant because it allows visitors to quickly and simply find what they are looking for. Therefore, anything that distracts from the reason people visit the site should be eliminated. Add too much information and it will compete for your audience's attention, distracting them from the resolution to the problem at hand—whether that's buying a book, reading relevant content, or subscribing to a service.

There are two dominant trends in website design, neither of which is particularly appealing. The first is sites that are cluttered with far too much text. I recently came across the site for a Florida company that makes custom gates and fences for homes and businesses. It was the ugliest site I had ever seen. The home page included more than thirty photographs of the company's fences and more than a thousand words. To put things in perspective, the Apple home page contains fewer than fifty words.

The second trend, slightly better but still troubling, is designers taking "minimalism" to an extreme. These site designers are so in love with their creativity that they create flash-based splash pages that are painfully slow to load and add no real value to the customer's experience. These techniques get in the way of what the customer intends to do when he or she lands on the site.

I enjoy listening to a local talk radio station. The hosts are very good about plugging the station's website, saying listeners can link to a featured book, article, or interview on the site. The trouble is I've tried several times to find information on the site and have failed each time. The designers have packed so much information onto the site—using up every square inch of the home page—that it is nearly impossible to find anything mentioned on a particular show. One time I got so frustrated that I went to the company website of the particular guest (he'd said he archives his radio interviews). Again, I could not find what I wanted. The guest had thrown every piece of content he could muster onto the home page. Thirty minutes later, I gave up.

You'd think that designing a simple site is easy. It's not. Simple design takes time and skill. It's easy to add clutter. Anyone can do it, and since many websites look as if they were designed by thirteen-year-olds, clutter is common. Designers are not considering the customer. It's ironic that adding clutter is easier than eliminating content that detracts from the focus of your site.

Too many choices can paralyze your customer. Columbia University professor Sheena Iyengar conducted an experiment that has become known as the famous "jam study." In a California gourmet market, Iyengar and her assistant set up a table to give away samples of jam. Every few hours, they reduced the number of samples from twenty-four to six. The customers who stopped by received a discount coupon to be redeemed at checkout should they decide to buy a jar before they left the store. The results were eye-opening. More customers stopped by the large assortment than stopped at the small sample size, so you would suppose that more sales were registered when customers had a larger range of choices. Wrong. Only 3 percent of customers who faced the large assortment bought the jam, while 30 percent of the customers who had the smaller sample bought the jam! Iyengar concluded that the presence of choice was appealing as a theory, but in reality, more choice was debilitating.

Iyengar's hypothesis makes much more sense to me now that I have young daughters. Give a three-year-old the choice of what to wear from a closet full of clothes and she will take a very long time to make up her mind. Offer only two choices and she makes up her mind immediately. Everyone is happy.

Now let's return to the discussion of the Apple website. Apple typically features one product on the home page, such as the iPad. If you want more choices, you can select from four other categories and that's all: Mac, iPod, iPhone, or iTunes.

When people go to your site, they are focused on a task: to learn something, read something, or order something. Having too much text or offering too many choices ultimately detracts from your customer's experience.

Losing a War One Slide at a Time

In principle seven we will focus much more on the role that effective communication plays in innovation, but for now keep in mind that complexity gets in the way of design—whether it be products, websites, or presentations. On Tuesday, April 27, 2010, the *New York Times* featured a front-page story about the U.S. military's use of PowerPoint. The title said it all: "We Have Met the Enemy and He Is PowerPoint."[6] The article recounted a story about General Stanley McChrystal, who at the time was the leader of the American and NATO forces in Afghanistan. McChrystal had been shown a PowerPoint slide about military strategy in the region. The slide had more than four hundred words and looked remarkably like a bowl of spaghetti. McChrystal said if he could understand the slide, America would win the war. It was meant as a joke, but some military leaders did not find anything funny about the PowerPoint problem. Some banned PowerPoint because they thought it was dangerous, literally stifling discussion and hampering critical thinking.

PowerPoint is not the problem. The problem is that the U.S. military leaders are not thinking in the manner of Steve Jobs, at least when it comes to communicating. Of course, any military operation is highly complex, with millions of moving parts, personnel, and equipment. The secret is to hide the complexity so your audience (Apple's customers; the military's soldiers) can quickly and simply understand what it is they need to focus on. Complexity stifles communication, understanding, and innovation. Remember, an idea or an invention becomes an innovation only when it moves society forward. If an idea cannot be acted on because of its complexity, it will never meet the criteria that innovation requires.

A Simple Way to Design the Life of Your Dreams

Is it possible to apply the Apple design philosophy to your life? Houston pastor Sal Sberna believes it is. In January 2006, Sberna created a series of four sermons for the Metropolitan Baptist Church titled "The Theology of the iPod." Sberna said he composed the sermons to help the young people of his congregation make the connection between the iPod and what God was trying to teach them. Sberna sent me his notes from the sermons. His key lesson involved the idea of simplicity. Sberna made the observation that the iPod is elegant and simple to use because of the way it was designed from the inside. God, he said, designed us to be simple on the inside as well. Sberna believes we have everything we need to stay connected to God, unless we allow outside influences to clutter that relationship.

You don't have to be religious to understand that designing your life the way Steve Jobs and Jonathan Ive design Apple products could actually increase your potential for success. Jim Collins, the bestselling author of *Good to Great*, discovered this powerful secret in a Stanford business class. Collins was taking a course on innovation and creativity when one of his teachers told him that he was an undisciplined and unfocused student. This comment caught Collins by surprise. He prided himself on setting three objectives at the beginning of every year and pursuing those goals (Big, Hairy, Audacious Goals—BHAGs) relentlessly. "Instead of leading a disciplined life," Collins's teacher told him, "you lead a busy life."[7]

The teacher gave Collins an assignment. She asked him to imagine that he had just inherited $20 million but he had only ten years to live. What would he do differently? More specifically, she asked: What would he "stop doing"? Collins said completing that exercise was one of the most important lessons of his life. After he contemplated his response to the question, he left a job at Hewlett-Packard. He loved the company but hated the job. Instead, he pursued his real passion, which was to become a business professor at Stanford. If Collins had not engaged in the "stop doing" exercise, millions of readers might never have enjoyed his writings, including two of the bestselling business books of all time: *Built to Last* and *Good to Great*. Collins says the exercise is so important for a successful life that he makes a "stop doing" list the cornerstone of his New Year's resolutions.

Collins offers a simple framework that will help you lead an extraordinary life. He suggests that you ask yourself three questions:

» What are you deeply passionate about?
» What are you genetically encoded for—what activities do you feel you are "made to do"?
» What makes economic sense—what can you make a living at?[8]

Collins then recommends that you take an inventory of your activities. If 50 percent of your time falls outside these three areas, then it's time to develop a "stop doing" list. "Make your life a creative work of art," Collins wrote in *USA Today*. "A great piece of art is composed not just of what is in the final piece, but equally important, what is not. It is the discipline to discard what does not fit that distinguishes the truly exceptional artist and marks the ideal piece of work, be it a symphony, a novel, a painting, a company, or, most important of all, a life."[9]

Apple designs products that are simple and elegant. These design goals have driven Steve Jobs for his entire career. Rip a page from the Steve Jobs innovation playbook: in business, set yourself apart from your competition not by what you add but by what you remove. In life, set yourself up for success not by how many projects you choose to tackle but by how many you choose to remove. Simple, isn't it?

iLessons

1 Ask yourself, "What is the deepest reason that people buy my product?" The answer should become your product's focus. Anything that detracts from that focus should be eliminated.

2 Review everything about your product or service from the perspective of your customer. Ask yourself, "What is the one thing our customers come to us for?" Make it easy for your customers to do or find the one thing. Look at everything—the product, the packaging, the website, the instruction manuals, the communications. Everything. Is it cluttered and confusing or simple and elegant?

3 As a New Year's resolution—or anytime during the year—create a "stop doing" list. Cut down on the time you spend on projects or tasks that do not advance your core purpose and fulfill your passion.

Create Insanely Great Experiences

People don't want to just buy personal computers anymore. They want to know what they can do with them, and we're going to show people exactly that.

—STEVE JOBS

CHAPTER 12

We're Here to Help You Grow

When we envisioned Apple's model we said it's got to connect with Apple. It was easy. Enrich lives. Enriching lives. That's what Apple has been doing for thirty plus years.

—RON JOHNSON, APPLE SENIOR VICE PRESIDENT, RETAIL OPERATIONS

There are no cashiers at an Apple Store. There are specialists, creatives—even geniuses—but no cashiers. There are no salespeople at an Apple Store, either. There are consultants, concierges, experts, and personal shoppers—but no salespeople. Although the Apple Stores have no commissioned sales staff, they generate more revenue per square foot than most other widely recognized brands. Apple's famous "glass cube" store on New York's Fifth Avenue reportedly generates higher sales per square foot than its neighbors Saks and Tiffany—significantly higher. Apple's revenue has been pegged at $4,032 per square foot a year. Compare that with Tiffany's at $2,600 or Best Buy at $930. Apple has become the world's best retailer by thinking differently from most shopkeepers. "People haven't been willing to invest this much time and money or engineering in a store before," said Steve Jobs in a 2007 interview for *Fortune* magazine. "It's not important if the customer knows that. They just feel it. They feel something's a little different."[1]

Apple opened its first retail store in 2001 at the Tysons Corner Center in McLean, Virginia. Less than five years later, it reached $1 billion in annual sales, hitting the magic number faster than any other retailer in history. Today, with 287 locations around the world, Apple Stores bring in more than $1 billion a quarter. Apple investors, employees, and customers should be thankful that Steve Jobs refused to listen to retail consultants such as David Goldstein, who said Apple would fail at retail. "I give them two years before they're turning out the lights on a very painful and expensive mistake," Goldstein predicted.[2] And now you know why Jobs doesn't hire consultants!

Skeptics misjudged the success of the Apple Stores because they were solely number crunchers. They failed to consider that Apple was not entering the business of building stores; it was in the business of creating experiences. Goldstein's mistake was comparing Apple to other PC retailers of the time, such as Gateway. He looked at gross margins in the PC retail business and concluded that Apple would have to generate $12 million a year to pay for its space. Gateway, he cited as evidence, was doing only $8 million at its stores. Goldstein's conventional analysis made sense on paper. In the real world, as you've learned from the previous principles, Steve Jobs does not think conventionally, nor does he underestimate the power of an emotional experience that doesn't always fit conveniently into a spreadsheet. Jobs launched an innovation in the retail space precisely because he had a bigger vision than his competitors. His customers would enter an Apple Store to shop for products and leave "feeling" inspired.

Enriching Lives

Apple entered the retail business out of necessity. In 2000, it was dependent on giant electronics retailers that simply pushed products, Apple or otherwise. Employees at companies such as Sears or CompUSA had little, if any, training on Apple products and what made them unique. Jobs said that buying a computer had replaced buying a car as the most dreaded purchasing experience.

He realized he had to improve the retail experience or risk losing even more market share (Apple's share of the U.S. computer market stood at 3 percent). "It was like, we have to do something, or we're going to be a victim of plate tectonics," Jobs said about his decision to enter retail. "We have to think different about this. We have to innovate here."[3]

Jobs knows what he doesn't know, and he didn't know retail. He asked Gap CEO Mickey Drexler to join Apple's board, and he hired former Target executive Ron Johnson, who shared Jobs's vision of creating beautifully designed, but affordable, products. Also in line with Jobs, Johnson realized that innovation could not take place without a clear, compelling vision. "To succeed in any business, you need an exceptionally clear vision," Johnson told a group of equity analysts gathered in San Francisco in September 2006. "And to me a vision is something that you can say in one sentence. The fewer words the better. When we started, the commonly accepted thing that retailers did was to sell stuff. So if you put Gateway's vision into words, it was to 'sell boxes.' They used to call it 'moving metal.' When we envisioned Apple's model we said it's got to connect with Apple. It was easy. Enrich lives. Enriching lives. That's what Apple has been doing for thirty plus years."[4]

When Johnson and Jobs decided that the vision for Apple's stores would be "enriching lives" instead of "moving metal," it allowed them to throw out the conventional retail playbook that dictated store design, location, and staffing decisions. Apple would build boutiques that offered solutions, a novel approach to selling computers. Jobs, giving a tour of the first Apple Store, said, "People don't want to just buy personal computers anymore. They want to know what they can do with them, and we're going to show people exactly that."[5]

Johnson asked his team, "What would a store that enriches lives look like?" Here's a hint: unlike anything else. After studying customer service champs outside of computer retail—such as The Four Seasons hotel—Johnson arrived at several criteria that would help the Apple Stores stand apart:

» **Design uncluttered stores.** The stores would be open, light, and airy and would use only three materials (stainless steel, glass, and

Scandinavian wood). Johnson said that Target had thirty-one toaster models. Williams-Sonoma, the experts in food preparation, had only two. He would model the Apple Stores on this concept of minimalism, reducing the number of products they would offer. Johnson did not have much of a choice. When he first met with Jobs, the iPod had not been created yet, so Apple had four products (two portables, two desktops) to fill six thousand square feet. Instead of panicking, Johnson saw it as the ultimate opportunity. He would fill the store not with products but with the ownership experience. It gave Apple the space to innovate.

» **Locate the stores where people live their lives.** Most Apple Stores are located in malls or shopping districts, not in the middle of giant parking lots or remote locations. "The real estate was a lot more expensive," said Jobs, "but it was worth it because people didn't have to gamble with 20 minutes of their time. They only had to gamble with 20 footsteps of time."[6]

» **Allow customers to test-drive products.** No computer retailer at the time would let you connect to the Internet and try out merchandise. Walk around in an Apple Store and you will find that all of the products are connected to the Internet. Customers are welcome to browse for as long as they like. They can read books on the iPad, play games on an iPod Touch, or listen to music on an iPod Nano.

» **Offer a concierge experience.** Johnson asked his team to tell him about the best customer service experience they had ever had. Most of them talked about hotels such as The Four Seasons. That gave Johnson the idea of building a "bar" in the store where customers could walk up and ask for help. Instead of dispensing alcohol, Apple would dispense advice. When Steve Jobs gave a tour of the first Apple Store, he said every product would be displayed in the first 25 percent of the store, and the rest would be devoted to solutions. Explaining the Genius Bar, Jobs said, "Wouldn't it be great if when you went to buy a computer or after you bought a computer, if you had any questions, you could ask a genius? This is our Genius Bar. There will be somebody here who can do service right in the store and will be able to answer any questions you've got. If that person doesn't know the answer [picks up red phone], they've got a hotline to call us directly at Apple headquarters in Cupertino, where we have somebody who does."[7]

» **Make it easy to buy.** There's no standing in long lines at an Apple Store to buy your merchandise, because, well, there are no cash registers. Every specialist wanders the floor with a special EasyPay, wireless credit-card reader that will get you on your way in no time. A receipt is sent to the customer via e-mail. Apple discourages the use of cash. Some stores have a $250 limit on cash purchases and some items cannot be purchased with cash unless converted to a gift card. This might sound unwieldy and has attracted some negative publicity, but the wireless purchase option does make it easy for the majority of Apple customers to check out quickly.

» **Offer one-to-one training.** Customers who buy a Mac online or in an Apple Store can sign up for one-to-one training with a "creative," someone who can teach them about any program they would like to learn about. On any given day, you're likely to see people young and old learning to write documents in Pages, create presentations in Keynote, organize photos in iPhoto, or learn instruments with GarageBand. The more people enjoy the programs Apple has to offer, the more likely they are to return.

Apple has innovated around the retail experience by changing people's expectations of what a retail experience could be.

No Reality Filters

Johnson once said that going from Target to Apple was an eye-opening experience, because Steve Jobs had no "reality filters." It was a perceptive insight that teaches us a lot about Steve Jobs, Apple, and innovation. Johnson said that from birth, people are taught that they can't do things. According to Johnson, "Innovation is this amazing intersection between someone's imagination and the reality in which they live. The problem is, many companies don't have great imagination, but their view of reality tells them that it's impossible to do what they imagine."[8]

Johnson cited an experience he had at Target. The chain carried essentially the same products as Wal-Mart. Johnson asked a famous designer, Michael Graves, to design something new

> *When I was young, the one thing I could do well was draw. My mother suggested I think about using drawing in a profession like architecture. I wasn't well informed about architecture and what it could mean in the cultural domain until I went to Rome. Then I understood architecture through a different kind of lens. Once you look at the work of an early Roman temple and see the role of the floor, the ceiling, the wall, the column, the roof, the window, it hits home in a way that you say, "Aha, these are the elements of an architectural composition."*[10]
>
> —MICHAEL GRAVES,
> ON THE IMPORTANCE OF
> SEEKING EXPERIENCES
> OUTSIDE OF
> CONVENTIONAL NORMS

and unique. Graves designed a teakettle that eventually became a huge hit for the store. He would go on to design hundreds of popular products for Target. At the time Johnson introduced the teakettle, though, Target executives suggested cutting back on the quality so they could sell it for $20 instead of $40. Johnson stuck to his guns, believing Target customers would appreciate everyday products that were well designed and still reasonably affordable. Design is now the cornerstone of Target's business and its differentiator, Johnson noted.

When Johnson got to Apple, he expected the same type of push-back but instead found a CEO who had "no reality filter" in regard to the value of great design, high-quality products, and a fervent imagination. "We let imagination win," said Johnson. "If you ask customers what they love about our stores, they love the things we imagined."[9] The lesson that Johnson's Target-versus-Apple experience teaches us is that conventional thinking leads to conventional ideas. If Target had tried to outdo Wal-Mart at its own game, it would have failed to develop a unique brand identity. If Apple had chosen to follow Gateway's strategy, it too would have failed to create an innovative retail experience. In both cases, the companies created successful innovations in retail because they looked outside of industry-accepted norms for inspiration: Target turned to designer Michael Graves, who was better known for his world-famous architecture than for everyday appliances, while Apple turned to The Four Seasons—a company that had nothing to do with computers and yet played a pivotal role in the Apple Store's success.

We're Here to Help You Grow

In February 2010, I walked into an Apple Store to purchase a new MacBook Pro for some creative tasks we needed to accomplish in our office. For the record, we are not "Mac heads" at Gallo Communications Group. We are very pleased with the performance of both Microsoft PCs and Macs. Our employees find that the two platforms serve different purposes. We are, however, really biased on the subject of an exceptional customer service experience and believe Apple does it exceptionally well.

I knew what I wanted, so I could have easily made my Apple purchase online without stepping foot in a store, but I wanted to get the full "Apple experience." As it turned out, I did begin the journey online by booking an appointment with a "personal shopper." Just as customer service champ Nordstrom has personal shoppers to help you select the right merchandise, Apple has personal shoppers to answer all your questions and to help you find the right fit. Once I selected a local Apple Store, Apple e-mailed me confirmation of my personal shopping appointment.

I arrived at the store and was greeted right on time by Dominick, a "specialist" who spent the next hour answering my questions and showing me Apple products. Dominick did not work on commission, which he told me early in our conversation. "We're here to help you grow," he said. On hearing that statement, I realized this would be a unique experience. That one sentence—we're here to help you grow—taught me why Apple has been able to create one of the most innovative environments in the retail category. Most retailers are in business to move product; Apple is in business to help you grow. Big difference.

"Dominick, I'm still debating whether to buy a Mac or a PC. Why should I make the switch to Mac?" I asked. (Although I knew the answer to this, I wanted to hear how my personal shopper would respond.)

"You mentioned that you give presentations," Dominick said. I noted by this comment that he was listening carefully to my remarks and evaluating my needs. "The Mac operating system is a Unix-based platform, which means it's incredibly stable and reliable. You don't want to experience technical problems in the middle of a presentation to three hundred people, do you?" he asked.

"Of course not," I responded.

"iLife comes preinstalled on all new Macs," Dominick continued. "You mentioned that you want to do more with photos and video. iLife gives you the best programs to organize, share, and enjoy your photos, movies, and music."

"Sounds great," I said, "but I would have to learn all new programs. I already know how to use a PC, and I've gotten very comfortable with it."

"That's OK. We can sign you up for personalized one-to-one training right here in our store," Dominick replied.

Apple had thought of everything. Dominick had been trained to listen to my needs, customize a solution, and predict what my hesitation might be—and to do it all in an approachable, friendly manner. I could have made my purchase on the spot, but I chose to see how far I could take the experience.

"Well, I'm still not sure," I said, shaking my head and putting on my best "I'm confused" look.

"Take your time," Dominick said. "If you think it would help, we can put you in touch with one of our business consultants."

I thanked Dominick for his time and asked for an appointment with a consultant. Dominick took my name and said someone would be in touch. When a typical retailer says someone will be in touch, it usually means you're unlikely to hear from that someone for days, if at all. Apple was different. By the time I returned to the office, I had a message from an Apple Store consultant who would help me with my decision. I returned to the Apple Store a few days later to meet with my consultant. Just as Dominick did, this person made it clear that he was not on commission. "I'm here to make you feel comfortable with our products. We want a customer for life," he said.

I asked the consultant the same series of questions I had asked my personal shopper, and the answers were largely the same—everyone at Apple is trained to speak from the same playbook. The messages are consistent. The consultant priced out an itemized list of products that would meet my needs and handed me a final cost sheet, which included $99 for a "one-to-one" training program, giving me access to a customized training session once a week for a year.

"Well, there is one more problem," I said. "I have a PC with a lot of stuff on it, and I'll have to transfer it to my Mac. How can I do it?"

"Just bring in your laptop at the time of purchase, leave it with us, and we'll transfer everything," the consultant said. "Then we'll schedule an appointment for you to pick up your old computer and meet your new one. We call it Meet Your Mac."

Again, Apple had thought of everything. Each time I raised an obstacle about switching to Mac, an Apple specialist or consultant offered a solution. They even scheduled a friendly, nonthreatening introduction to my new computer—Meet Your Mac. It was like being set up for a date: I was introduced to the system by someone I "knew" (a specialist), I was guaranteed that she (the computer) would have all the qualities I was looking for (including low maintenance!), and I could "meet" her in a casual setting. Once we met, we could get to know each other through personalized training sessions every week for an entire year. Anyone this deep into a relationship would find it hard to separate. And that's the key to Apple's successful innovation in retail. Where most retailers are moving product, Apple is establishing a lifelong relationship.

Be forewarned: building deep emotional relationships with your customers could lead to some strange, unintended

> " We do no market research. We don't hire consultants. The only consultants I've ever hired in my 10 years is one firm to analyze Gateway's retail strategy so I would not make some of the same mistakes they made. But we never hire consultants, per se. We just want to make great products."
>
> —STEVE JOBS

consequences. On Valentine's Day in 2010, Joshua and Ting Li decided to tie the knot and profess their love for each other in front of friends and family. Getting married on Valentine's Day is not uncommon. Getting married on Valentine's Day at the Apple Store on New York's Fifth Avenue is quite unusual. The "minister" was dressed like Steve Jobs, complete with a black mock turtleneck sweater, blue jeans, and running shoes. The couple read their "iDo's" from an iPhone, and the video was edited and posted on YouTube (likely edited on a Mac).[12]

Yes, strange things happen when your customers fall in love with your brand. Even stranger things happen when two people fall in love with each other because your brand brought them together!

As Disney's largest shareholder, Steve Jobs is often called on for advice to help the media giant improve its business. When an executive charged with reinventing Disney's retail stores asked Jobs for his input, Jobs said, "Dream bigger."

No better advice has ever been given.

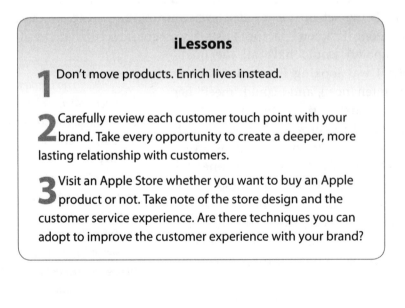

iLessons

1 Don't move products. Enrich lives instead.

2 Carefully review each customer touch point with your brand. Take every opportunity to create a deeper, more lasting relationship with customers.

3 Visit an Apple Store whether you want to buy an Apple product or not. Take note of the store design and the customer service experience. Are there techniques you can adopt to improve the customer experience with your brand?

CHAPTER 13

Think Differently About Your Brand Experience

If you just think about what makes customers and employees happy, in today's world that ends up being good for business.

—TONY HSIEH, FOUNDER, ZAPPOS.COM

Robert Stephens started a billion-dollar enterprise with an initial investment of $200, a bicycle, and a dream to create an innovative customer experience. While attending college, Stephens rode his bike to people's houses to fix their computer problems. Stephens always saw himself as a brand. He had a call center (a cell phone) and a supply chain (a mountain bike). When it came time to expand his empire in 1994, Stephens had no money for advertising, so he "stole" ideas from customer service experts. Drivers for United Parcel Service always wore uniforms, so Stephens decided that his repair experts would also dress in uniforms. Since the employees were self-described computer geeks, the uniforms had to fit the part—white button-down short-sleeve shirts, a clip-on black tie, black pants, white socks, and a metallic police-style badge just like a special agent's. In keeping with the special agent theme, Stephens purchased Volkswagen

Beetles for his staff and had them painted in black and white, similar to police cruisers. He liked the flat-rate pricing he found at an oil-change chain, so he adopted similar fees for his computer services.

By now you might have guessed that Stephens is the founder of Geek Squad, the computer repair and electronics service company purchased by Best Buy in 2002. Since then, Geek Squad has grown from sixty employees and $3 million in revenue to more than $1 billion in annual revenue. Geek Squad service departments are set up in all of Best Buy's 1,143 U.S. stores, and its iconic "Geekmobiles" still cruise around neighborhoods making house calls. Geek Squad's twenty-four thousand "agents" are still dressed in the nerdy uniforms that Stephens first adopted to help his brand stand out.

Geek Squad might never have become synonymous with Best Buy had it not been for forward-thinking Best Buy vice president Sean Skelley. As electronics components, computers, and gadgets became more complex and harder to set up, Skelley had been thinking about ways to get closer to customers and to make a more satisfying connection with them. Geek Squad had built a reputation for superior customer service that Skelley knew would complement the Best Buy chain.

An Internet search for "computer repair" returns twenty-seven million links. Imagine how hard it must be for computer repair firms to differentiate themselves. Geek Squad's Robert Stephens could have been one of the thousands of computer repair experts around the country who carve out a modest living serving a handful of clients. But he dreamed bigger. Fulfilling that dream required that he think differently about the experience customers had with his brand.

Delivering Happiness

The founder of online shoe and clothing retailer Zappos.com, Tony Hsieh, has a lot in common with Apple founder Steve Jobs. Both started their successful businesses from a spare bedroom, both were committed to improving the customer service experience, and both changed the meaning that a brand's products could have with its customers. By reinventing the customer experience, Zappos has achieved extraordinary success (acquired by Amazon for $1.2 billion in 2009) and has been named by *Fortune* magazine as one of the best places to work in the country.

After I interviewed Hsieh for a *BusinessWeek* article, he invited me to visit the Zappos headquarters in the Las Vegas area. (Zappos is located in Henderson, Nevada, about fifteen minutes from the Vegas strip.) I did just that in December 2009. I have never experienced anything like the Zappos culture, at least in corporate America. Its employees are genuinely thrilled to come to work, and its customers are rabid fans (75 percent of Zappos.com's transactions are repeat purchases). The "secret" to Zappos.com's success is that Hsieh never set out to sell shoes. His vision was to build an innovative corporate culture that would deliver happiness to employees and customers alike.

An Inside Look at the Zappos Experience

"You name it. I make it happen," said Roz Searcy when I asked her what she did at Zappos.[1] Roz, who is shuttle driver, receptionist, and go-to girl, picked me up from my hotel in Las Vegas for the short drive to Henderson, where I toured the crazy, fun, and wacky world of Zappos.com. Zappos has made a name for itself as one of the best places to work in the country. It's easy to see why. Everyone—from the CEO to the receptionist—lives the brand's values. Following are five principles that have made Zappos the gold standard for innovative customer service.

1. TREAT EVERYONE LIKE FAMILY

The tour started with a Zappos shuttle bus showing up right on time outside my hotel. I was the only passenger on the bus. Nobody knew I was there to write a story for BusinessWeek.com. I don't think it would have mattered. What mattered most to Zappos employees was that I wanted to learn about their culture, and they were eager to share it.

"Why did you drive all the way to my hotel just to pick me up?" I asked Roz.

"We treat our customers as family. If you had a family member in town, wouldn't you pick them up from their hotel or the airport? That's what we do for customers or anyone who wants to learn more about our culture!"

Always remember that everyone in your company—*everyone*—represents your brand. Enter an Apple Store and you'll be greeted by friendly, knowledgeable staff. The same holds true at Zappos. From the shuttle driver to the receptionist to the call center operators, everyone at Zappos represents the company's culture.

2. HIRE FOR CULTURAL FIT

Everyone I met at Zappos had an outgoing personality. Our tour guide, Jonathan Wolske, exuded passion and enthusiasm. He was having fun telling the Zappos story. Folks in the call center would take a break and say hello, blow whistles, and enthusiastically greet us as we walked by their cubicles. (I say "cubicles," but they are more like pods of creativity, as employees are allowed to express their individuality in their personal work spaces.) Hsieh told me that the company hires for cultural fit. For example, one of the company's ten core values is to "create fun and a little weirdness." So, representatives ask prospective employees a question: "On a scale of 1 to 10, how weird are you?" If you're a 1, you're probably too straitlaced for Zappos, and if you're a 10, you may be a little too nutty. It's not the number that's important but how people react to it. Zappos looks for people who have fun with others. I was given a "culture book" at the end of the trip that contained unedited observations from hundreds of employees. The word *love* is probably the most common term used to describe the work experience. Hire people who love your brand and what it stands for. You can teach them the rest.

3. TRUST YOUR TEAM

Hsieh innovated in the call center business by breaking from the status quo. Instead of following a script, as most call center employees are required to do at other companies with a large online presence, Zappos employees have no scripts and no time limits. Their only mission is to "wow" customers and create an emotional connection with them. Every employee has a supply of postcards sitting next to the phone. Employees are encouraged to build a relationship with each customer and drop the caller a handwritten note. For example, one employee asked a customer why she was buying flip-flops. The customer said she was leaving for Fiji. The Zappos employee sent her a note that read, "Enjoy your trip!"

These are simple gestures that help attract a customer for life. In another example, Hsieh told me that an employee had once spent four hours on the phone with a customer. He never asked the employee, "Why did you spend so much time?" Instead, he asked, "Was the customer wowed?"

Get it? Innovative customer service isn't brain surgery. It is simply courtesy, common sense, and the desire to treat everyone—customers, partners, and employees—like family.

4. SHARE EVERYTHING

All financial and performance information is shared daily with employees—average call times, sales numbers, profits, and the like. In fact, Zappos is so open with its performance information that results are posted on a board for all to see. The staff even encouraged me to take video of the board and to share it with others on my blog. Public relations professionals, take note: there was no PR person monitoring me during my tour. I was completely free to take photographs and video and to talk to employees. Zappos has nothing to hide. The company reached more than $1 billion in annual sales during the worst retail sales environment in decades. It did so because it trusts its employees to do the right thing for the customer.

5. HAVE FUN!

During our tour, an employee interrupted the tour guide to tape some segments for the company blog. Everyone was cheering and high-fiving one another. I have never seen another group of people having so much fun with each other. Zappos employees are not afraid of having fun because their bosses might look down on them. Fun is encouraged. Fun becomes a problem only when Zappos employees are *not* having it.

In many industries, superior customer service is your only sustainable advantage. Now think about the basic lessons Zappos teaches us about customer service: hire for cultural fit, treat your employees like gold, trust them, encourage deeper relationships with customers, and have fun. Is this rocket science? No, it's not. But it's done so rarely in the retail space today that Zappos is considered to have one of the most innovative company cultures in the United States.

The most important similarity between Zappos and Apple is that both have changed the meaning their customers associate with their brands. In order to create a culture devoted to providing an innovative customer service experience, you must begin by asking yourself, "What am I really selling?" For example, Apple is not in the business of selling computers; Apple "enriches lives." Zappos is not in the business of selling shoes; Zappos "delivers happiness."

What business are you in?

A Touch of Vegas in the Chicago Suburbs

In the Chicago suburb of Glenview, Illinois, you'll come across customers who have driven a hundred miles to purchase computers, TVs, MP3 players, digital cameras, or washer-dryers from Abt Electronics. There are plenty of other places to buy electronics in Chicago, including Best Buys. Still, even the Geek Squad experience can't compare to the unique experience that welcomes customers to Abt.

Mike Abt, one of the four brothers who run the store, told me that the vision for Abt Electronics is to create a unique experience for people who buy electronics.[2] If your vision is to offer an innovative experience in your business, then you should look outside your industry for inspiration. Just as Apple's Ron Johnson looked for inspiration at The Four Seasons and Robert Stephens turned to UPS, Mike Abt also sought insight from outside his industry. In Abt's case, he turned to Las Vegas.

When I first saw Abt's lobby—its atrium—it reminded me of the magnificent Bellagio hotel in Vegas. (See Figure 13.1.) Abt has palm trees, attractive storefronts (stores-within-a-store, much like what you find in a high-end shopping mall), and a water fountain that moves to music. Just as with the famous water show set to Andrea Bocelli music at the Bellagio, Abt water shows are scheduled on the half hour. "This looks really familiar," I said to myself. Sure enough, I learned that Mike Abt had also visited the Bellagio and decided to bring a touch of Vegas to Glenview.

Abt knew that in order to compete against the big-box retailers such as Best Buy, Wal-Mart, and Sears, he had to offer a unique experience, far more exciting and enticing than anyone else. The fountain show is just one aspect of the Abt experience that attracts shoppers from miles around. The store offers unique architecture and artwork that please the eye while freshly baked cookies are pleasing to the nose. Attractions are abundant. Children and adults alike love the seventy-five-hundred-gallon aquarium—another Vegas-inspired attraction, based on the giant aquarium behind

FIGURE 13.1 Abt Electronics atrium

FIGURE 13.2 Abt Electronics aquarium

the check-in desk at the Mirage. (See Figure 13.2.) A diver cleans the large tank, which, as with the fountain show, has become a must-see attraction for people in the store. The tank is positioned near the high-definition video cameras, so customers testing the cameras have something beautiful and colorful to point at. Local schools even schedule field trips to the Abt aquarium.

Apple, Geek Squad, and Abt all offer a lesson about innovating around the customer service experience: it's OK to "steal" ideas from customer service experts in other industries and to adapt those ideas to your business. Stealing ideas from your competitors may work for the short term, but it's unlikely to turn you into an innovation leader. You're simply copying the leader. That's not innovation. Innovation is seeing what exists in another industry and applying what you learn to improve the customer experience.

A Pizza Place That Can't Be Topped

Americans love pizza. Pizza is a $30 billion-a-year industry in the United States, dominated by such giants as Little Caesar's, Domino's, Pizza Hut, and Papa John's. Who of sound mind would open a pizza place in the face of such entrenched competition? Someone who thinks along the lines of Steve Jobs.

Ask any eighteen- to thirty-four-year-old in Madison, Wisconsin, to name his or her favorite pizza and the answer is likely to be Toppers. Based in the nearby town of Whitewater, Toppers Pizza has opened twenty-six stores in the upper Midwest, often taking market share from the established pizza chains in the towns where it decides to locate a new franchise. It also earns more revenue per square foot than stores affiliated with national pizza chains. Toppers outperforms the competition by creating an innovative customer experience.

By now you know that innovation begins with a vision. "Our core purpose was to build an extraordinary company that brings together families, friends, and fanatics for food and fun," Toppers director of marketing Scott Iversen told me.[3] *Fun* is the key word. If the Toppers vision had been to "make great pizza," the company would have had a difficult time attracting a rabid following. First, Toppers has a very specific target market in mind. Where the national pizza chains appeal to everyone, Toppers knew it had to carve out a niche for itself, so its founders focused on the youth market, opening stores in college towns in Wisconsin. Apple did serve as an inspiration. Although Apple products are enjoyed by people of all ages, Apple products are "hip" with young people. The founders of Toppers asked themselves, "How can we be cool with the college crowd?" Among the innovative answers:

> » **Use fresh ingredients.** The national pizza chains truck in their dough to individual outlets. Toppers makes its dough fresh daily at each store. The key is to communicate this distinction consistently in all of the company's marketing and promotions.
> » **Provide menu variety.** Toppers carries unique pizzas that gain a fanatical following among young people, who often share their experiences on their social networks. Its most popular creations include a Mac 'N Cheese pizza and a "Hangover Helper," a pizza that has omelet-style ingredients.
> » **Empathize with your customer.** Most college kids are on a budget. They may be eager to try the famed Mac 'N Cheese pizza but may be reluctant to spend $17 for a large. Toppers took care of that with "MyZa," individual, trial-size pizzas that sell for $7. Toppers also

learned that young people like to share items off the menu, so it cre-ated "ToppersStix," cheesy-covered breadsticks that come for less than $10.

» **Hang out with your customers.** Toppers embraces social media. The chain maintains profiles on Facebook and Twitter. Although the franchise has only twenty-six stores, it has eleven thousand Facebook fans. The chain has its own YouTube page, where it posts funny videos of its customers spoofing other pizza chains. Toppers has fun with its customers, engaging them where they live their lives.

» **Have fun.** When a Toppers delivery driver shows up at your door, you're handed everything you need to enjoy your pizza, including plates, napkins, and packets of red pepper. Oh, and one more thing: green army guys or lollipops. "Why do you do that?" I asked Iversen. "Why not? It's fun. It's memorable. And our customers talk about it!" Toppers is fun and irreverent at every point in the customer interaction.

» **Hire for culture fit.** As is the case with Zappos and Apple, Toppers hires for personality. Trainers can teach anyone how to make pizza, but they can't teach friendliness. You may be able to make a killer pizza, but if you're a grump, Toppers doesn't want you. Also as with Apple, everyone is trained to know the products. Every employee at Toppers can describe any item on the menu and make sugges-tions based on a customer's preferences. This approach creates an environment where people feel welcome instead of dismissed as just another "transaction."

According to Iversen, "Where the big guys offer mediocre qual-ity and don't care about you as a person, we want our customers to know that we offer a superior product in terms of quality and freshness, but also that we want to have a personal relationship with them. People love brands that connect with them personally." Toppers cannot compete by being liked. It needs to be *loved* and fanatically so. Based on the rabid following it seems to generate in its markets—and its record revenue in 2009, one of the worst years for restaurants in the country—Toppers is in the early stages of a long-lasting love affair.

Innovation That Won't Break the Bank

As you can tell by now, innovation need not be expensive. Business journals are filled with stories of how much companies spend on R&D, as if spending and innovation go hand in hand. As Steve Jobs has said, innovation has nothing to do with how much you spend. It's all about creating great products, services, or experiences your customers will love. During a visit to the Olympic city of Vancouver, British Columbia, I dropped by a store that had been written up in *Fast Company* for its innovative customer service—Everything Wine. Founder Paul Clinton wanted to find a way to compete against the big-box wine retailers such as Costco and BevMo. Those chains have tiny markups, so it's nearly impossible to compete on price if you want to stay in business. Clinton decided to innovate around the experience.

Everyone at Everything Wine is a wine expert. Just as there are no cashiers at Apple, there are no "cashiers" at this unique wine-shop. Everyone is trained to be a specialist and to answer questions about specific wines and suggest food pairings. Customers need to feel appreciated. They will not feel appreciated if, when they ask a question, they get this response: "I don't know. I just work here." What surprised me most was the fact that Everything Wine won an award by the Vancouver Chamber of Commerce as the most innovative local business. This award reminded me how few companies there are that do customer service well: when a store does something as basic as training all of its employees to be experts, it gets recognized as being an innovation leader. Innovation need not be expensive. But it does require a commitment to serve the customer.

On the same trip to Vancouver, I chatted with a young lady who worked for the Westin hotel where I was staying. Her "passion" was graphic design. How do I know? Her passion was written on her name badge. When I discovered this little item about her life, we talked, and I learned that she was taking classes in computer design. I've had similar conversations with Westin employees at other hotels. I've talked about travel experiences with a waiter in Dallas and movies with a bellhop in Kansas City.

In 2008, Westin Hotel and Resorts decided to launch an innovative initiative designed to encourage deeper relationships between hotel employees and guests. The stroke of genius: new name tags. The twist was that under the person's name, the tag included this phrase: "My passion is _____." Westin executives told me that the "passion tags" open a dialogue between the company's fifty thousand employees and its guests, and when guests start talking, they are much more forthcoming about any issues that concern them during their stay. In the hotel business, if a hotel simply "meets" a guest's needs, the hotel receives a good loyalty score from that particular guest. On the other hand, if the guest has a problem and it gets resolved satisfactorily, the guest's "intent to return," an important indicator for the hotel, rises dramatically. A simple phrase on a name tag encourages guests to talk and engage, and they tend to leave with a pleasurable experience in their minds. Now, I don't know what the going rate is for name tags, but as an innovation, they probably cost a lot less than remodeling a hotel lobby.

An innovative customer experience can be simple, inexpensive, and relatively easy to introduce, and whether it's Apple, Geek Squad, Abt Electronics, Toppers, Everything Wine, or Westin, the vision is the same: to enhance and enrich the connection between the brand and its customers.

---

iLessons

1 Look outside your industry for ideas on how to stand out from your competitors.

2 Hire for cultural fit, and train everyone to be an expert in that "culture."

3 Have fun. Passion is contagious. If your employees aren't having fun, your customers won't be either.

Master the Message

You've baked a really lovely cake, but
then you've used dog shit for frosting.

—STEVE JOBS

CHAPTER 14

The World's Greatest Corporate Storyteller

Steve Jobs is the ultimate showman who keeps the audience excited the whole way leading up to the reveal.

—DAVID BLAINE, MAGICIAN

On January 27, 2010, Steve Jobs introduced yet another Apple innovation, concluding the presentation by summing up the product in one sentence: "Our most advanced technology in a magical and revolutionary device at an unbelievable price." He had just unveiled the iPad, giving the audience a full tour of the tablet computer's capabilities, which span video, music, games, e-mail, newspapers, books, and more. And just as he does for every new product, Jobs offered his audience a one-sentence, Twitter-friendly description that positions the product exactly as Apple wants the world to see it.

If you missed the presentation, no problem. Apple immediately posted the video link to its website and issued a press release at the conclusion of the presentation. The headline on the press release announced, "Apple introduces iPad, a magical and revolutionary device at an unbelievable price. If you missed the press release, you could visit the home page of the Apple website, which carried a photograph of the iPad alongside text that read, "iPad is here, a magical and revolutionary product at an unbelievable price." If you missed the presentation, the press release, and the website, Apple had one more platform from which to reach you: the Apple Stores. The entrance of each store had a poster with a photo of the iPad. Alongside the photograph, the poster read, "A magical and revolutionary product at an unbelievable price." Apple's positioning of the product was ubiquitous and unmistakable.

Conduct an Internet search for the keywords iPad + "magical and revolutionary" and you will find that it returns nearly nine million links! And no, most of those links do not take you back to the Apple website. A CNN headline blared, "Apple unveils the magical iPad." A ZDNet headline read, "Jobs was right: iPad is magical and revolutionary." A popular blogger wrote, "3 reasons iPad is magical and revolutionary." Apple had made the product description so concise, compelling, and consistent that it had been picked up by thousands of analysts, reporters, and customers who were searching for a way to talk about the new device.

Convincing Others That Your Great Idea Is Really a Great Idea

The iPad's presentation and marketing messages proved once again that Steve Jobs is the world's supreme corporate storyteller. For more than three decades, he has turned the product launch into an art form. Although Jobs's slides are elegantly designed, his presentations go far beyond the slide show. They are meant to inform, educate, and entertain.

In 2009, McGraw-Hill published *The Presentation Secrets of Steve Jobs*, which revealed the exact techniques that make a Jobs presentation so awe-inspiring. The iPad presentation occurred after the book had been released, but bloggers who were familiar with its content wrote about how closely the presentation followed the template outlined in the book.

This fact underscores an important point: if Steve Jobs can follow the same template for his presentations, then you can adopt the very same techniques to make your ideas stand out, get noticed, and generate buzz. And please don't tell me, "My product isn't as sexy as an iPad." Bull. As long as you have an idea that improves someone's life or moves society forward, then you have a story to tell. It's up to you to communicate your story in a way that inspires, energizes, and excites your listeners.

Emory University neuroscience professor Gregory Berns has said, "A person can have the greatest idea in the world—completely different and novel—but if that person can't convince enough other people, it doesn't matter."[1] Storytelling has always mattered to Steve Jobs. He thinks differently about his message and how he presents it to his employees, investors, customers, and the general public.

Companies, executives, and entrepreneurs around the world are trying to deconstruct the magic behind Apple's success. They take apart Apple's products to learn clues about their unique designs. They study Steve Jobs for clues to his thinking. Each of the components is a part of the story—one of seven parts—but the last part, the seventh principle underlying breakthrough success, may be the most important. Steve Jobs has mastered the message, communicating his ideas so brilliantly that he persuades investors, employees, and customers to back his vision and to join him on his journey.

Countless ideas will never see the light of day, let alone move society forward, if their stories are not told effectively. Steve Jobs has been thinking differently about telling the Apple story since the beginning, at least as far back as 1981 when he was a twenty-six-year-old entrepreneur with a big dream and a flair for articulating that dream.

Author Jeffrey Young calls 1981 a watershed year for Apple. At the beginning of the year, fewer than 10 percent of Americans had even heard of Apple. By the end of the year, Apple's name recognition had risen to 80 percent. Apple generated this publicity by positioning itself as the only real competition to IBM, which had entered the market for personal computers. Young believes that IBM's entrance was one of the best things that could have happened to Apple, because the move legitimized the market for personal computers.

Apple took out an audacious full-page ad in the *Wall Street Journal* and the *New York Times* "welcoming" IBM to the space and reminding IBM (and readers) that Apple had invented the personal computer system:

WELCOME IBM.
SERIOUSLY.

Welcome to the most exciting and important marketplace since the computer revolution began 35 years ago. And congratulations on your first computer. Putting real computer power in the hands of the individual is already improving the way people work, think, learn, communicate, and spend their leisure hours . . . We look forward to responsible competition in the massive effort to distribute this American technology to the world. And we appreciate the magnitude of the commitment. Because what we are doing is increasing social capital by enhancing individual productivity. Welcome to the task.[2]

Although Apple's 1984 television spot for Macintosh that ran once during the Super Bowl ranks among the most famous ads in television history, some commentators have asserted that Apple's 1981 newspaper ad was its most effective and influential, because Apple successfully positioned itself as the legitimate contender to IBM, a company that was ten times bigger than the fledgling start-up. (Today Apple's market cap is larger than IBM's, and Apple is worth more than Intel and Hewlett-Packard combined.)

The human imagination has always been inspired by a David-and-Goliath story, the little guy facing overwhelming odds who manages to beat back the bad guy using guile, skill, and an unwavering belief in himself. Every great story or movie has a hero and a villain, and so, too, does Apple's narrative. And nobody tells it better than Steve Jobs.

"If, for some reason, we make some big mistake and IBM wins, my personal feeling is that we are going to enter a computer Dark Ages for about 20 years," Steve Jobs said in a *Playboy* interview. "Once IBM gains control of a market sector, they always stop innovation—they prevent innovation from happening . . . Apple is providing the alternative."[3]

A Business Plan That Ignited a Board's Enthusiasm

In addition to the IBM ad, 1981 saw Apple's first real business plan, which Jobs himself had written. In the plan, Jobs introduced the metaphor of Macintosh as the "crankless computer," as discussed in Chapter 6. The following description appeared in Apple's business plan, and according to Young, the language "caught fire" in the boardroom when Jobs presented it; the excerpt demonstrates Jobs's mastery at telling a story:

> Personal computers are now at the stage where cars were when they needed to be cranked by hand to get started . . . Personal computers are simply not complete, as cars were not at the crank stage. The crank for personal computers is the awkward human interface. Users need to learn a host of unnatural commands and operations in order to make the computer do what they want it to do. The turn of this decade saw a lot of manufacturers, some very big ones, jump on the personal computer bandwagon. Some personal computers have more memory than others, some have more mass storage, some have color, others have more columns, but they all need to be hand cranked.[4]

Effective communication is a key ingredient behind the commercialization of successful innovations. Steve Jobs had an idea for an approachable computer that would replace the command-line interface with icons and a mouse, but he had to "sell" the idea to the Apple board. According to Young, the power of Jobs's vision carried the day, and the executive staff and company board gave the project the green light. It's intriguing to ask: would Steve Jobs's ideas have been translated into world-changing innovations had it not been for his ability to persuasively communicate the vision behind those ideas? Of course, we'll never really know the answer, but I would argue that those ideas would have been less likely to see the light of day without an extraordinary storyteller.

And We're Calling It . . . iPad

On the foggy January morning of Steve Jobs's iPad presentation at San Francisco's Yerba Buena Events Center, I was standing outside the building waiting for the presentation to begin and sharing my insights live for viewers of Fox Business News. Few outsiders knew exactly what Jobs would unveil that morning (although a tablet had been long rumored), and I did not have any inside information to share with the television reporter, despite her best efforts to get a scoop. But I could, and did, predict exactly how Jobs would present the new product, regardless of what it might be. I could predict the presentation accurately because Jobs's previous presentations have given us a crystal ball that reveals his approach. The following sections highlight several ingredients that Steve Jobs incorporated to bring the iPad to life. In doing so, he sold his audience on the vision, the benefits, and the excitement behind Apple's latest innovation. And if I had to bet, I would say Jobs will include these very same elements in future product launches.

A TWITTER-FRIENDLY HEADLINE

As described at the beginning of this chapter, Steve Jobs positioned the iPad in one sentence, calling it a "magical and revolutionary" product. He said the phrase twice. It was one of the first things he said as he walked onstage and the last message he left with his audience. Innovative ideas are, by definition, new. Customers typically require some help to understand where the product fits into their lives. Steve Jobs always provides a one-sentence description that is so concise that it easily fits within a 140-character Twitter post. What's an iPod? "It's one thousand songs in your pocket." What's a MacBook Air? "It's the world's thinnest notebook." One sentence speaks volumes.

AN ANTAGONIST

Every Steve Jobs presentation has a hero and a villain, an antagonist as well as a protagonist. The iPad presentation was no different. Although IBM played the role of the antagonist in the early 1980s, a villain need not be a competitor. It's often not. In many cases, Jobs will introduce the villain as a problem in need of a solution. Of course, in the Jobs narrative, Apple always plays the hero.

During the iPad presentation, a category of devices called "netbooks" played the role of the villain. Jobs showed a slide with two images: an iPhone on the left side and a notebook computer on the right side. A question mark appeared in between them. Jobs introduced the problem like this:

> In order to create a new category of devices, those devices are going to have to be far better at doing some key tasks. Better than the laptop, better than the smartphone. What kind of tasks? Well, things like browsing the Web. Doing e-mail. Enjoying and sharing photographs. Watching videos. Enjoying your music collection. Playing games. Reading e-books. If there's going to be a third category of device it's got to be better at these kinds of tasks than either a laptop or a smartphone. Otherwise, it has no reason for being. Now, some people have thought, that's a netbook. The problem is that netbooks aren't better at anything. They're slow, low-quality displays and run clunky old PC software. They're just cheap laptops. We don't think they are a third category of device. But we think we've got something that is and we'd like to show it to you today for the first time. We call it the iPad.[5]

THE RULE OF THREE

Neuroscientists are finding that humans can process only three or four chunks of information in short-term memory. If that's the case, why deliver ten message points when three is likely all your audience can absorb in one sitting? Jobs will often explain new products and ideas by focusing on three key points and no more. He used this approach during the iPad presentation, as illustrated in Table 14.1.

VISUAL SIMPLICITY

Steve Jobs understands that his audiences retain information more effectively when ideas are presented in words and pictures instead

TABLE 14.1 iPad Presentation Content Divided into Three Key Points[6]

iPAD PRESENTATION CONTENT	1	2	3
Apple gets its revenue from three product lines:	iPhones	iPods	Macs
Apple has three competitors in the mobile devices category:	Nokia	Samsung	Sony
Netbooks have three problems:	Slow	Low-Quality Displays	Clunky PC Software
Customers will have access to three stores in the iPad:	iTunes	App	iBookstore
The iPad will come bundled with the choice of three data plans and price points:	16GB ($499)	32GB ($599)	64GB ($699)

of words alone. For example, there were no bullet points on any of the slides in the iPad presentation. There were words and pictures—plenty of pictures—but no bullet points. Take a look at Table 14.2. In the first column, you will read what Jobs actually said during one portion of the iPad presentation. The second column describes the slide that accompanied his words.

AMAZINGLY ZIPPY WORDS

Steve Jobs's enthusiasm for Apple's products is reflected in the emotive words he uses to describe a product's features. He avoids the buzzwords, jargon, and corporatespeak so prevalent in business today—empty, meaningless words that are vague and nonemotional. While many marketers fill their conversations with nonsense, phrases such as *best-of-breed*, *paradigm shift*, and *share of voice* are simply not found in the Jobs vocabulary. Few business professionals have the confidence to phrase ideas the way Jobs does. He once said the buttons on an Apple computer screen look so good, "you'll want to lick them." Jobs described the speed of the iPhone 3GS as "amazingly zippy." Here are some other examples of amazingly zippy ways Jobs chose to describe the iPad:

TABLE 14.2 Jobs's Words with Corresponding Slide Descriptions from the iPad Presentation[7]

JOBS'S WORDS	CORRESPONDING SLIDE DESCRIPTION
The iPad is really thin. It's just half an inch thin.	Side view of iPad Text reads, "0.5 inches thin"
It's got a gorgeous 9.7-inch IPS display. It's gorgeous.	Photo of iPad Text reads, "9.7-inch IPS display"
iPad is powered by our own custom silicon. We have a chip called A4, the most advanced chip we've ever done. It screams.	Photo of iPad Text reads "1GHZ Apple A4 chip"
We've been able to achieve 10 hours of battery life, which means I can take a flight from San Francisco to Tokyo and watch video the whole way on one charge.	Artistic rendering of a battery, fully charged Text reads, "10 hours"

» "It's so much more intimate than a laptop and so much more capable than a smartphone."
» "It's the best browsing experience you've ever had."
» "It's a dream to type on."
» "It's that simple."
» "It's awesome."
» "It's a screamer."[8]

Whether it's the words he uses, the slides he designs, or the messages he delivers, Steve Jobs takes nothing for granted when telling the story about a new product. Even the actual "set" is designed. When Jobs introduced the iPad, he shared the stage with two items, neither of which was a lectern. A comfy leather chair and a small circular table were the only "props" that Jobs would need. He sat down in the chair, picked up the iPad that had been placed on the table, and, as his audience watched, proceeded to demonstrate the iPad's capability. The staging was brilliant. The iPad is not intended to be a third device that you carry in your purse or briefcase, along with a laptop and a phone. It is intended to make your life more comfortable and entertaining, such as during those times when you're in the kitchen and you want to browse movie reviews and order tickets on Fandango, or when you want to plop down on your comfy couch and pick up where you left off in the book you've been reading. Although he never explicitly pointed out the set, the staging acted as a subtle indication of how Apple sees the iPad's role in your life.

Steve Jobs is one of the world's premier storytellers. He knows that excellent design and customer service will take you only so far. Innovation requires positive buzz, and positive buzz is spread by inspired evangelists who understand the vision and share the excitement emotionally and effectively.

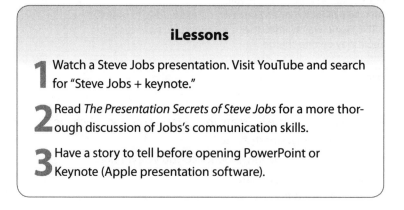

iLessons

1 Watch a Steve Jobs presentation. Visit YouTube and search for "Steve Jobs + keynote."

2 Read *The Presentation Secrets of Steve Jobs* for a more thorough discussion of Jobs's communication skills.

3 Have a story to tell before opening PowerPoint or Keynote (Apple presentation software).

CHAPTER 15

Think Differently About Your Story

> **Ideas are not really alive if they are confined only to a person's mind.**
>
> —NANCY DUARTE, AUTHOR, *SLIDE:OLOGY*

Former General Electric CEO Jack Welch tells of embarking on a road trip to learn more about GE's divisions in the early stages of his leadership. During an especially confusing presentation, Welch raised his hand to ask a question. He did not understand some of the terms the speaker was using. The speaker turned to Welch and said, "How do you expect me to teach you in five minutes what has taken me 25 years to learn?"[1] According to Welch, the manager didn't last long.

The world is filled with bright, innovative individuals whose ideas are falling on deaf ears because the individuals fail to communicate those ideas effectively. The brain does not pay attention to boring things, and if your story is boring, it is less likely to win over converts.

According to the authors of *Innovation*, "Ideas have always been a dime a dozen, but never more so than today in the exponential economy. We are all bombarded with the new 'new' thing. Getting the attention needed for success requires that you distinguish your ideas by their clarity and value. If you are the champion of a new innovation, one of your jobs is to raise the financial and human resources to get your project completed. This always means that you must convince someone—a company president, a board of directors, a venture capitalist, or a government program manager—that you have a good idea."[2]

This observation reminds me of a conversation I had with a manager at a Fortune 500 company. This particular manager had one of the brightest people in the company on his team, but the employee wasn't rising as quickly as one would expect.

"Why isn't he more successful within the company?" I asked the manager.

"Because he can't give a presentation," the manager said. "He's boring and confusing, yet he's the brightest guy in the room by far!"

Unfortunately, poor presentation skills can kill a career. Communication counts. If you do not believe it, there will be plenty of competitors who will eat your lunch, not because they necessarily have better products or ideas but because they understand the importance of telling a better story. Steve Jobs gets this, and communication skills have mattered to him for the last three decades.

Spreading the Gospel of Cloud Computing

Salesforce.com founder and cloud computing pioneer Marc Benioff credits storytelling as one of the primary contributors to his company's rapid success. In an interview for a *BusinessWeek* article, Benioff told me, "Communication is probably the most essential part of my job."[3]

After starting salesforce.com in the bedroom of a San Francisco apartment, Benioff grew the company into a $1 billion-a-year enterprise in less than a decade. During those ten years of growth, Benioff understood that in order to get noticed, he would have to make friends with reporters and bloggers who would help him spread the gospel of cloud computing.

Despite a hectic schedule, Benioff always responded quickly and directly to reporters. Few media requests ever went unanswered. Although he had a PR firm, Benioff often fielded requests directly. (I know firsthand because he unfailingly returned my e-mails when I was working as a business reporter, and usually within twenty-four hours.) Benioff decided early in his career that he would not treat the media as adversaries. Instead, he would treat them as a pivotal part of his marketing strategy. "Journalists immediately think of me as a resource for a quote or a comment because they know that I will be available to offer fresh insight and to meet their deadlines," Benioff told me.[4]

Benioff says that social media have turned customers into "content creators." This means that successful entrepreneurs must feed the need for fresh content and insights. According to Benioff, "The future of communicating with customers rests in engaging with them through every possible channel: phone, e-mail, chat, Web, and social networks. Customers are discussing a company's products and brand in real time. Companies need to join the conversation."[5]

Three Keys to Communicating Value

Benioff and Steve Jobs are a lot alike when it comes to communicating a brand story. Here are three techniques that both entrepreneurs have used successfully, techniques that you can adopt today to improve the way you communicate the value behind your idea.

TELL CLASSIC STORIES

Most reporters could not care less about a tiny start-up in some guy's bedroom, and that's why Benioff never positioned himself as such. He told a classic David-versus-Goliath story. "We gave the media something different. We gave them something new. We always positioned ourselves as revolutionaries. We went after the largest competitor in the industry or the industry itself. We made our story about change. We were about something new and different that was good for customers, and good for the community. We talked about the future."[6]

Sound familiar? It should. If not, reread the previous chapters!

KEEP EVERYONE ALIGNED

Consistency of message is critical. Everyone in the organization must speak from the same playbook. At salesforce.com, Benioff made sure staffers could effectively convey what they did and what they stood for in one sentence. He created a laminated "cheat sheet," with one sentence on the front and benefits of the service on the back. Salesforce.com employees and partners were even provided training on the subject so that they could all deliver the message effectively and consistently. Throughout much of salesforce.com's history, the sentence read simply, "The End of Software."

ENCOURAGE PRESENTATION SKILLS DEVELOPMENT

Want a job at salesforce.com? It helps to be a good presenter. Some candidates are required to give a presentation in addition to answering tough questions. "Presentation skills are key," says Benioff. "People who work for you represent your brand. You want them to present themselves—and represent you—in a certain way. Whether employees realize it or not, everyone in a company interfaces with customers in one way or another, and their attitude will affect the brand. That's why we work so hard to make sure we have the right people representing our brand, and that everyone is in alignment once they get here."[7]

I've taken a slight detour with Marc Benioff's techniques to reinforce the point that most successful entrepreneurs share Steve Jobs's commitment to telling a compelling brand story. They also use very similar techniques to tell those stories.

Seven Guidelines for Selling Your Ideas the Steve Jobs Way

Since the release of *The Presentation Secrets of Steve Jobs*, companies and individuals around the world have changed the way they present the vision and the benefits behind their brand, product, services, or ideas. I've heard directly from executives in virtually every industry: automobiles, health care, manufacturing, pharmaceuticals, technology—even nuclear weapons! If you have an idea, you will stand a far greater likelihood of persuading others to embrace that idea if you adopt just some of the techniques that have made Steve Jobs a master storyteller. Now here are seven techniques that you can use today to sell your ideas the Steve Jobs way.

1. CREATE A "HOLY SMOKES" MOMENT

Every Steve Jobs presentation has one moment that leaves people in awe—the holy smokes moment. These bits are scripted ahead of time to complement his slides, the Apple website, press releases, and advertisements. Often these moments occur as adjuncts to the formal product presentation. For example, in 2008, Jobs pulled the MacBook Air out of a manila interoffice envelope to show everyone just how thin it was. Bloggers went nuts, and the image of Jobs and the envelope turned out be the most popular photograph of the event.

On September 9, 2009, the subject of the holy smokes moment wasn't a product at all. It was Steve Jobs himself walking onstage after a long, health-related absence for a liver transplant. He told the audience he now had the liver of a mid-twenties person who died in a car crash and was generous enough to donate vital organs. "I wouldn't be here if it wasn't for such generosity," he said.

Whether you use Microsoft PowerPoint or Apple Keynote presentation software, script the "holy smokes" moment ahead of time, before you even open the software tool. For example, I was working with scientists at a well-known weapons lab. They were creating presentations to seek funding for "focused lethality munitions"—more advanced weaponry that can pinpoint targets with increased accuracy, saving the lives of innocent people in war zones. (The information is public, so I'm comfortable documenting it, although I will leave out the name of the organization and its participants.) One such weapon would wipe out enemy combatants in a small area while leaving the family next door unharmed. We decided to create a memorable moment outside of the PowerPoint slides by placing a circle of brightly colored tape on the floor and another circle of tape in a second color several yards farther out. At a key juncture in the presentation, the speaker would point to the tape and announce that anyone sitting within the first circle of tape would have been killed by the bomb, while anyone outside the second circle of tape would be unharmed. What do you think the audience will remember—the slides or the tape?

Think outside the slide. Ask yourself, "How do I make this content jump off the page (or the slide)?" Create emotionally charged events to persuade your listeners to take up your cause.

2. STICK TO THE RULE OF THREE

The rule of three is one of the most powerful concepts in writing. It's the reason Goldilocks saw three bears. It's the reason most plays are written in three acts. The human mind, as previously noted, can retain only three or four "chunks" of information, and Jobs is well aware of this principle. A Steve Jobs presentation is typically divided into three parts. On September 9, 2009, Jobs walked onstage and told his audience he would cover three product categories: iPhone, iTunes, and iPod. Jobs has even been known to have fun with the principle. At Macworld 2007, he introduced "three revolutionary products": an MP3 player, a phone, and an Internet communicator. After repeating the three products several times, he disclosed the big reveal—all three would be wrapped up in one product, the iPhone. The rule of three turned into the "holy smokes" moment.

Ask yourself, "What are the three things I want my audience to know?" Not twenty things, just three. You can get away with more points in written form (such as an article or a book), but stick to three in public presentations and oral conversations.

3. SHARE THE STAGE

Jobs rarely gives an entire presentation himself. Usually he surrounds himself with a supporting cast. He had a large supporting cast at the iPad presentation in January 2010. After Jobs took the audience for a tour of the product's features, he introduced several Apple executives to discuss other elements of the new products, including Scott Forstall, Apple senior VP of iPhone software, and Phil Schiller, Apple senior VP of product marketing. Apple executives then introduced non-Apple speakers such as game developers. In all, Jobs shared the stage with seven others for a one-and-a-half-hour presentation. If you can share your presentation with a team member (or customer), by all means, do so. Remember, though, as with any type of performance, presenters need to practice when they tag-team to ensure they get all the transitions and "scene changes" executed seamlessly.

4. INTRODUCE HEROES AND VILLAINS

Every great drama has a hero and a villain. As illustrated in the preceding chapter with the discussion of the iPad introduction, Steve Jobs is a master at creating drama. We see this technique as far back as 1984 when Apple introduced the Macintosh. Jobs set up the product launch by painting a picture of IBM—"big blue"—bent on "world domination." Apple, he said, would be the only company to stand in its way. The crowd went nuts. One can also interpret the well-known "I'm a Mac, I'm a PC" ads as hero-versus-villain vignettes played out in thirty-second installments. Stellar presentations have an antagonist—a common enemy—so the audience can rally around the hero. Your brand and your product play the role of the hero.

5. THINK VISUALLY

Apple presentations are strikingly simple and visual. As we also discussed in the previous chapter, there is very little text on a Steve Jobs slide, and there are no bullet points. This technique puts to use what psychologists call "picture superiority," which simply means that ideas are more easily recalled when presented in both text and images rather than in text alone. This concept has profound implications for your presentations. Do not clutter your slides with extraneous information that distracts from your message. Sometimes all you need is one word or one photograph to make your point. Remember that the slides themselves are meant to complement your message. Your story should take center stage. Do not use your slides as notes to read from. If you want further insight into creating more visually engaging presentations, read *The Presentation Secrets of Steve Jobs* and books by design experts Nancy Duarte, Garr Reynolds, and Cliff Atkinson.

6. CREATE TWITTER-FRIENDLY HEADLINES

Apple makes it simple for its customers to talk about its products—the company writes the headlines for them. What's the MacBook Air? "The world's thinnest notebook." If you can't describe your company, product, service, or idea in one sentence that fits within a Twitter post, go back to the drawing board. Don't announce it until you can.

7. SELL DREAMS, NOT PRODUCTS

Steve Jobs is passionately committed to changing the world, and his passion shows in every presentation. Anyone can learn the specific techniques he uses to come up with visually creative slides, but those slides will fall flat if delivered without passion and enthusiasm. When Jobs introduced the iPod in 2001, he said that music was a transformative experience and that in its own small way, Apple was changing the world. Where most observers saw a music player, Jobs saw an opportunity to create a better world for his customers. That's the difference between Jobs and the vast majority of mediocre leaders—Jobs is genuinely committed to changing the world, and he's not afraid to say it.

None of your ideas will turn into world-changing innovations if they remain confined to the inside of your head. At some point you will have to persuade someone else to invest, buy, participate, join, or evangelize. You would be surprised at how many people fail to understand the importance of this step. These individuals seem to believe that their ideas will change the world regardless of how hard they are to comprehend. Unfortunately, you will never hear about most of them. I often wonder how many truly revolutionary ideas are never given a chance to succeed because the brilliant mind that produced the idea could not tell the story behind it.

You have extraordinary ideas to share. Don't let poor communication sabotage the ultimate success of those ideas. A great presentation can transform minds, start movements, and grow companies. Start building your empire today. Let Steve Jobs show you how.

iLessons

1 Tell your story early and often. Make communication a cornerstone of your brand every day.

2 Make your brand story consistent across all platforms: presentations, website, advertising, marketing materials, social media.

3 Think differently about your presentation style. Study Steve Jobs, read design books, and pay attention to awe-inspiring presentations and what makes them different from the average PowerPoint show. Everyone has room to raise the bar on delivering presentations, but rising to the challenge requires a dedicated commitment to improve and an open mind.

One More Thing ...

Don't Let the Bozos Get You Down

**Self-confidence is the surest way of obtaining
what you want. If you know in your own heart you
are going to be something, you will be it. Do not
permit your mind to think otherwise. It is fatal.**

—GENERAL GEORGE S. PATTON

Innovation sits in a lonely place because very, very few people have the courage to pitch radically new ideas and the self-confidence to stick to their convictions. Innovation takes confidence, boldness, and the discipline to tune out negative voices. Few individuals have such courage, which is why so few can or will be able to innovate on a grand scale the way Steve Jobs does. The next great ideas, companies, and movements will come from those rare individuals who have the courage to believe in their principles and to stand up for them in the face of overwhelming odds.

In 1977, when Apple had begun selling a new personal computer, the Apple II, Ken Olsen, the founder of Digital Equipment, said, "There is no reason why anyone would want a computer in their home." Thank goodness Steve Jobs had the faith to believe in his vision to put a computer into the hands of everyday people.

Nearly all successful entrepreneurs have battled their share of skeptics. Imagine how hard it must have been for one young man in particular to hear the following:

"We don't need you. You haven't gotten through college yet."

"Get your feet off my desk; get out of here. You stink and we're not going to buy your product."

"Your stores won't work. Maybe it's time you stop thinking so differently."

"Your problem is that you still believe the way to grow is to serve caviar in a world that seems pretty content with cheese and crackers."

These remarks were all directed at one time or another to a man who would later be recognized as the master of innovation—Steve Jobs. Jobs and Woz faced plenty of "bozos" who did not appreciate what the two entrepreneurs were attempting to do—create simple-to-use tools for people who wanted to change the world. They refused to listen to naysayers. In 2005, Jobs had this advice for the graduates of Stanford University: "Don't let the noise of others' opinions drown out your own inner voice."

Woz summed up the secret to success in his book, *iWoz*. When asked, "How do you set about changing the world?" Wozniak answered:

First, you need to believe in yourself. Don't waver. There will be people—and I'm talking about the vast majority of people, practically everybody you'll ever meet—who just think in black-and-white terms . . . Maybe they don't get it because they can't imagine it, or maybe they don't get it because someone else has already told them what's useful or good, and what they heard doesn't include your idea. Don't let these people bring you down. Remember that they're just taking the point of view that matches whatever the popular cultural view of the moment is. They only know what they're exposed to. It's a type of prejudice, actually, a type of prejudice that is absolutely against the spirit of invention.[1]

It's very difficult for most people to embrace the unknown, yet the unknown is a world in which innovators feel the most at home.

According to analyst Tim Bajarin, who understands Apple better than almost anyone else on the planet, most professionals do not share the Steve Jobs approach to business. "Most corporations try to predict what customers want twelve to eighteen months out. Steve is more interested in what technology will allow people to do ten years from now," says Bajarin.[2]

Individuals who do think that far into the future inevitably run up against the headwinds of short-term corporate mind-sets, the kind of pressure that Bajarin believes is so prevalent in corporate America today. Jobs put his head down and ran straight into those headwinds, facing hurdles and skeptics with passion, conviction, and an unbending belief in his long-term vision.

One of the highest compliments ever paid to Steve Jobs came from an unlikely source, Microsoft cofounder Bill Gates. In May 2007, Gates and Jobs shared the stage in a rare joint appearance at D: All Things Digital. Gates was asked about Apple's greatest contribution to the computer industry. He responded:

> What Steve has done is quite phenomenal, and it goes back to 1977 and the Apple II computer and the idea that it would be a mass-market machine. The bet that was made by Apple uniquely was that this could be an incredible and empowering phenomenon. Apple pursued that dream. One of the most phenomenal things was the Macintosh. *That was risky.* People may not remember that Apple really bet the company on it. Steve gave a speech once that was one of my favorites. He said, we build products that we want to use ourselves. He has pursued that with incredible taste and elegance, and it has had a huge impact on the industry, innovation, and risk taking.[3]

"I do believe there is such a thing as dreaming the dream of a grand vision," Bajarin told me. "Great entrepreneurs are focused on today, but the most innovative have a road map of where they will be tomorrow. Steve Jobs takes care of the short term and satisfies what the customer wants today, but he dreams about and anticipates what the customer will want in the future."[4]

In 1997, when Apple was on the verge of collapse, Jobs called a meeting of his employees and, dressed in shorts and a black turtleneck, gave them a pep talk that would remind everyone why Apple must not be allowed to fail. Jobs said, "What we're about is not making boxes for people to get their jobs done. We believe that people with passion can change the world for the better."[5] Jobs had been away from the company that he founded for more than ten years, yet his vision had never wavered. Nothing seemed impossible.

Steve Jobs says he looks in the mirror every morning and asks himself, "If today were the last day of my life, would I want to do what I am about to do today?"[6] If the answer is "no" for too many days in a row, Jobs knows it is time to change something. Have you been saying "no" for too long? If so, what do you think Steve would do in your situation? I hope that the seven principles presented in this book will give you some guidance.

In America, between the years of 1980 and 2005, virtually all net new jobs were created by firms that were five years old or less, according to *New York Times* columnist Thomas Friedman. Friedman proposes that for a nation to thrive, it needs more start-ups, not bailouts. "If we want to bring down unemployment in a sustainable way, neither rescuing General Motors nor funding more road construction will do it. We need to create a big bushel of new companies—fast . . . But you cannot say this often enough: Good-paying jobs don't come from bailouts. They come from start-ups. And where do start-ups come from? They come from smart, creative, inspired risk takers."[7]

Perhaps the ultimate lesson that Steve Jobs has taught us is that risk taking requires courage and a bit of craziness. See genius in your craziness. Believe in yourself and your vision, and be prepared to constantly defend those beliefs. Only then will innovation be allowed to flourish, and only then will you be able lead an "insanely great" life.

Notes

INTRODUCTION

1. Thomas L. Friedman, "More (Steve) Jobs, Jobs, Jobs, Jobs," *New York Times*, January 24, 2010, nytimes.com/2010/01/24/opinion/24friedman.html?page wanted=print (accessed January 25, 2010).
2. Andy Serwer, "The '00s: Goodbye (at Last) to the Decade from Hell," *Time*, November 24, 2009, time.com/time/printout/0,8816,1942834,00.html (accessed January 30, 2010).
3. Bill Gates, "The Key to a Bright Future Is Innovation," *Financial Times*, January 29, 2010, ft.com/cms/s/2/a4810bb2-0c75-11df-a941-00144feabdc0.html?catid= 11&SID=google (accessed January 29, 2010).
4. Barry Jaruzelski and Kevin Dehoff, "Profits Down; Spending Steady," *Strategy + Business*, Winter 2009, 46.
5. Barry Jaruzelski and Richard Holman, "Innovating Through the Downturn: A Memo to the Chief Innovation Officer," Booz & Company, Inc., study, 2009, booz.com/media/uploads/Innovating_through_the_Downturn.pdf (accessed May 22, 2010).
6. Rick Hampson, "In America's Next Decade, Change and Challenges," *USA Today*, sec. 1A, January 5, 2010.
7. Tapan Munroe, Ph.D., economist (author, *What Makes Silicon Valley Tick?*), in discussion with the author, February 5, 2010.
8. Ibid.
9. Curtis Carlson and William Wilmot, *Innovation* (New York: Crown Business, 2006), 17.
10. Munroe, in discussion with the author.
11. Robert Kiyosaki, "We Need Two School Systems," *USA Today*, The Forum, sec. 1, February 9, 2010.
12. Michael Moritz, *Return to the Little Kingdom* (New York: The Overlook Press, 2009), 106.
13. Stanford University, "'You've Got to Find What You Love,' Jobs Says," *Stanford Report*, June 14, 2005, http://news.stanford.edu/news/2005/june15/jobs06150 .html?view=print (accessed January 22, 2010).

CHAPTER 1

1. Rob Walker, "The Guts of a New Machine," *New York Times Magazine*, November 30, 2003, nytimes.com/2003/11/30/magazine/30IPOD .html?pagewanted=all (accessed May 23, 2010).
2. Curtis Carlson and William Wilmot, *Innovation* (New York: Crown Business, 2006), 13.
3. Paul Krugman, "The Big Zero," *New York Times*, December 27, 2009, nytimes .com/2009/12/28/opinion/28krugman.html (accessed May 23, 2010).
4. Adam Lashinsky, "Why Him?" *Fortune*, November 23, 2009, 90.
5. Morten T. Hansen, Herminia Ibarra, and Urs Peyer, "The Best Performing CEOs in the World," *Harvard Business Review*, January–February 2010, http://hbr .org/2010/01/the-best-performing-ceos-in-the-world/ar/1 (accessed May 23, 2010).
6. Michael Arrington, "What if Steve Jobs Hadn't Returned to Apple in 1997?" *TechCrunch*, November 26, 2009, http://techcrunch.com/2009/11/26/steve -jobs-apple-1997 (accessed May 23, 2010).
7. Junior Achievement Study, "Steve Jobs Bigger than Oprah!" October 13, 2009, ja.org/files/polls/Teens-Entrepreneurship-Part-2.pdf (accessed May 23, 2010).
8. Peter Burrows, "The Seed of Apple's Innovation," *BusinessWeek*, October 12, 2004, businessweek.com/bwdaily/dnflash/oct2004/nf20041012_4018_db083 .htm (accessed May 23, 2010).
9. YouTube, "Apple—Crazy Ones," YouTube, youtube.com/watch?v=XUfH -BEBMoY (accessed May 23, 2010).
10. Nancy Koehn, "His Legacy," *Fortune*, November 23, 2009, 110.
11. Michael Moritz, *Return to the Little Kingdom* (New York: The Overlook Press, 2009), 293.
12. Lee Brower and Jay Paterson, "Money Talks, Meaning Whispers," *Motivated,* Spring 2010, 65.
13. Moritz, *Return to the Little Kingdom*, 153.

CHAPTER 2

1. Stanford University, "'You've Got to Find What You Love,' Jobs Says," *Stanford Report*, June 14, 2005, http://news.stanford.edu/news/2005/june15/jobs -061505.html?view=print (accessed January 22, 2010).
2. Ibid.
3. Ibid.
4. Ron Baron, "Ron's Conference Speech: Eighteenth Annual Baron Investment Conference," *Baron Funds Quarterly Report,* September 30, 2009.
5. Ibid.
6. Daniel Morrow, "Excerpts from an Oral History Interview with Steve Jobs," Smithsonian Institution (Oral and Video Histories), April 20, 1995, http:// americanhistory.si.edu/collections/comphist/sj1.html (accessed May 23, 2010).
7. Steve Wozniak with Gina Smith, *iWoz* (New York: W. W. Norton & Company, 2006), 150.

8. Michael Moritz, *Return to the Little Kingdom* (New York: The Overlook Press, 2009), 106.
9. Leadership, "Steve Wozniak—Apple Innovation: Innovation Inspiration with the Co-Founder of Apple Computer, Inc.," *London Business Review*, October 1, 2008, londonbusinessforum.com/events/apple_innovation (accessed January 5, 2010).
10. Morrow, "Excerpts from an Oral History Interview with Steve Jobs."
11. Stanford University, "'You've Got to Find What You Love,' Jobs Says."
12. Ibid.
13. Jessica Livingston, *Founders at Work: Stories of Startups' Early Days* (Berkeley: Apress, 2008), 57.
14. Wikipedia, "Steve Jobs," Wikiquote, http://en.wikiquote.org/wiki/Steve_Jobs (accessed May 23, 2010).

CHAPTER 3

1. Bill Strickland, president and CEO, Manchester Bidwell Corporation, in discussion with the author, February 16, 2010.
2. Ibid.
3. Hannah Clark, "James Dyson Cleans Up," *Forbes*, Face Time, August 1, 2006, forbes.com/2006/08/01/leadership-facetime-dyson- cx_hc_0801dyson_print .html (accessed February 19, 2010).
4. Chuck Salter, "Failure Doesn't Suck," *Fast Company*, December 19, 2007, fastcompany.com/node/59549/print (accessed February 19, 2010).
5. Clark, "James Dyson Cleans Up."
6. Sharon Aby, founder, Beyond Ideas, in discussion with the author, January 13, 2010.
7. RachaelRayShow.com, "Maria Shriver's Women's Conference" [video], October 28, 2008, rachaelrayshow.com/show/segments/view/rachael-maria-shrivers -womens-conference (accessed May 23, 2010).
8. Ibid.
9. Carmine Gallo, "From Homeless to Multimillionaire," *Bloomberg BusinessWeek*, July 23, 2007, businessweek.com/smallbiz/content/jul2007/ sb20070723_608918.htm (accessed May 22, 2010).
10. Ibid.
11. Ibid.
12. Ken Robinson, *The Element: How Finding Your Passion Changes Everything* (New York: Viking Press, 2009), 1.
13. Ibid.
14. Ibid., 20.
15. Darren Vader, "Biography: Steve Jobs," The Apple Museum, theapplemuseum .com/index.php?id=49 (accessed May 23, 2010).
16. Jonathan Mahler, "James Patterson Inc.: How a Genre Writer Has Transformed Book Publishing," *New York Times Magazine*, January 24, 2010.
17. Ibid.

18. Michael Moritz, *Return to the Little Kingdom* (New York: The Overlook Press, 2009), 72.
19. Wikipedia, "Intrapreneurship," includes Jobs quote, http://en.wikipedia.org/wiki/Intrapreneurship (accessed May 23, 2010).
20. Craig Escobar, CEO, Show America, in discussion with the author, January 14, 2010.

CHAPTER 4
1. Rob Campbell, CEO, Voalté, in discussion with the author, February 5, 2010.
2. Ibid.
3. Jeffrey S. Young, *Steve Jobs: The Journey Is the Reward* (Glenview, IL: Scott, Foresman and Company, 1988), 176.
4. Computer History Museum, "The Computer History Museum Makes Historic Apple Documents Available to Public," press release, June 2, 2009, computerhistory.org/press/Apple-IPO-and-Macintosh-Plans.html (accessed May 22, 2010).
5. Ibid.
6. Ibid.
7. Steve Wozniak with Gina Smith, *iWoz* (New York: W. W. Norton & Company, 2006), 150.
8. Bloomberg, "Voices of Innovation: Steve Jobs," *Bloomberg BusinessWeek*, October 11, 2004, businessweek.com/print/magazine/content/04_41/b3903408.htm?chan=gl (accessed February 15, 2010).
9. Leander Kahney, *Inside Steve's Brain* (New York: Portfolio, 2008), 7.
10. Ibid.
11. Bobbie Johnson, "The Coolest Player in Town," *The Guardian*, September 22, 2005, guardian.co.uk/technology/2005/sep/22/stevejobs.guardianweekly technologysection (accessed May 22, 2010).
12. Wozniak with Smith, *iWoz*, 151.
13. Alltop, "1994 *Rolling Stone* Interview of Steve Jobs," Alltop, February 5, 2010, http://holykaw.alltop.com/1994-rolling-stone-interview-of-steve-jobs (accessed May 23, 2010).
14. *Triumph of the Nerds*, PBS documentary written and hosted by Robert X. Cringely (1996, New York).
15. Ibid.
16. Ibid.
17. Guy Kawasaki, *The Macintosh Way* (Glenview, IL: Scott, Foresman and Company, 1990), 18.
18. Ibid.
19. Sharon Aby, founder, Beyond Ideas, in discussion with the author, January 13, 2010.
20. The Pixar Touch, "Steve Jobs Thinks Different, 1997," The Pixar Touch History of Pixar, November 8, 2009, http://thepixartouch.typepad.com/main/2009/11/steve-jobs-shareholder-letter-1997.html (accessed March 3, 2010).

21. Ibid.
22. YouTube, "Steve Jobs Introduces the 'Digital Hub' Strategy at Macworld 2001," YouTube, youtube.com/watch?v=9046oXrm7f8 (accessed May 22, 2010).
23. Microsoft News Center, "Gates Showcases Tablet PC, Xbox at COMDEX; Says New 'Digital Decade' Technologies Will Transform How We Live," news press release, November 11, 2001, microsoft.com/presspass/press/2001/Nov01/11-11 Comdex2001KeynotePR.mspx (accessed May 23, 2010).
24. Dick Brass, "Microsoft's Creative Destruction," *New York Times*, February 4, 2010, nytimes.com/2010/02/04/opinion/04brass.html (accessed May 22, 2010).
25. Tim Bajarin, president, Creative Strategies, in discussion with the author, February 4, 2010.
26. Young, *Steve Jobs: The Journey Is the Reward*, 187.
27. Ibid., 121.
28. Apple.com, "Macworld San Francisco 2007: Keynote Address," apple.com/ quicktime/qtv/mwsf07 (accessed May 23, 2010).

CHAPTER 5

1. YouTube, "John F. Kennedy's Moon Speech to Congress—May 25, 1961," YouTube, youtube.com/watch?v=Kza-iTe2100 (accessed May 23, 2010).
2. Ibid.
3. YouTube, "1983 Apple Keynote—The '1984' Ad Introduction," YouTube, youtube.com/watch?v=lSiQA6KKyJo (accessed May 22, 2010).
4. Guy Kawasaki, *The Macintosh Way* (Glenview, IL: Scott, Foresman and Company, 1990), 100.
5. Ibid.
6. Ibid.
7. Nancy Mann Jackson, "Wanted: Fully Engaged Employees," *Entrepreneur*, April 26, 2010, entrepreneur.com/humanresources/managingemployees/ article206318.html (accessed May 23, 2010).
8. Jeffrey S. Young, *Steve Jobs: The Journey Is the Reward* (Glenview, IL: Scott, Foresman and Company, 1988), 328.
9. Gary Hamel, "The Hole in the Soul of Business," *Wall Street Journal*, January 13, 2010, http://blogs.wsj.com/management/2010/01/13/the-hole-in-the-soul-of -business (accessed May 23, 2010).
10. Lev Grossman, "How Apple Does It," *Time*, October 16, 2005, time.com/time/ printout/0,8816,1118384,00.html (accessed February 15, 2010).
11. Carmine Gallo, *Fire Them Up! 7 Simple Secrets to: Inspire Colleagues, Customers, and Clients; Sell Yourself, Your Vision, and Your Values; Communicate with Charisma and Confidence* (Hoboken, NJ: John Wiley & Sons, Inc., 2007), 41.
12. Ibid.
13. Gallo, *Fire Them Up*, 193.
14. Jacqueline Edelberg, Ph.D. (author, *How to Walk to School*), in discussion with the author, February 22, 2010.
15. Ibid.

16. Ibid.

17. David Sheff, "*Playboy* Interview: Steven Jobs," *Playboy*, February 1985, 58.

18. Roberto Verganti, "Having Ideas Versus Having a Vision," *Harvard Business Review* blog, March 1, 2010, http://blogs.hbr.org/cs/2010/03/having_ideas _versus_having_a _vision.html (accessed May 23, 2010).

19. America's Most Admired Companies, "Steve Jobs Speaks Out"[Strategy], *Fortune*, March 7, 2008, http://money.cnn.com/galleries/2008/fortune/0803/ gallery.jobsqna.fortune/3.html (accessed May 23, 2010).

CHAPTER 6

1. Steve Wozniak with Gina Smith, *iWoz* (New York: W. W. Norton & Company, 2006), 173.

2. Jeffrey H. Dyer, Hal Gregersen, and Clayton Christensen, "The Innovator's DNA," *Harvard Business Review*, Spotlight on Innovation (Reprint R0912E), December 2009, 3.

3. Ibid.

4. Ibid.

5. Ibid.

6. Leander Kahney, *Inside Steve's Brain* (New York: Penguin Group, 2008), 73.

7. Ibid., 74.

8. YouTube, "Steve Jobs: Good Artists Copy Great Artists Steal," YouTube, youtube.com/watch?v=CW0DUg63IqU (accessed May 22, 2010).

9. Gregory Berns, *Iconoclast* (Boston: Harvard Business Press, 2008), 8.

10. Ibid.

11. Ibid., 33.

12. Ibid., 54.

13. Wikipedia, "Steve Jobs," includes quote on Bill Gates, http://en.wikiquote.org/ wiki/Steve_Jobs (accessed May 23, 2010).

14. Jeffrey S. Young, *Steve Jobs: The Journey Is the Reward* (Glenview, IL: Scott, Foresman and Company, 1988), 236–37.

15. David Sheff, "*Playboy* Interview: Steven Jobs," *Playboy*, February 1985, 58.

16. Young, *Steve Jobs: The Journey Is the Reward*, 226.

17. Ibid., 227.

CHAPTER 7

1. Jeffrey H. Dyer, Hal Gregersen, and Clayton Christensen, "The Innovator's DNA," *Harvard Business Review*, Spotlight on Innovation (Reprint R0912E), December 2009, 3.

2. Brigham Young University, "Innovators Practice 5 Skills the Rest of Us Don't, Says BYU, INSEAD and Harvard B-School Study," news release, January 19, 2010, http://news.byu.edu/archive09-Dec-dyerinnovation.aspx (accessed March 21, 2010).

3. Ibid.

4. Dyer et al., "The Innovator's DNA," 4.

5. Gary Wolf, "Steve Jobs: The Next Insanely Great Thing," *Wired*, wired.com/ wired/archive/4.02/jobs_pr.html (accessed May 23, 2010).

6. Michael Moritz, *Return to the Little Kingdom* (New York: The Overlook Press, 2009), 98.

7. Ibid., 118.

8. Steve Wozniak with Gina Smith, *iWoz* (New York: W. W. Norton & Company, 2006), 290.

9. Gregory Berns, *Iconoclast* (Boston: Harvard Business Press, 2008), 21.

10. Dyer et al., "The Innovator's DNA," 3.

11. Adriana Herrera, principal and founder, ERA Communications, in discussion with the author, March 11, 2010.

12. Ken Robinson, *The Element: How Finding Your Passion Changes Everything* (New York: Viking Press, 2009), 50.

CHAPTER 8

1. YouTube, "Macworld Boston 1997—Full Version," YouTube, youtube.com/ watch?v=PEHNrqPkefl (accessed May 23, 2010).

2. *Wired* News Staff, "The Best of *Wired* on Apple," *Wired*, March 30, 2003, wired .com/gadgets/mac/news/2006/03/70538 (accessed May 23, 2010).

3. YouTube, "Macworld Boston 1997—Full Version."

4. YouTube, "Apple—Crazy Ones," YouTube, youtube.com/watch?v=XUfH -BEBMoY (accessed May 23, 2010).

5. Steven Levy, *The Perfect Thing: How the iPod Shuffles Commerce, Culture, and Coolness* (New York: Simon & Schuster, 2006), 118.

6. Wikipedia, "TheGlobe.com," includes Stephan Paternot quote, http:// en.wikipedia.org/wiki/TheGlobe.com#cite_note-5 (accessed May 23, 2010).

7. America's Most Admired Companies, "Steve Jobs Speaks Out"[Strategy], *Fortune*, March 7, 2008, http://money.cnn.com/galleries/2008/fortune/0803/ gallery.jobsqna.fortune/3.html (accessed January 2, 2010).

8. Ibid. [iPhone].

9. Rob Enderle, "When You Should Never Listen to Your Customers," *ITBusinessEdge*, April 9, 2010, itbusinessedge.com/cm/blogs/enderle/when -you-should-never-listen-to-your-customers/?cs=40585 (accessed May 23, 2010).

10. The Creative Leadership Forum, "The Cultural Importance of the Leader Around Innovation—Robert Verganti—Author of *Design-Driven Innovation*," March 26, 2010, thecreativeleadershipforum.com/creativity-matters-blog/ 2010/3/26/the-cultural-importance-of-the-leader-around-innovation-robe .html (accessed April 14, 2010).

11. Ibid.

12. YouTube, "Apple Music Event 2001—The First Ever iPod Introduction," YouTube, youtube.com/watch?v=kN0SVBCJqLs (accessed May 23, 2010).

13. YouTube, "Apple Music Event 2003—iTunes Music Store Introduction," YouTube, youtube.com/watch?v=B2n86TROxzY (accessed May 22, 2010).

14. Ibid.

15. Ibid.

16. Roberto Verganti, *Design-Driven Innovation* (Boston: Harvard Business Press, 2009), 76.

17. Ibid., 51.

18. Lev Grossman, "Invention of the Year: The iPhone" [The Best Inventions of 2007], *Time*, November 1, 2007, time.com/time/specials/2007/article/0,28804,1677329_1678542,00.html (accessed May 23, 2010).

19. Apple.com, "Macworld San Francisco 2007: Keynote Address," apple.com/quicktime/qtv/mwsf07 (accessed May 23, 2010).

20. America's Most Admired Companies, "Steve Jobs Speaks Out" [iPhone], *Fortune*, March 7, 2008, http://money.cnn.com/galleries/2008/fortune/0803/gallery.jobsqna.fortune/index.html (accessed January 2, 2010).

21. Nick Spence, "Apple's Woz: iPad Great for Students, Grandparents," *PCWorld*, April 3, 2010, pcworld.com/article/193329/apples_woz_ipad_great_for_students_grandparents.html (accessed May 23, 2010).

22. Dan Lyons, "Think Really Different," *Newsweek*, March 26, 2010, newsweek.com/id/235565 (accessed May 23, 2010).

23. Jesus Diaz, "iPad Is the Future," Gizmodo blog, April 2, 2010, http://gizmodo.com/5506692/ipad-is-the-future (accessed May 23, 2010).

24. YouTube, "Apple iPad: Steve Jobs Keynote January 27, 2010—Part 1," YouTube, youtube.com/watch?v=OBhYxj2SvRI (accessed May 23, 2010).

25. Ibid.

26. Katherine M. Hafner and Richard Brandt, "Steve Jobs: Can He Do It Again?" *BusinessWeek*, August 27, 1988, businessweek.com/1989-94/pre88/b30761.htm (accessed May 23, 2010).

27. Sharon Aby, founder, Beyond Ideas, in discussion with the author, January 13, 2010.

28. Leander Kahney, "How Apple Got Everything Right by Doing Everything Wrong," *Wired*, March 18, 2008, wired.com/techbiz/it/magazine/16-04/bz_apple?currentPage=2 (accessed March 30, 2010).

29. Leander Kahney, *Inside Steve's Brain* (New York: Penguin Group, 2008), 63.

CHAPTER 9

1. Adrian Salamunovic, cofounder, DNA 11, in discussion with the author, April 7, 2010.

2. Alain Breillatt, «You Can't Innovate like Apple,» *Pragmatic Marketing* 6, no. 4, pragmaticmarketing.com/publications/magazine/6/4/you_cant_innovate_like_apple (accessed May 23, 2010).

3. Matthew Boyle, "The Accidental Hero," *Bloomberg BusinessWeek*, November 5, 2009, businessweek.com/magazine/content/09_46/b4155058815908.htm (accessed May 23, 2010).

4. Carmine Gallo, *10 Simple Secrets of the World's Greatest Business Communicators*, (Naperville, IL: Sourcebooks, 2005), 19.

5. David Meerman Scott, *Worldwide Rave* (Hoboken, NJ: John Wiley & Sons, Inc., 2009), 24.

6. Ibid.

7. Carmine Gallo, *Fire Them Up! 7 Simple Secrets to: Inspire Colleagues, Customers, and Clients; Sell Yourself, Your Vision, and Your Values; Communicate with Charisma and Confidence* (Hoboken, NJ: John Wiley & Sons, Inc., 2007), 23.

CHAPTER 10

1. YouTube, "Steve Jobs Keynote Macworld 1998—Part 2," YouTube, youtube .com/watch?v=LWuR88AIKLg (accessed May 23, 2010).

2. Ibid.

3. Peter Burrows, "The Seed of Apple's Innovation," *BusinessWeek*, October 12, 2004, businessweek.com/bwdaily/dnflash/oct2004/nf20041012_4018_db083 .htm (accessed May 23, 2010).

4. YouTube, "Objectified—Jonathan Ive Talks About Mac Design," You Tube, youtube.com/watch?v=t0fe800C2CU (accessed May 23, 2010).

5. YouTube, "Oct. 14—Apple Notebook Event 2008—New Way to Build—2/6," YouTube, youtube.com/watch?v=7JLjldgjuKI (accessed May 23, 2010).

6. Ibid.

7. YouTube, "Objectified—Jonathan Ive Talks About Mac Design."

8. Ibid.

9. Sheryl Garratt, "Jonathan Ive: Inventor of the Decade," *The Observer*, November 29, 2009, guardian.co.uk/music/2009/nov/29/ipod-jonathan-ive-designer/print (accessed January 4, 2010).

10. Ibid.

11. Rob Walker, "The Guts of a New Machine," *New York Times*, November 30, 2003, nytimes.com/2003/11/30/magazine/30IPOD.html?pagewanted=all (accessed May 23, 2010).

12. Ibid.

13. Steven Levy, *The Perfect Thing: How the iPod Shuffles Commerce, Culture, and Coolness* (New York: Simon & Schuster, 2006), 77–78.

14. Ibid., 74.

15. Ibid.

16. Om Malik, "User Experience Matters: What Entrepreneurs Can Learn from 'Objectified,'" Gigaom blog, January 3, 2010, http://gigaom.com/2010/01/03/ objectified-design (accessed May 23, 2010).

17. YouTube, "Introducing the New iPhone—Part 1," YouTube, youtube.com/ watch?v=ftf4riVJyqw (accessed May 23, 2010).

18. Ibid.

19. Matthew E. May, *In Pursuit of Elegance* (New York: Broadway Books, 2009), 79.

20. David Pogue, "Buzzing, Tweeting and Carping," *New York Times*, February 17, 2010, nytimes.com/2010/02/18/technology/personaltech/18pogue. html?pagewanted=all (accessed May 23, 2010).

21. Malik, "User Experience Matters."

22. Todd Lappin, "What My 2.5-Year-Old's First Encounter with an iPad Can Teach the Tech Industry," bNet, April 7, 2010, http://industry.bnet.com/technology/10006827/what-my-25-year-olds-first-encounter-with-an-ipad-can-teach-the-tech-industry (accessed May 23, 2010).

23. Andy Ihnatko, "Review: iPad Is Pure Innovation—One of Best Computers Ever," *Chicago Sun-Times*, March 31, 2010, suntimes.com/technology/ihnatko/2134139,ihnatko-ipad-apple-review-033110.article (accessed April 5, 2010).

24. Steve Chazin, "Apple: Do One Thing, Better," MarketingApple.com, February 23, 2010, marketingapple.com/marketing_apple/2010/02/apple-do-one-thing-better.html (accessed May 23, 2010).

25. Dan Frommer, "Apple COO Tim Cook: 'We Have No Interest in Being in the TV Market,'" *Business Insider*, February 23, 2010, businessinsider.com/live-apple-coo-tim-cook-at-the-goldman-tech-conference-2010-2 (accessed May 23, 2010).

26. Noah Robischon, "Steve Jobs' Advice to Nike: Get Rid of the Crappy Stuff" [video], *Fast Company*, April 26, 2010, fastcompany.com/video/mark-parker-nike-and-steve-jobs-apple (accessed May 23, 2010).

27. Leander Kahney, *Inside Steve's Brain* (New York: Portfolio, 2008), 61.

28. America's Most Admired Companies, "Steve Jobs Speaks Out" [on Apple's focus], *Fortune*, March 7, 2008, http://money.cnn.com/galleries/2008/fortune/0803/gallery.jobsqna.fortune/6.html (accessed May 23, 2010).

29. Jeffrey S. Young, *Steve Jobs: The Journey Is the Reward* (Glenview, IL: Scott, Foresman and Company, 1988), 153.

30. May, *In Pursuit of Elegance*, 23.

CHAPTER 11

1. Carmine Gallo, "Lessons in Simplicity from the Flip," *Bloomberg BusinessWeek*, February 17, 2010, businessweek.com/smallbiz/content/feb2010/sb20100217_244373.htm (accessed May 23, 2010).

2. Ibid.

3. Mick Mountz, founder and CEO, Kiva Systems, in discussion with the author, January 21, 2010.

4. The Creative Leadership Forum, "The Cultural Importance of the Leader Around Innovation—Robert Verganti—Author of *Design-Driven Innovation*," March 26, 2010, thecreativeleadershipforum.com/creativity-matters-blog/2010/3/26/the-cultural-importance-of-the-leader-around-innovation-robe.html (accessed April 14, 2010).

5. Arik Hesseldahl, "Senuous Sound Machine," *Bloomberg BusinessWeek*, May 3–May 9, 2010, 78.

6. Elisabeth Bumiller, "We Have Met the Enemy and He Is PowerPoint," *New York Times*, April 27, 2010, nytimes.com/2010/04/27/world/27powerpoint.html (accessed May 23, 2010).

7. Jim Collins, "Best New Year's Resolution? A Stop Doing List," *USA Today*, December 29, 2003, usatoday.com/news/opinion/editorials/2003-12-30 -collins_x.htm?loc=interstitialskip (accessed May 23, 2010).

8. Ibid.

9. Ibid.

CHAPTER 12

1. Jerry Useem, "Apple: America's Best Retailer," *Fortune*, March 8, 2007, http:// money.cnn.com/magazines/fortune/fortune_archive/2007/03/19/8402321/ index.htm (accessed May 23, 2010).

2. Cliff Edwards, "Commentary: Sorry, Steve: Here's Why Apple Stores Won't Work," *BusinessWeek*, May 21, 2001, businessweek.com/magazine/ content/01_21/b3733059.htm (accessed May 23, 2010).

3. Jerry Useem, "Apple: America's Best Retailer."

4. ifoAppleStore.com, "Think Equity Conference 2006," includes Ron Johnson quote, September 13, 2006, ifoapplestore.com/stores/thinkequity_2006 _rj.html (accessed May 23, 2010).

5. YouTube, "Apple—Steve Jobs Introduces the First Apple Store Retail 2001," YouTube, youtube.com/watch?v=OJtQeMHGrgc (accessed May 23, 2010).

6. ifoAppleStore.com, "Think Equity Conference 2006."

7. YouTube, "Apple—Steve Jobs Introduces the First Apple Store Retail 2001."

8. ifoAppleStore.com, "Think Equity Conference 2006."

9. Ibid.

10. YouTube, "Autodesk (corporate documentary)," YouTube, youtube.com/ watch?v=Hz8-WfBW3qU (accessed May 23, 2010).

11. America's Most Admired Companies, "Steve Jobs Speaks Out" [on choosing strategy], *Fortune*, March 7, 2008, http://money.cnn.com/galleries/2008/ fortune/0803/gallery.jobsqna.fortune/7.html (accessed May 23, 2010).

12. UPI.com, "Couple Enjoys Wedding with Apple Theme," February 20, 2010, upi .com/Odd_News/2010/02/20/Couple-enjoys-wedding-with-Apple-theme/UPI -44951266688299 (accessed May 23, 2010).

CHAPTER 13

1. Carmine Gallo, "An Inside Look at the Zappos Experience," Talking Leadership blog, January 11, 2010, http://carminegallo.com/talking-leadership/an-inside -look-at-the-zappos-experience (accessed May 23, 2010).

2. Mike Abt, co-owner, Abt Electronics, in discussion with the author, May 7, 2010.

3. Scott Iversen, director of marketing, Toppers, in discussion with the author, May 6, 2010.

CHAPTER 14

1. Woodruff Health Sciences Center, Emory University, "Neuroscientist Reveals How Nonconformists Achieve Success," press release, September 25, 2008,

http://whsc.emory.edu/press_releases2.cfm?announcement_id_seq=15766 (accessed May 23, 2010).

2. Jeffrey S. Young, *Steve Jobs: The Journey Is the Reward* (Glenview, IL: Scott, Foresman and Company, 1988), 237.

3. David Sheff, "*Playboy* Interview: Steven Jobs," *Playboy*, February 1985, 70.

4. Young, *Steve Jobs: The Journey Is the Reward*, 236.

5. Apple.com, "Apple Special Event January 2010," apple.com/quicktime/qtv/specialevent0110 (accessed May 23, 2010).

6. Ibid.

7. Ibid.

8. Ibid.

CHAPTER 15

1. Jack Welch with John A. Byrne, *Straight from the Gut* (New York: Warner Business Books, 2001), 72.

2. Curtis Carlson and William Wilmot, *Innovation* (New York: Crown Business, 2006), 129.

3. Carmine Gallo, "Storytelling Tips from Salesforce's Marc Benioff," *Bloomberg BusinessWeek*, November 3, 2009, businessweek.com/smallbiz/content/nov2009/sb2009112_279472.htm (accessed May 23, 2010).

4. Ibid.

5. Ibid.

6. Ibid.

7. Ibid.

ONE MORE THING . . . DON'T LET THE BOZOS GET YOU DOWN

1. Steve Wozniak with Gina Smith, *iWoz* (New York: W. W. Norton & Company, 2006), 289.

2. Tim Bajarin, president, Creative Strategies, in discussion with the author, February 4, 2010.

3. YouTube, "Steve Jobs and Bill Gates Together—Part 1," YouTube, youtube.com/watch?v=_5Z7eal4uXI&feature=fvw (accessed May 23, 2010).

4. Bajarin, in discussion with the author.

5. YouTube, "Steve Jobs on Marketing and Passion," YouTube, youtube.com/watch?v=c2cDQw-Cmd4 (accessed May 23, 2010).

6. Stanford University, "'You've Got to Find What You Love,' Jobs Says," *Stanford Report*, June 14, 2005, http://news.stanford.edu/news/2005/june15/jobs-061505.html (accessed May 23, 2010).

7. Thomas L. Friedman, "More (Steve) Jobs, Jobs, Jobs, Jobs," *New York Times*, January 24, 2010, nytimes.com/2010/01/24/opinion/24friedman.html?pagewanted=print (accessed January 25, 2010).

Index